D0146805

# The Post-Industrial Utopians

BORIS FRANKEL

# The
# Post-Industrial Utopians

The University of Wisconsin Press

Published in the United States of America by
The University of Wisconsin Press,
114 North Murray Street, Madison,
Wisconsin 53715

Published in Great Britain by Polity Press in association
with Basil Blackwell

Editorial Office:
Polity Press, Dales Brewery, Gwydir Street
Cambridge, CB1 2LJ, UK

Basil Blackwell Ltd
108 Cowley Road, Oxford, OX4 1JF, UK

Printed in Great Britain

Library of Congress Cataloging-in-Publication Data

Frankel, Boris.
   The post-industrial utopians.
   Includes index.
   1. Socialism.   2. Economic policy.   3. Social
   policy.   4. Environmental policy.   I. Title.
HX73.F73   1987      335      87–6147
ISBN 0–299–10810–4
ISBN 0–299–10814–7 (pbk.)

# Contents

# Contents

# Contents

# Preface

In an age when political and social organizations focus on single issues just as narrowly as do academic specialists, there is a pressing need to take a larger overview. This book follows on from my earlier *Beyond The State? Dominant Theories and Socialist Strategies* (1983), and discusses a number of issues such as social welfare, defence policy and cultural developments which were there neglected for reasons of space. The exhaustion of mainstream Left parties has also prompted me to devote more attention to the ideas and practices of many of those groups and individuals working in the alternative, small-is-beautiful and Green movements. I have long been dissatisfied with the fragmentation of anti-capitalist social movements – especially the open hostility between Red and Green movements. But whereas *Beyond The State?* analysed the weaknesses in orthodox Marxist theory and mainstream Left alternative economic programmes (especially those advocated by Labour and Socialist parties in Western Europe), *The Post-Industrial Utopians* subjects the non-Marxist radical and alternative theories to a critical analysis. If the mainstream Left fails to listen to the eco-feminist and eco-pacifist critiques of existing societies, it will be condemning itself to a future of political conservatism and marginalization. But without the political economic strength and experiences of the labour movement, the Green and alternative movements are equally doomed to snapping at the heels of those conservative political forces which threaten the future of the whole planet.

With all the talk about post-industrial society – whether in the form of Rightwing restructuring and futurology or non-Marxist alternatives to the theoretical bankruptcy and sclerosis of parliamentary Left parties – it is regrettable that so many on the Left prefer to dwell in the past rather than face up to the present and the immediate future. For too long Labour, Socialist and Communist parties (with some minor exceptions) have attacked, disregarded or at best given token lip-service to environmentalists and feminists, while continuing the old conservative practices. Disasters such as Chernobyl have momentarily shaken even these ossified parties and unions into concerned reflection. But unless there is a serious attempt to develop genuinely eco-socialist policies and break down the ignorance and hostility between the traditional Left and new social movements, the old and new Right will continue to set the pace and determine the agenda and framework of public discourse. There is nothing more myopic ('pragmatic') than a Labour or Socialist party on the verge of electoral victory or trying to get re-elected. During these periods, the whole labour movement is silenced into 'electoral solidarity' or mobilized into open hostility to 'ultra-Left' and Green criticisms. The temporary 'electoral solidarity' is soon replaced by open intra-party factional divisions between Left and Right, while the possibility of creating new alliances with alternative social movements is once more overlooked or postponed until the next eco-social crisis.

Over the last century, the socialist movement has theorized over and struggled with the problem of how to develop class consciousness in the majority of workers. The problems faced by radicals are even more difficult today. Not only is there the perennial problem of how to mobilize the working class into anti-capitalist action, but there is also the need to make Left parties and unions conscious of the extremely limited and often quite conservative nature of their programmes and practices. Little wonder that many members of the Green and others alternative movements regard the traditional Left as part of the problem rather than part of the solution. Are we destined to see continued hostility between the traditional Left Red and the new alternative Green forces, or is there a third way? There is first a need to take extremely seriously the ideas and practices of both groupings. It is hoped that this book will be read and discussed by both Red and Green activists as well as by all those interested in the possible futures confronting us all.

I would like to thank the following people for their invaluable help in writing this book. First, special thanks to Alan Roberts who laboured hard and long to improve the text. Peter Beilharz, Richard Tanter, John Wiseman and Julian Triado read all or parts of the text and made important suggestions and critical comments. I would also like to thank Tony Giddens for his help and encouragement and Polity Press and Basil Blackwell (especially Anna Oxbury) for all their assistance in producing the book. Special thanks to Lori Graham and Gabby Moretti who laboured hard on the word processor. Finally, I would like to thank my mother Tania who once again provided the vital support without which this work could not have been written.

Boris Frankel
June 1986

The very prevalence of these futurist images that now rain upon us from television, bookstalls and the press induces us to take them seriously. They represent capital's utopia, its promised post-industrial land: a futuristic mirage so tantalizingly discernible to those now thirsting in the economic desert. One can readily see the ideological role of this planned, post-industrial society, in so far as it represents a dangerous disguise which permits a spurious escape from the anxieties surrounding the decisions and happenings of the present. By offering a potential exit from the ills of the present, electronic futurism floods in to fill an ideological vacuum. More than this, however, it is modelled upon, and becomes a caricature of, the image of a socialist society.

Frank Webster and Kevin Robins,
'Information Technology: Futurism,
Corporations and the State' *The Socialist Register 1981*

But I believe that even Marx was still too tied to the notion of a continuum of progress, that even his idea of socialism may not represent, or no longer represent, the determinate negation of capitalism it was supposed to. That is, today the notion of the end of utopia implies the necessity of at least discussing a new definition of socialism. The discussion would be based on the question of whether decisive elements of the Marxian concept of socialism do not belong to a now obsolete stage in the development of the forces of production.

Herbert Marcuse, 'The End of Utopia',
*Ramparts*, April 1970

# Introduction

It is tempting to draw parallels between the first few decades of the nineteenth century, and the 20 years we have just lived through. Imagine what they were like, those first years of industrial capitalist development. Whether the growth of new technology and new social relations instilled exhilaration, dismay or anxiety, it was still possible to approve the works of Saint-Simon, Fourier or Owen. But if, by the late 1840s, the work of Marx and Engels was accepted as showing that the new industrial society could not be transformed in the manner advocated by these utopian socialists, it was then necessary to study much more deeply the way the present had developed from the past, in order to estimate what future was possible, and how it could come about.

Since the 1960s there has been both a revival of, and reaction against, utopian thought. It has become somewhat of a cliché to say that we are living through the dawn of an new epoch. The flow of writings on the nature of the new phase of history has been unceasing. Krishan Kumar, one of the better surveyors of this recent literature, notes:

> The diversity of names for the new society similarly indicates both variety and convergence: variety in the bases from which the changes are viewed, as well as in the singling out of the principal forces promoting the change; convergence of the idea that the industrial societies are entering on a new phase of their evolution, marking a transition as momentous as that which a hundred years ago took European societies from an

agrarian to an industrial social order. Thus Amitai Etzioni speaks of 'the post-modern era', George Lichtheim of 'the post-bourgeois society', Herman Kahn of 'post-economic society', Murray Bookchin of 'the post-scarcity society', Kenneth Boulding of 'post-civilized society', Daniel Bell simply of 'the post-industrial society'. Others, putting the point more positively have spoken of 'the knowledge society' (Peter Drucker), 'the personal service society' (Paul Halmos), 'the service class society' (Ralf Dahrendorf), and 'the technetronic era' (Zbigniew Brzezinski). Taken as a whole, these labels tell us what it is in the past that has now been or is being suspended – e.g. scarcity, the bourgeois order, the predominance of the economic motive; and also what can be expected to be the main principle of the future society – e.g. knowledge, personal services, the electronic technology of computers and telecommunications.[1]

Whether we are moving into a post-industrial society is highly debatable. Scarcity, along with the predominance of the economic motive, profit maximization and the bourgeoisie, still hold sway. However, I will not be devoting much space to a demonstration that Rightwing analysts such as Kahn, Bell et al. – despite their classless labels such as 'technetronic era' and 'the knowledge society' – are in fact ideological defenders of the dominant corporate order; this critique has been successfully carried out by others.[2] Nor am I particularly interested in futurology as science or science fiction. Rather, I want to focus on the various schools of post-industrial thought which have emerged in recent decades as harbingers of potentially liberating social relations and institutions. Given the great variety of post-industrial theorists – from Right to Left – it is a mistake simply to dismiss these analysts as ideologists, utopians or romantics. It is not hard to establish that this literature promotes a great deal of bourgeois ideology and utopianism. But this is no reason for us to blind ourselves to the significant developments in new technology, with their accompanying occupational changes and general shifts in the whole gamut of socio-political relations. From a socialist perspective, the choice is either to interpret these new developments as relatively superficial, leaving unaltered the historical relations between labour and capital, or to attempt to explain and anticipate how these new developments will affect capitalist societies. Despite the incompatible ideological perspectives that clash within post-industrial theory, there has been significant cross-fertilization of themes and issues. I would therefore like to survey briefly the more important exponents of post-industrial theory, liberal and radical environmentalism and neo-Marxist thought, called here 'the post-industrial utopians'. Following this, I will discuss the relevance of utopian thought and outline why I have focused on particular problems and broader themes.

## RIGHTWING RESPONSES TO INDUSTRIAL CLASS CONFLICT

If we overlook the historical context which gave rise to Rightwing post-industrial literature, our understanding of it will be defective, sanitized and a-historical. Most of the leading American post-industrial theorists developed their arguments against a background in which Cold War polemics were followed by the tumultuous upheavals of the civil rights, counter-culture and anti-war movements of the 1960s and early 1970s. Later works were written in the spirit of containment and the readjustment of Carter and Trilateralism or, later still, in the more recent climate of aggressive New Right monetarism, Moral Majority puritanism and super-patriotism. The 'end of ideology', proclaimed in the 1950s,[3] was succeeded by the 'cultural contradictions of capitalism',[4] as widespread dissent and conflict shook American post-war society. The old pre-1960s pluralist certainties about the growing irrelevance of class conflict soon gave way to the 'crisis of democracy' and the 'democratic distemper',[5] as capitalist classes battled to 'lower the political temperature' and leave politics in the safe hands of 'technetronic era' managers.

By the 1980s, post-industrial writing was simultaneously aggressively optimistic – 'the coming boom' and 'the resourceful earth' – and yet suffering from an inferiority complex vis-à-vis the Japanese.[6] On the one hand, there was a need to answer a new generation of anti-war and pro-environmental activists; on the other, there was widespread concern among political and business groups that the USA was losing the post-industrial race against Japan. The old 'Commie' menace of the 1950s had to be refought in the New Cold War with the two-edged sword of high technology – 'Star Wars'; the 'Commies' might still be the leading public enemy, but the other edge would serve to maintain American dominance over the Japanese and Europeans.

Putting aside the cruder Rightwing partisans of post-industrialism (like Herman Kahn), it is important to understand why people such as Daniel Bell look forward to the 'coming of post-industrial society'. If Bell could agree with Marxists that industrial society has been characterized by the rule of industrialists and the conflict between labour and capital, what could answer them more crushingly, than a prognosis that the proletariat is disappearing! Even better, how could one more easily expunge nagging doubts – perhaps even guilt – over defending a capitalist system, than by prophesying the replacement of this very capitalist class by the new knowledge-based elites. In a society based on consensus and the rational application of advanced technical knowledge, class conflict falls into the historical dustbin, and post-industrial theorists can champion 'participation' and 'reason' without revolution, while decision-making is left in the safe hands of technocratic managers.

As the theorist *par excellence* of post-industrial society, Daniel Bell displays an erudite knowledge of conventional and radical social theory. Unlike aggressive Rightwingers such as Herman Kahn, Bell is sensitive to the deep-seated contradictions of existing societies. According to Bell, 'three realms – the economy, the polity, and the culture – are ruled by contrary axial principles: for the economy, efficiency; for the polity, equality; and for the culture, self-realization (or self-gratification). The resulting disjunctions have framed the tensions and social conflicts of Western society in the past 150 years.'[7] These are themes which have been also taken up by the Left (for example, Habermas on modernity)[8] and the

Moral Majority (pro-family, anti-feminist), and will be discussed in a later chapter.

At the end of *The Coming of Post-Industrial Society*, Bell notes that:

> For most of human history, *reality was nature,* and in poetry and imagination men sought to relate the self to the natural world. Then *reality became technics*, tools and things made by men[sic] . . . Now *reality is primarily the social world* – neither nature or things . . . Inevitably, a post-industrial society gives rise to a new Utopianism, both engineering and psychedelic. Men[sic] can be remade or released, their behaviour conditioned or their consciousness altered. The constraints of the past vanish with the end of nature and things.[9]

While Bell is generally optimistic, such brief glimpses of unconstrained technological nightmares are downright threatening to activists in the Green and Red alternative environmental and socialist feminist movements. At least Bell is aware that purely technocratic solutions to contemporary economic problems can clash sharply with the cultural and political needs of people no longer prepared to suffer the repression and domination which characterized pre-industrial and, in Bell's terms, 'industrial society'.

Although Bell's work has been very influential, he is by no means the dominant guru of Rightwing post-industrial theory. Given the changing socio-political environment since the 1950s, it is revealing to consider how the old and New Right respond to the challenge of 'post-industrialism'. While there is a common belief in the virtues of free enterprise and high technology, the earlier emphasis on technocratic management has been modified to make room for current demands like deregulation of the capitalist market.[10] Similarly, the earlier liberalism of the 1960s has given way to anti-welfare, pro-militarist and anti-egalitarian images of post-industrial society. On the other hand, one section of the New Right has attempted to appropriate the language and values of the alternative technology and small-is-beautiful movements. For example, Peter Shack, a Rightwing

Australian politician, has sung the praises of post-industrial society in a 'dry' key:

> The post-industrial future is essentially a rejection of bigness, centralization, and bureaucracy. Its motto is 'small is beautiful'. It is the antithesis of 'bureaucratic civilization'. On the contrary, it is anarchistic and communistic in the real sense. It is not socialistic in the sense of 'big government': it is 'small government' (where the State has withered away). Nor is it capitalistic in the sense of a predominance of large-scale capitalist enterprise and control. It is small-scale, co-operative and self-employment [sic] in which each worker (or a local community) owns (or shares in owning) the means of production. Value emphasis in the post-industrial society moves to the search for liberty, individualism, truth, beauty, identity and goodness – in the optimistic vision because material needs have become easy to meet. It is a society which is compassionate, resourceful and free . . . This is what 'dry' economics is on about! This is what 'wet' liberal thinking on social issues wishes to achieve![11]

Like Nozick and other Rightwing anarchists,[12] Shack has taken over the vocabulary of the Left (for example, the withering away of the state), so that New Right symbolism can provide a mask for the reality of increasing poverty, corporate gigantism (in the form of takeover mania), and the growth in authoritarianism. The twin strands of technocratic management and 'small government' thus constitute uneasy and contradictory responses (on the part of New Right and Old Right theorists) to contemporary socio-economic crises.

## SMALL-IS-BEAUTIFUL AND ATARI DEMOCRATS

The fact that various members of the New Right have borrowed the language of small-is-beautiful and alternative technology movements, should not blind us to clear differences between the latter and the New Right. The influence of writers and activists such as Schumacher,[13] Illich,[14] Galtung,[15] and Nader is considerable.[16] In the past 20 years there has been a significant growth in movements, parties, journals and individual campaigns focusing on humane alternatives to the ugly reality of impersonal bureaucracies, exploitation of Third World peoples, the arms race, dangerous new technology, unsafe products, irrational health, education and transport systems, economic growth which destroys the environment, and agribusiness profits in a world of mass starvation.

This diverse group includes individuals who espouse conventional liberal or centre politics, as well as many others who have a close affinity with radicals on various issues. 'Atari Democrat' is a label applied to those politicians and theorists who combine technocratic solutions with the rhetoric of small-is-beautiful. They are generally strong admirers and promoters of high tech such as Senator Gary Hart in the USA, David Owen in the UK, Simon Nora and Alain Minc in France,[17] or many of the technocrats who work for MITI, the OECD and the EEC. Their supporters are often 'Yuppies', tertiary-educated professionals or the owners of small businesses. They are sensitive to many of the critiques of authoritarian education, conventional medicine, high cholesterol diets, and exploitative North–South relations. In their self-image and their public relations projections, they often distinguish themselves from traditional big business and big labour; they are the 'democratic vanguard' of the new information society. Rejecting the aggressive campaigns of the Moral Majority or the confrontationism of Thatcherism and Reaganism, the 'Atari Democrats' present the 'human face' of new technology, and stress the need for educated citizen initiatives, tolerance, consensus and personal awareness – while they leave largely unchallenged most of the existing practices of the corporate sector.

In contrast, those groups and individuals who take small-is-beautiful almost religiously, are often committed activists against the worst aspects of capitalist societies. Distinguishing themselves from the traditional Marxist Left, many alternative technology environmentalists, believers in small-is-beautiful, pacifists, Third World 'alternative development' activists, Friends of the Earth and others, reject the conservative organizational methods and personal

consumption of the 'Atari Democrats' and the labour movement – just as much as they reject the commodity fetishism of
capitalist consumerism. Committed Christians are especially
evident in promoting anti-war campaigns, co-operatives such
as Mondragon, alternatives to brutal regimes in the Third
World, 'convivial tools' and new supranational relations in
the form of 'World Order' models,[18] 'new internationalism',[19] and non-alienated, small-scale relations.
Despite their major differences with the orthodox Left, there
has been a significant cross-fertilization of ideas as many
have combined Western Marxist critiques with the values of
Gandhi, Nyerere, liberation theologists, Schumacher and
Illich. Their image of post-industrial society has a great
affinity with the programmes of the various Green
movements.

## LEFT SOURCES OF POST-INDUSTRIALISM

The term 'post-industrial' was first coined by Authur Penty,
an English Guild Socialist.[20] Penty, a follower of William
Morris and John Ruskin, believed in a decentralized, small
artisan or craft-based society. It is interesting to note that
Rudolf Bahro, in the 1980s, also calls for a post-industrial
socialism on similar lines. The difference is that Penty
rejected the new industrialism, while Bahro, Peter Fuller and
other admirers of craft socialism wish to go forward beyond
capitalism, rather than backwards.[21] But both schools, in
their admiration for a post-industrial socialism which is
essentially rural based, or at least free of large conurbations,
break with the radical tradition of post-scarcity socialism
articulated by Marcuse, Bookchin and many others in the
1960s.[22] The latter writers' belief in abundant material
resources, a new science to replace technical rationality, and
the liberation of humanity from surplus repression and
surplus labour, differ sharply from Bahro's radical fundamentalist 'industrial disarmament'. But the anarchist tradition, Bloch, the Frankfurt School, Reichs' views and other
radical streams helped lay the foundations of contemporary
post-industrial socialist thought in reviving utopian socialist

ideas and in their radical rejection of existing capitalist and Communist societies.

While there were numerous radical critiques of Bell and other Rightwing post-industrial theorists, the notion of post-industrial society was beginning to be taken seriously by a small number of Left theorists. At the beginning of the 1970s, Alain Touraine published *The Post-Industrial Society*,[23] in which he warned of the division between the humanists and technocrats in the new 'knowledge class' of the 'programmed society'. Writing in the wake of the 1960s student revolt, Touraine, like other Left analysts of that period, tended to overestimate the importance of universities. Apart from Touraine there were other individuals and groups interested in post-industrial society and futurology. Radovan Richta headed a group of over 40 researchers at the Institute of Philosophy in Prague during the 1960s. Their report, *Civilization at the Cross-Roads*, was a strange mixture of humanist Marxism, technocratic planning and post-industrial futurology.[24] Johan Galtung and Robert Jungk also flirted with futurology as they attempted to integrate peace research with analyses of the state of the world in the year 2000.[25]

Not all the Left looked forward to the post-industrial society as an age of post-scarcity and tranquility. Christopher Lasch, in his earlier radical phase, argued that post-industrial society would be inherently unstable.[26] New classes would emerge, and it would see the decay of the industrial city, increased waste consumption and global military states of emergency. Like Touraine, Lasch also over-emphasized the importance of the university and incorrectly forecast (in 1971) that poverty would no longer be a general and pervasive condition.[27] The interest in future forms of social welfare could also be seen in the post-industrial analyses of Larry Hirschhorn. In several monographs written for the Institute of Urban and Regional Development at Berkeley, Hirschhorn focused on the social crisis in the service sector.[28] According to Hirschhorn, 'the post-industrial revolution is reflected in a social crisis of work and consequent crisis of daily life.'[29] In the areas of education, health, social welfare and other services, standards were being subjected to profound questioning and their legitimacy undermined. Accordingly, the post-Keynesian period would be characterized by an anarchy of *ad hoc* solutions and crisis managment. Interpreting Bell in a radical perspective, Hirschhorn traced the historical changes in the capitalist labour process and the corresponding developments in social services. As the production of goods is replaced by the production of services, material reality becomes less visible to workers engaged in these services as well as to their clients.[30] The classical adjustment of men and women to job and family through the social service nexus has been undermined by a new turn in social development itself. Administration, management and manipulation are replacing production as the determinants of social structure. But the new subjectivity emerges alongside yet against the new manipulation; herein is born the social service crisis. However, this crisis cannot be solved within the social service institutions themselves.[31]

Hirschhorn and others at the stillborn Center For Post-Industrial Studies at Berkeley were also involved with the Kapitalistate Group (James O'Connor, Erik Wright et al.) and attended Claus Offe's seminar in 1974.[32] The emphases on social services and new forms of production were related to other concerns such as the 'fiscal crisis of the state' and the crisis of crisis management. Hirschhorn's analysis is dated by its over-emphasis on 1960s dissent and the phenomenon of drop-outs. Yet it is also visionary, in that his crisis of social services anticipated later developments which are still to be fully played out in leading OECD countries.

By the late 1970s, the aftermath of the so-called 'crisis of Marxism' included two new developments. At a theoretical level, post-Marxist and anti-Marxist theorists such as Baudrillard,[33] and Lyotard,[34] engaged in debate with Marxists over the nature of modernism, post-modernism and 'post-industrial culture'. In recent years this debate on modernity – involving such authors as Habermas, Jameson, Rorty, Davis, Berman,[35] etc. – has in many ways become an explicit debate over the nature of culture and social production in the emerging 'post-industrial' society. The dispute over aesthetics and epistemology is paralleled by the debate over the working class and the role of social movements, initiated by Gorz, Touraine,[36] Bahro and others. If the traditional labour movement and its parties were failing to address the crucial issues of the new period – issues troubling feminists, environmentalists and peace activists – could the proletariat still be cast as the revolutionary subject of history? How could the Left respond to the resurgent New Right and the deep-seated malaise in leading capitalist economies? Were the European social democratic and Communist parties locked into a high technology race with Japan and the USA regardless of massive unemployment and stagnant social welfare budgets? These and other major questions about the reorganization of social agendas in the 1980s marked a distinct break with both the earlier forms of utopian socialism and the pragmatism of Eurocommunism and Eurosocialism.

At the political level, the emergence of the various Green and ecological parties gave added impetus to the growth of post-industrial socialist theory. Despite the substantial differences between the various strands of the Green movement – from former New Leftists to former Christian Democrats – there is no doubt that the electoral successes of the Green movement in West Germany, plus the mobilization of the peace movement, have stimulated new interest in utopian strategies seeking alternatives to existing forms of industrialism.[37] In many ways, the earlier works of Illich, Marcuse, Schumacher, etc., have been revived in conjunction with feminism, alternative food production theories, and a profound radical commitment to environmental conservation and grass roots democracy. Meanwhile, in France, the UK, North America, Japan, Australia and other OECD countries, the structural bias of electoral systems, the dominance of existing Left parties, or threats to the very existence of the Left, have meant that the Green movements have had far less impact there than in West Germany. The moves to the right of the French, Italian, Spanish and Japanese Socialist parties and the Australian and British Labour parties, have furrowed out an ever-increasing gap in these countries between Red and Green movements and the parties which attract a large number of working-class voters.

## WHO ARE THE POST-INDUSTRIAL UTOPIANS?

In this book, I focus particularly on those writers and movements who, while not necessarily socialists, are supporters of greater equality, tolerance, a peaceful environment and an end to mass waste and irrational social production and distribution. As I have indicated in my survey of Right and Left sources of post-industrial theory, there has been a significant cross-fertilization of ideas and practices. The writers upon whom I concentrate are, in many respects, representative of the various currents of left of centre radical theory. These writers express, to a greater or lesser extent, most of the popular notions of the past 20 years concerning small-scale, decentralized democratic alternative lifestyles, new technology, the environment, North–South relations, peace, and images of new cultural and domestic social relations. The utopian elements in their writings do not necessarily stem from their being radical. In fact, the less radical theorists like Barry Jones and Toffler are just as utopian as the more radical figures such as Bahro and Gorz. I will explain my attitude to utopian writers shortly. For the moment, it is enough to state my belief that many on the Left need to give much more attention to the issues these utopians treat.

In positing questions which everyone needs to consider – for example, what are the desirable forms of production, environment policy, gender relations, political institutions and welfare services – the post-industrial utopians express views which appear to win greater popular attention than traditional Marxist themes. Of course, it would be ludicrous to deny that most of these concerns have also been expressed in many contemporary Marxist writings. But it has become increasingly clear over the past 20 years that a new generation of socially aware citizens see Marxism as far less relevant to their concerns than the issues and theories advanced by various social movements. Moreover, it is currently fashionable to argue that class conflict is irrelevant, that central planning can only be authoritarian, that market socialism or other market mechanisms are necessary, and that revolution is obsolete. But even if we assumed universal acceptance of the social changes proposed by the post-industrial theorists (in existing capitalist and Communist countries), this would still not guarantee that these imaginative proposals were necessarily viable.

Whether the various economic, political and cultural alternatives advocated by our post-industrial utopians are reformist or revolutionary, the urgent need is to discuss seriously their *feasibility*. While it is true that there is less interest in contemplating or experimenting with radical alternatives than in the late 1960s, it is also true that with deeper experience rigorous examination of them has tended to replace their unreflective acceptance. It is increasingly recognized that moral exhortation is just not enough, if radicals cannot answer the serious questions as to feasibility, organization and finance.

But even if we rightly criticize the utopians for their failure to demonstrate the feasibility of their ideas in the areas of their concern, this would be no excuse for ignoring the need for radical changes. This is especially true of those critiques which base themselves upon economic criteria drawn essentially from the need to maintain the operation of existing capitalist societies. Although I discuss aspects of the works of Galtung, Sale, Stonier, Gershuny and other writers,[38] I have decided to concentrate on the views of Rudolf Bahro, Andre Gorz, Barry Jones and Alvin Toffler. A brief biographical note on each of these theorists may help to explain my choice of post-industrial utopians.

## Rudolf Bahro

Born in Germany during the Third Reich, Bahro grew up in East Germany and became widely known after his imprisonment by East German authorities for dissident activities. His book, *The Alternative*,[39] was a Marxist critique of 'actually existing socialism' and was hailed by many Western Leftists in the late 1970s. Released from jail in 1979 (after much international protest), Bahro moved to West Germany where he became closely associated with the fundamentalist wing of the Green Party. In the last ten years he has moved from Marxism to radical Green fundamentalism, mixed with quasi-religious alternative forms of consciousness.

### André Gorz

Born in Austria in 1924, Gorz was closely associated with Sartre and others on *Les Temps modernes* in the French political culture of pre-1968. His analysis *Strategy for Labor* (1964) became very influential over the next ten years.[40] Gorz was also well known for his critique of technical rationality, his writings on ecology and his many articles as a journalist for *Le Nouvel observateur*. He is one of the few Leftists to survive the pre-1968 and post-1968 generations of intellectual fashion in France. With the publication of *Farewell to the Working Class* (1980), Gorz established himself as one of the leading voices of post-Marxist, post-industrial socialism. If Bahro embodies many of the radical environmentalist, counter-cultural influences of the past 20 years, Gorz combines the interests of radical syndicalism, Western Marxism and French post-1981 anti-Marxism or post-Marxism.

### Barry Jones

A long-time member of the Labor Party and a well-known figure in Australia, Jones (born in 1932) is a strong campaigner for social welfare reform, penal reform and educational advancement. He has been an enthusiastic supporter of the Australian film industry, and is an avid digestor of nearly every type of reading material available. As Minister for Science in the Hawke government after 1983, Jones has been the main publicist for a post-industrial society through his writings such as *Sleepers, Wake!* (1982) and his many speeches and activities. In setting up the Commission for the Future, Jones has translated his interests in new technology into an agency which will help educate and prepare the Australian public for the 'coming post-industrial society'. Well known for his quiz king victories on television and his theoretical eclecticism, Jones represents a combination of 'Atari Democrat' and traditional Fabian values mixed with a dash of radical theory.

### Alvin Toffler

Like Jones, Alvin Toffler is a well-known eclectic whose inspirational sources run from Gramsci to Milton Friedman.

An ex-Marxist, Toffler still shows the influence of his old teacher – managerialist James Burnham – despite his familiarity with more recent writings of Western Marxists. Toffler has been closely associated with giant corporations (for example, *The Adaptive Corporation* was a report written for AT & T in 1972)[41] and was associate editor of *Fortune*. Best known for *Future Shock* (1970), Toffler represents the centre Right to centre Left perspectives. His work *The Third Wave* (1980) is both a continuation of earlier themes and a more radical departure on Toffler's part. This latter work has not prevented Toffler from being invited to the White House by Reagan or fêted by governments in China and elsewhere. In publishing a book of interviews with Toffler (*Previews and Premises*)[42] the Leftwing publishing house South End Press felt (correctly) that, despite Toffler's Rightwing background and strong corporate and government connections, his analysis in *The Third Wave* would be of importance to Leftwing readers. With Gorz and other members of the Left singing the praises of *The Third Wave*, it is clear that the cross-fertilization of Right and Left post-industrial views is well exemplified by Toffler's work.

The writings of Bahro, Gorz, Jones and Toffler give one ready access to a range of views – from liberalism through to social democracy, Marxism and radical environmentalism – which runs the gamut of contemporary post-industrial utopianism. Despite the major differences between, for example, Bahro and Toffler, all four post-industrial theorists are implicitly advocating, at the very least, new social relations which are anti-capitalist. And while it is true that Toffler and Jones, alongside Stonier, Sale and others, are also theorizing and rationalizing post-industrial modifications to private enterprise societies, there is a strong undercurrent in their writings which points to the emergence of a post-capitalist social formation. One can also justify including the works of Jones and Toffler on the grounds that each shares with Bahro and Gorz a strong desire to create a much more egalitarian, democratic and enlightened world – regardless of their current political affiliations and practices. It is precisely the glaring contradictions between what Toffler

and Jones value, and their support for policies and governments that work against achieving these values, which I will
be discussing in later chapters. As for Bahro and Gorz, they
raise questions and discuss issues which Marxists cannot afford
to ignore. Coming from a Marxist background, Bahro and
Gorz share with Jones and Toffler a recognition that many of
the values and concepts once championed by the labour
movement have proved to be less relevant in recent years.
Reckoning as they do with modern phenomena like mass
unemployment, increasing automation and environmental
destruction, their image of a post industrial society is based
upon revolutionizing work patterns and dominant forms of
consumption. The key question is: Are their analyses and
political strategies any better than the traditional goals and
strategies pursued by the orthodox Left?

## CRITICIZING AND DEFENDING UTOPIAN THOUGHT

It is no accident that I have called our theorists post-industrial
utopians. Gorz has entitled his vision of a new society: 'Utopia
for a Possible Dual Society'.[43] Bahro says of himself: 'From
scientific socialism I have returned to utopian socialism, and
politically I have moved from a class-dimensional to a populist
orientation.[44] Barry Jones would probably agree with Toffler
in disclaiming that he was a utopian,[45] even though Toffler is
very sympathetic to the Utopian Socialists and acknowledges
that his notions of post-industrial life may be seen to be
utopian.[46] Actually, Toffler states that the Third Wave society
is no 'anti-utopia': We glimpse here instead the emergence of
what might be called 'practopia' – neither the best nor the
worst of all possible worlds, but one that is both practical and
preferable to the one we had. Unlike a utopia, a practopia is
not free of disease, political nastiness, and bad manners.
Unlike most utopias, it is not static or frozen in unreal perfec-
tion. Nor is it reversionary, modelling itself on some imagined
ideal of the past . . . In short, a practopia offers a positive,
even a revolutionary alternative, yet lies within the range of
the realistically attainable.'[47]

Much has been written on utopian thought and the relevance of utopia. I do not propose to cover this area once again. Instead, I would like to discuss briefly some of the Left attitudes to utopian thought, and also indicate my own attitude to the term 'utopian'. Alain Touraine has written: 'Utopian thought is indispensable as a stage in the process of social and cultural change.'[48] Oscar Wilde was even more adamant when he pronounced: 'A Map of the World that does not include Utopia is not worth even glancing at.'[49] In proclaiming that Fourier was more radical than Marx, Herbert Marcuse (in 1970) reasserted the importance of utopian socialist thought to contemporary activists for social change.[50] According to Marcuse, utopias could be impossible because the objective and subjective historical conditions were immature. They could also be considered unfeasible because they contradicted certain physical and biological laws, for example, the desire for eternal youth. 'I believe', Marcuse says, 'that we can now speak of utopia only in this latter sense, namely when a project for social change contradicts real laws of nature. Only such a project is utopian in the strict sense, that is, beyond history . . .'[51]

I referred earlier to the similarity between the beginning of industrial societies and the last 20 years. An ambivalence towards utopian theorists is clearly evident in Marx and Engels's writings. In the *Communist Manifesto* they are scathing in their criticisms of the utopian socialists. This hostility to utopianism is well expressed by the young Lukács writing before 1919. According to Lukács: 'Marxist social theory put an end to the unbridgeable dualistic separation of social reality and human objectives which had made the previous theories of the great Utopians (Fourier, Owen) so hopelessly unattainable. Every Utopian scheme, however penetrating a critique of the given social situation it may have offered, however desirable it may have appeared as an ideal to be attained, has failed to determine the mode and the means necessary for its realization and has therefore come to nothing. Utopia has always remained a pious wish, the acceptance or rejection of which necessarily remained a voluntary decision on the part of each individual human being.'[52] (For a more contemporary example of this Marxist tradition, it is worth recalling Herb Gintis's penetrating critique of Ivan Illich's *Deschooling Society*.)[53]

But as they grew older, Marx and Engels were more appreciative and defensive of the Utopian Socialists. Engels wrote that the 'utopians could be nothing else at a time when capitalist production was as yet so little developed. They necessarily had to construct the outlines of a new society out of their own heads, because within the old society the elements of the new were not as yet generally apparent.'[54] Marcuse, Bahro and Gorz – though not Lukács – would have gained comfort from Engels's 1870 defence of utopianism: 'German theoretical Socialism will never forget that it stands on the shoulders of Saint-Simon, Fourier and Owen, three men who despite their fantasies and utopianism are to be reckoned among the most significant minds of all times, for they anticipated with genius countless matters whose accuracy we now demonstrate scientifically.'[55]

In citing the ambivalent attitudes of Marxists to utopian thought, I wish to declare my own ambivalence. Throughout this book I will use the concept 'post-industrial utopian' in a highly critical manner. For I agree with Lukács that no matter how desirable the post-industrial ideas may be, they remain pious wishes if not linked to concrete plans of action and organization. On the other hand, I am highly sympathetic to the utopian tradition as a vibrant source of inspiration, a rejection of the pedestrian and the resigned acceptance of irrationality and the impoverishment – in its broadest sense –of everyday life. Compared with the mainstream Left parties of today, many radical utopian ideas positively shine and challenge; moreover, many ideas which a mere ten years ago were regarded approvingly, are now dismissed by Left parties as 'ultra-Left' and 'utopian' as these parties move to the Right in response to the resurgence of New Right political forces and economic crisis tendencies. It is therefore necessary to remain within the radical utopian tradition, while at the same time subjecting these same utopian ideas to rigorous scrutiny and evaluation.

## THEMES TO BE DISCUSSED

It is important to make clear that this book is not essentially an exposition of post-industrial theory. While I devote considerable space to outlining particular views of the post-industrial utopians, there is no attempt to cover thoroughly the entire works of any specific thinker, for example, those of Gorz or Toffler. Rather, the book is organized around themes, based on the areas and issues of importance to all who are interested in social change. As the post-industrial utopians are representative of diverse strands of thought, this book aims to analyse the feasibility and desirability of various alternative socio-economic objectives. In this sense it is not an exercise in the history of ideas, nor a detailed historical case study of the transition to post-industrialism.

I begin my analysis with a discussion of the alternative economies proposed by the post-industrial theorists. How do these theorists see the new forms of production and exchange? What are the particular emphases that they give to co-operatives, informal work processes, decentralized production, do-it-yourself production and so forth? Are the analyses of existing capitalist societies adequately related to the new sources of post-industrial economies? What importance do the post-industrial theorists attach to planning, stateless communes or mixtures of local, national and supra-natural organization and exchange? Are markets to remain decisive or be superseded? Most importantly, what are the implications of greater integration or greater self-sufficiency?

Central to the problem of an alternative post-industrial economy is the whole issue of alternative welfare services. Most advocates of social change are rightly critical of existing bureaucratic welfare states. However, there is no agreement on whether they should be replaced by a stateless form of self-help services, a decentralized welfare system or something else again. Many radicals would like a situation where poverty and neglect were eliminated and yet the individual had maximum choice as to whether she or he worked or was cared for free of income and other worries. The concept of a guaranteed minimum income is regularly put forward as an alternative to existing welfare schemes. In chapter 2, I discuss the various guaranteed income schemes put forward by the post-industrial utopians. I also query the degree of commitment these theorists show to feminist critiques of existing economic and welfare practices, and enquire whether women would benefit from living in 'basic communes' or under market-socialist conditions. If the neglect of women, the aged, children and the poor (most of whom are women) is a hallmark of existing societies, then a post-industrial socialism deserves this name only if it adequately confronts the issues which many on the traditional Left have ignored.

After discussing alternatives to welfare states, I proceed to analyse the other burning issues of disarmament and North–South relations. Can there be a post-industrial society cleansed of the major military-industrial complexes? What positions do people like Gorz, Jones and Toffler hold on nuclear weapons? Is Bahro able to reconcile his advocacy of nuclear disarmament with his goal of industrial disarmament? Is an alternative defence system technologically feasible, given the implementation of small-is-beautiful, decentralization and appropriate technology? Are the post-industrial theorists preoccupied with the North to the neglect of countries in the Third World? Or can post-industrial societies be realistically envisaged, only with a resolution of the crises in the South, and a dismantling of the military machines?

After examining the feasibility of decentralized, co-operative, non-bureaucratic and non-aggressive economic, social welfare and defence alternatives, the next task is to analyse the nature of alternative cultural and political relations proposed by the post-industrial utopians. If new technology gives rise to greater numbers of people working at home, what are the implications for family structures, gender roles and so forth? If existing political, religious, educational and media institutions are overtly shaped by centralized and hierarchial social structures, what kind of post-industrial public and private relations can promote greater democracy, tolerance and equity? Can life be organized at local and global levels without the existence of mediating institutions at the national level? Is it possible to have universal values in education, law, etc., without central state institutions, or will a new wave of parochialism and refeudalization follow when political and cultural institutions are decentralized? Can socialist pluralism and grass-roots democracy survive without state planning, national sovereignty and cultural institutions which reproduce non-parochial values?

Finally the social and political strategies suggested by our theorists must be examined, quite apart from how plausible or desirable their various goals may be. How valid are their various attacks upon, and criticisms of class analysis and labour movement strategy? Are Green movements the model of post-industrial politics in contrast to Leninist vanguard parties? Or are social movements which reject state power and participation in electoral politics doomed to ineffectiveness? If the prevailing historical economic, political and military trends are in the direction of greater global and regional integration, how can decentralization and democratic autonomy triumph without semi-autarkic political-economic objectives? These and other pertinent questions will be discussed, in an attempt to bring together many of the issues which have troubled Left parties, alternative social movements and other radicals of all colours.

Self-management is not possible in communities of more than a few hundred people. But who is to control relations between the different self-managed communities? And who controls the *system of relations* between all the communities which make up a country? And the relations between these systems of relations? Either you reply 'no one', and thus abandon these relations to what are called 'market forces', which are actually relations of competing powers. Or you can try to civilize, to regulate these relations by public rules which maximize the sphere of autonomy. And in that case you need a legal system, and a state. There is no third way. Self-management is an aspiration whose effective sphere can be very wide, but it isn't a solution to everything. As an individual, I really don't want to be constantly bothered by all the problems of society, from international exchange to transport and communications systems, from monetary circulation to the police. I don't believe anyone should be forced to spend all their time worrying about such things.

André Gorz, *Paths to Paradise*

If I may pick an arbitrary figure, let us take an area fifty by a hundred kilometres wide. It must be possible to organize reproduction at this level: food, homes, schools, clothing, medicine, perhaps as much as ninety per cent of what we need. For another nine per cent we could deal on a national or provincial level, and for a further one per cent we would be dependent on a world market . . . I may have exaggerated in talking of a reduction from 100 to 1. Some countries may need external trade to the magnitude of, say, ten per cent. But, to carry this to its logical conclusion, it already makes economic sense to think of producing certain types of necessary goods at one particular point in the world, from which global distribution could then take place. What I want to underline is the principle of contraction and the dissolution of the world market as we know it. If we want to achieve equilibrium and stability, we may have to re-create the original structure of the world market, which was limited to a small quantity of surplus and luxury goods.

Rudolf Bahro, *From Red to Green*

# 1

# More Integration or More Autarky
## *The Incompatible Paths of Economic Restructuring*

In a biting critique of the New Left, Irving Kristol makes the perceptive observation that 'the identifying marks of the New Left are its refusal *to think economically* and its contempt for bourgeois society precisely because this is a society that does think economically'.[1] While there have been numerous Left critiques of existing bourgeois economic theories and policies, there have been very few comprehensive and coherent radical economic alternative programmes. The problem is quite complex. On the one hand, the failure of many radicals to explain how socialist societies would maximize equality and freedom, without repeating the lessons of existing Communist and capitalist societies, is directly linked to the widespread failure to think economically. On the other hand, too many people think economically, but in narrow productivist terms. Yet there has never any shortage of imaginative alternative ideas concerning the redistribution of wealth, power and privilege. Like earlier social reformers and revolutionaries, the authors discussed below also put forward many exciting and suggestive visions of an alternative future. But how viable are these alternatives? Will their alternative socio-economic structures actually promote and achieve the objectives of a decentralized, egalitarian, environmentally and culturally tolerant social order? These and other questions will be asked of the post-industrial theorists. Although I do not believe that one should separate conceptions of economic structures from vital problems such as social welfare, in this chapter I will concentrate on some of the key aspects of post-industrial economies as envisaged by our utopian theorists. Following an outline of the main characteristics of these future economies, I will then proceed to evaluate the strengths and weaknesses of these alternatives to contemporary deindustrializing, decaying and problem-ridden capitalist societies.

## MAIN CHARACTERISTICS OF POST-INDUSTRIAL ECONOMIES

On first impression, all the post-industrial theorists advocate an economy which is based on renewable energy resources, decentralized, small-scale enterprises, co-operatives, non-bureaucratic and diverse socio-economic institutions and cultural practices. On closer inspection, however, it becomes clear that there is fundamental disagreement between Toffler, for example, who believes in transnational post-industrial corporations, and Bahro who advocates a radical anti-capitalist and anti-industrial economy. In fact, there is little agreement between Bahro, Gorz, Jones, Toffler and others concerning the geographical or territorial scale of the post-industrial society (whether it will be based on local, national or supra-national levels). There is also no agreement on whether it will be based upon a mixture of market and plan, predominantly centrally planned, a non-market but monetarized economy, or a non-market, self-sufficient autarky. Furthermore, there is no agreement on whether post-industrial economies should have high growth rates or zero growth, how they will relate with pre-industrial and industrial economies in the Third World, or whether computerized 'electronic cottages' are compatible with socialist solidarity and feminist objectives. But this is to anticipate some of the major issues to be discussed in later chapters.

Alvin Toffler and Barry Jones construct their image of a post-industrial economy from an eclectic mixture of sources fused together by an anti-Marxist methodology. Rudolph Bahro and Andre Gorz rely on a number of non-Marxist sources, but approach these in a manner which still indicates the lasting influence of their Marxist heritage. Regardless of whether the post-industrial utopians have a Marxist or non-Marxist past, there is no clear indication that this background has resulted in predictable conclusions concerning their respective images of a post-industrial economy. But it does help to explain their analyses of existing industrial societies as well as their theories of how the transition to a post-industrial society will take place.

Whereas Marxists tend to divide societies into pre-capitalist and capitalist modes of production (or social formations which have a combination of both modes), Jones and Toffler are theoretically closer to Bell and other non-Left post-industrial analysts. This is evident in their subdivision of history into agricultural or land-based pre-industrial societies, secondary goods or industrial societies, and information-based or post-industrial societies. While there are significant differences between Bell, Kahn and Brzezinski on the one hand,[2] and Toffler and Jones on the other, they conceive a post-industrial society as having a capitalist or 'mixed economy' of public and private sectors. Jones actually adds the further stage of post-service society (a term he borrows from American post-industrial theorist Bertram Gross)[3] which could be 'a golden age of leisure and personal development based on the co-operative use of resources'.[4] While not arguing that a post-industrial and post-service society is inevitable, Jones's analysis of past and present societies has a high technological determinism built into his theory of social evolution. According to Jones, humanity has passed through the Neolithic agricultural revolution and the industrial revolution. Pre-industrial societies were characterized by the movement from nomadic pastoral life to settled, systematic food production, while industrial societies have gone through the steam, electric and atomic revolutions.[5] The division of social life into technical stages is complicated by Jones's attempt to use Kondratiev's Long Wave theory of economic expansion, stagnation and renewed expansion. There are more than enough problems with Long Wave theory,[6] and Jones himself admits that Kondratiev's periodization of successive Waves of economic change does not seem to fit his own phases of the steam, electronic and atomic revolutions.[7]

Alvin Toffler is also captivated by Waves. But his Waves are quite different to those theorized by Kondratiev. According to Toffler, we have already witnessed two major Waves in human history. The First Wave is broadly synonymous with all the various pre-industrial, agrarian and hunting societies. The Second Wave signifies the development of a set of social practices and modes of thought which transcend the narrow notion of industrialism. Regardless of whether the society has a capitalist or Communist political economy, Toffler argues that Second Wave nations are characterized by the development of giant bureaucracies which in turn are based on 'hierarchical, permanent, top-down, mechanistic organization, well designed for making repetitive productive products or repetitive decisions in a comparatively stable industrial environment'.[8] We are, claims Toffler, on the threshold of a new Third Wave in human history. This third Wave brings with it

> a genuinely new way of life based on diversified, renewable energy sources; on methods of production that make most factory assembly lines obsolete; on new, non-nuclear families; on a novel institution that might be called the 'electronic cottage'; and on radically changed schools and corporations of the future. The emergent civilization writes a new code of behaviour for us and carries us beyond standardization, synchronization, and centralization, beyond the concentration of energy, money and power.
>
> This new civilization, as it challenges the old, will topple bureaucracies, reduce the role of the nation-state, and give rise to semi-autonomous economies in a post-imperialist world. It requires governments that are simpler, more effective, yet more democratic than any we know today. It is a civilization with its own distinctive world outlook, its own ways of dealing with time, space, logic and causality.[9]

Toffler's image of future Third Wave societies is a mixture of current socio-economic practices in capitalist countries and an anti-market use-value, democratic and egalitarian

post-industrial utopia. The continuation with capitalist practices is evident in Toffler's belief that Third Wave societies
will be based upon transnational corporations, while at the
same time having extensive forms of decentralized socio-
economic institutions.[10] In this scenario, Toffler envisages
private transnational corporations operating as new, multipurpose institutions ('small-within-big is beautiful');[11] in the
new global economy—which requires a new planetary consciousness—Toffler sees the emergence of a whole variety of
new ways of thinking, working, interacting, managing, producing and distributing. The mass, standardized products
and institutions of Second Wave societies give way to small,
diversified and demassified products and processes.[12] A dual
process of larger, transnational, economic, political, cultural
and scientific institutions develops at the same time as
regional and local forces emerge to decentralize economic
and political decision-making—both trends weaken and
transform the nation state and the national economy as we
have known them in Second Wave industrial societies. Global
interaction links small, demassified institutions and products
across the former boundaries of the old, centralized nation
state.

In contrast to this image of a new, multipurpose and
demassified capitalist Third Wave, Toffler also envisages an
alternative set of social developments (which he attempts to
pass off as a coherent and fully integrated vision of the Third
Wave). The reason why these other elements of the Third
Wave appear as an alternative to his multipurpose corporation, is that their dynamo or reproductive process is envisaged
by Toffler to reside outside the domain of market forces and
market values. According to Toffler, economies have been
divided into production for use and production for exchange
(Toffler's debt to Marx?). In First Wave societies most people
consumed what they produced, while in Second Wave societies
most production was for exchange rather than direct consumption.[13] With the growth of Third Wave societies,
Toffler sees a new shift taking place between use-value and
exchange-value goods and services. Although he does not see
the market immediately withering away, Toffler believes that

post-industrial societies will be based on an extensive do-it-yourself, non-market economy and social structure of individual and communal goods and services.[14] The growth of 'prosumers' (that is, people who both produce and consume their own goods and services), narrows dependence on the traditional exchange-market economy thus leading to a process of demarketization.[15] A small-scale institutional structure, demassification, the emergence of a home-based 'electronic cottage' economy oriented to renewable energy sources and convivial tools and services (the influence of Ivan Illich?), self-help or 'prosumer-activated' technology and values–all suggest 'the end of the process of marketization, if not in our time, then soon after'.[16] Toffler's post-industrial society is a paradoxical mixture of transnational industries and communication linking the parochial 'electronic cottage' with the outside global or 'planetary consciousness'.[17] In rejecting isolated, self-sufficient pre-market economies, Toffler puts forward an image of radical social diversity and decentralization which will eventually be based on the 'withering away of the market'. Toffler is to be praised for championing a world characterized by more global or universalistic values (in contrast to existing parochial prejudices) as well as new forms of production which are unalienated and environmentally sensitive. But how such a 'prosuming' social order can survive simultaneously, at both local and global levels, without either the market or socialist production and distribution, is the utopian imaginary which Toffler shares with some of our post-industrial theorists.

The desire to eliminate the difference between production and consumption was put forward earlier by Paul and Percival Goodman in their book *Communitas: Means of Livelihood and Ways of Life*.[18] The goal of self-sufficiency is also a familiar theme in many anarchist, environmentalist and radical alternatives to existing capitalist and Communist societies. It is important to distinguish two types of post-industrial literature. On the one hand, we have several examples of self-sufficient, home-based or co-operative based images of production, distribution and social reproduction. These old and new theorists of self-sufficiency range from anarchists such as Bookchin and Goodman, to radical alternative technologists such as Dickson as well as Bahro and many members of Green parties in Europe.[19] Included in these attractive images of self-sufficiency are various transitional practices which ultimately point to the new society.

The development of intermediate technologies, intermediate economies, the growth of the Third sector (between market and state) or informal and invisible economic exchanges based on household repairs, barter, moonlighting, cashless exchanges and unregulated work, are constantly cited by a whole range of writers as indications of the signs of the future. The emphasis is nearly always on the virtue and desirability of small, personalized exchanges in these informal or Third sectors. On the other hand, writers such as Jones, Toffler and Gershuny see home-based, service-sector economies developing as a consequence of the computer revolution and the move to a small, diversified set of social exchanges.[20] According to Jones, the development of a fifth economy sector (domestic production) is related to the need to recognize the unpaid and paid nature of various forms of work in the domestic sphere.[21] Post-industrial societies will be much more oriented to the household—whether in the form of paying millions for labouring and caring for others in a domestic environment, or in images of 'electronic cottages' hooked up to the outside world, or a regeneration of simple technologies, arts and crafts, food production and other small-scale production. Whereas anarchists such as Bookchin, or Greens such as Bahro wish to replace capitalist societies with a socialist small-scale and decentralized social order, Jones, Stonier and other non-radical post-industrial theorists wish to allocate significantly more public and private funds to a wholesale re-education, retraining and reorientation of capitalist societies to a computerized, domestic-based, post-service economy and a greater leisure-based 'mixed economy' of public and private sectors.[22]

While it is possible that Bahro might agree with a number of the images of a post-industrial society contained in the works of Jones and Toffler, it is also clear that he would be strongly opposed to the notion of high-technology, multi-purpose transnationals or large, statist educational and social welfare service economies. Both Gorz and Bahro approach the need for a radical, post-industrial economy from different starting-points from Toffler, Jones and others. Bahro is correct in evaluating everything in the future according to whether it breaks with or continues the disastrous trends of environmental abuse, labour exploitation and irrational consumption carried on at present. In Bahro's words, 'we support everything that (a) minimizes the supply of labour, i.e. makes it relatively scarce, and above all (b) loosens time structures in every way, so as to increase the free time available to people.'[23]

André Gorz is also primarily interested in the relationship between production and environment, work time, alienation and autonomy. For Gorz, a

> drastic reduction of the duration of work is, however, not intrinsically liberatory, any more than the automation which makes it possible . . . In the current social environment, only work, however ungratifying it may otherwise be, offers men and women occasions for association, communication and exchange. The non-work sphere is the sphere of solitude, isolation, enforced idleness for all those who dwell on the periphery and in the suburbs of the great metropolitan agglomerations. Liberated time will be nothing else but empty time unless there are (a) a politics of collective equipment which endows communes, cities or large buildings, with places for meetings, exchange, and autonomous activities (b) a politics of cooperation and voluntary association permitting the development, on a local and non-market basis, of all types of collective services which are more effective, better adapted, more flexible, and are less expensive where they do not have an institutional and state character (aid to the aged, child-care cooperatives, transportation co-operatives, etc.).[24]

Leaving the issue of social services until the next chapter, it is clear that both Bahro and Gorz promote the admirable objective of overthrowing the role of work as it exists under present, capitalist and Communist societies. The crucial question is whether a post-industrial society would permit the institutionalization of the self-management of time which Gorz advocates. In return for a guaranteed lifetime salary, workers (according to Gorz) could arrange to work flexible hours, days, weeks, months or other periods of time so long as they performed a minimum number of work hours during their working lives.[25]

Given their Marxist backgrounds, it is not surprising that Bahro and Gorz undertake a simultaneous assault on the capitalist work ethic as well as on the narrow workerism and wage militancy of orthodox Marxist revolutionary parties. In their political strategy, as well as in their ultimate vision of a post-industrial society, Bahro and Gorz break with conventional notions of socialist society – a society which orthodox Marxists have conceived too narrowly as being based on increased productive forces and social relations at odds with the environmentalist images to be found in the works of Bahro and Gorz. It would be a mistake, however, to believe that Rudolf Bahro shares a notion of the future which matches Gorz's post-industrial society. Gorz's commitment to a mixture of state-planned aspects of the economy as well as radical decentralization, makes his post-industrial society read like a mixture of Marx, Toffler, Green as well as traditional French socialism. For example, it is clear that Bahro and Gorz are quite opposed on military issues, nuclear power and the general role of state institutions in the present and the future.

As one of the main spokespersons for a fundamental revision of the bases of industrial society, Bahro articulates a consistent hostility to all forms of statism, industrial growth and high technology. His post-industrial society is literally a post-industrial society – a unilateral deindustrialization or the abolition of industrial growth as we know it today. It is not clear whether Bahro sees a role for low energy using new computer technology and how this technology could be produced in small communes. Gorz, on the other hand, is much closer to Toffler in his desire to utilize new technology in his environmentally balanced, socialist society. What is clear about Bahro is his advocacy of autonomous 'basic communes'. In Bahro's words, these 'basic communes' 'will produce their basic needs for food, clothing, accommodation, education and health to a large extent internally; they will decide on certain specialized production mainly for barter in the vicinity, and contribute to maintaining the general communications and conditions of production (transport and information) either in this way or by seconding labour-power for that purpose.'[26]

Up until this point I have tried to present a brief overview of some of the major conceptions of post-industrial economies. Summarizing the varying conceptions of a post-industrial society, one can categorize the differences between our theorists along the following lines. First, it is necessary to recognize those writers such as Jones, Toffler, etc., who envisage post-industrial societies as more integrated or globally connected than present national industrial societies. For the latter, socio-economic developments will take place in connection to the present and future role of governments in promoting a post-service society or in nation states being broken up by radical decentralizing policies. Accordingly, post-industrial societies will not necessarily be socialist, will not be self-sufficient autarkies, and will not be possible without the extension on a massive scale of new technology which renders obsolete existing national and local Second Wave industries. Toffler and Jones do not believe that political and social struggles over new technology and other Third Wave forms will be irrelevant. But their conception of post-industrial economies and lifestyles is optimistic in the sense that they believe post-industrial production and consumption can satisfy local diversity and autonomy at the same time as sustaining transnational, multipurpose corporations and/or transformed public and private sectors which are capable of eliminating mass unemployment and depression.

Second, authors such as Gorz go one step further than the 'mixed economy' post-industrial theorists. Advocating neither self-sufficiency nor multipurpose corporations, Gorz's image of post-industrial socialism rests on a combination of socialist planning by the state, decentralized production (based on a mixture of new labour-saving technology and simple traditional labour-intensive, environmentally safe crafts), plus a vague international connection to other societies which is never clearly spelt out. Gorz is both an opponent of the market as the primary co-ordinating mechanism, and yet at the same time, an advocate of non-parochial structures which would be much more democratic than current bureaucratic regulation of economic and political practices.

Finally, we have a third group of post-industrial theorists who stress self-sufficiency and opposition to current industrial and post-industrial growth which in their view means more damage to the environment, more centralization of power in the hands of supranational political institutions (for example, the EEC) or more power to transnational corporations. This school of thought believes that post-industrial economies are not possible without a radical devolution of economic power, a radical disengagement of workers and parties from the current restructuring of industries along imperialist lines (that is, moving industries to Third World countries for cheap global production). The difference between the various advocates of radical autarky mainly revolves around the role of market mechanisms. In Bahro's as well as earlier anarchist writings, self-sufficiency is conceived as a socio-economic order which operates principally along simple forms of moneyless barter, decentralized planning and information exchanges, or other such non-capitalist market mechanisms or non-monetarized exchanges. Little is said about international economic exchanges, relations between affluent societies and Third World countries and so forth. In opposition to this non-market conception of post-industrial autarky (although simple barter is itself a market mechanism), is an image of radically decentralized communities maintaining their self-sufficiency through market mechanisms and the continued use of money. This scenario has a long tradition in American politics (the attempt to revive the old New England town) and is best theorized in recent works such as *Human Scale* by Kirkpatrick Sale.[27] Self-sufficiency is based on small-scale enterprises and communities. While market mechanisms continue to flourish, there is a deep opposition to both statism and large corporate control of economic processes. A radical environmentalism is combined with the best traditions of democratic participation and free enterprise.

Both the market and non-market versions of post-industrial autarky challenge the images of post-industrial economies put forward by Toffler, Jones, Gorz and others. It is therefore necessary to analyse some of the major problems and assumptions embodied in the varying notions of how all of these post-industrial societies work. Before carrying out a more detailed evaluation of post-industrial theories, it is also necessary to emphasize that nearly all the writers examined below display either a total neglect of, or minimal interest in, the following key issues and areas:

(1) the structure and role of state institutions in post-industrial societies;
(2) the political economic consequences of women's liberation;
(3) institutional mechanisms which will not only redistribute wealth, but provide adequate income or sustenance for existing and future unpaid workers and dependents;
(4) the future of military technology and production;
(5) the domestic and international implications of either global integration or local autarky.

All of these issues have been addressed by at least one or two of our post-industrial theorists, but their prescriptions, as well as their comprehension of the range of problems involved, leave a lot to be desired. Most of these neglected issues will also be discussed in subsequent chapters (especially the nature of social welfare and the status of women). I would like to devote the remaining part of this chapter to exposing some of the major weaknesses in the varying conceptions of how decentralized, demarketized, small-scale and egalitarian post-industrial economies (no matter how desirable) would actually work.

## DEMASSIFIED CAPITALISM OR DEMARKETIZED THIRD WAVE SOCIALISM?

Any concerned person, whether socialist or social reformer, must not only become aware of the incompatible consequences of more global integration or more autarky, but must also be able to identify those trends and policies in existing societies which are most likely to promote one type of economic development as opposed to another form of economic future. The incompatibility of greater transnational integration or greater self-sufficiency is constantly evident in many contemporary versions of market socialism, small-is-beautiful literature and other images of alternative societies. Alvin Toffler's *The Third Wave* is a good example of how attractive alternative lifestyles rest on a set of inconsistent assumptions and economic practices. I have already mentioned that Toffler puts forward a scenario consisting of new, transnational multipurpose corporations and the growth of non-market 'prosuming' which eventually leads to the withering away of the market. There are several major problems with this image of the future. First, Toffler's analysis of contemporary capitalist practices ignores the worst aspects and exaggerates the innovative potentials. Second, Toffler fails to show how the very same economic and technological forces which bring into being the new global economy, will not in themselves nullify or seriously undermine the industrial basis and economic viability of local, 'prosuming' non-market sectors. Third, Toffler provides no convincing analysis of how a demarketized global world comes into being, nor how it remains a viable mixture of local and transnational economic exchanges.

The utopian quality of Toffler's post-industrial society has very much to do with his naïve and unreal analysis of capitalist enterprises. Toffler would dearly like to see private corporations implement 'social accounting' (that is, maximize equality, environmental protection, etc., and not just maximize profits). Accordingly, Toffler sees the multipurpose corporation through those rose-coloured glasses designed especially to read corporate public relations handouts. While there is a minority of corporations which have slightly modified their public profiles, hiring practices and interior design – in order to minimize criticism from minorities or maximize productivity by providing more congenial work conditions – these corporations are few and far between. In fact, Toffler's whole methodology in *The Third Wave* is based on extrapolating from a small range of socio-economic examples and treating these as the norm for the future. This method of trend projection and impressionistic analysis results in Toffler combining an eclectic mixture of excellent insights with speculative ideas of a highly questionable kind. Thus his whole analysis of the break-up of nation-states, demassification of products, decentralization of political processes, etc., is itself a consequence of exaggerating and misreading the nature of conflict in contemporary societies, plus exaggerating the actual degree of centralization, standardization and synchronization achieved within capitalist societies. While there is no doubt that enormous bureaucracies and much standardization and centralization of decision-making characterize contemporary societies, many of the fine illustrations which Toffler provides of decay, neglect, political and economic conflict in Second-Wave societies, are in fact examples of lack of control, lack of synchronization, and lack of standardization. It is precisely the *desynchronization* of social forces and institutions at local, regional, national and supranational levels (a theme which I have analysed at length)[28] which makes Toffler's transition to a post-industrial society so problematical. In fairness to Toffler, he does argue that the transition to Third Wave societies will be far from smooth (he even warns of violence), but his conception of social struggle seems strangely incongruous with his benevolent view of capitalist enterprises.

In claiming that capitalist corporations were abandoning existing forms of standardized, mass products for diverse, one-off, quality products, Toffler appears to ignore all those key industries which either cannot diversify, or are actually increasing the mass quality of their products. I am referring here to the leading corporations in car production, steel, aluminium, oil, rubber, chemicals and electronics. These leading corporations are engaged in the production of commodities (for example, oil and steel) which provide minimal opportunities for diversified products (that is, small-within-big is beautiful); while these industries have suffered from overproduction, fluctuating profit rates recessions and mild recoveries in the past ten years, it is clear that demassification is not a viable option open to all major industries. Certainly it is possible to produce steel and other key commodities in small-scale enterprises, for example, Mao's 'backyard foundries' or small businesses in Italy. But small scale is not equivalent to product diversification, or an option open to all large capitalist corporations.

Faced with increasing challenges at national and international levels, many major corporations have in fact pursued the opposite strategy to that of diversification. An increasing number of corporations have diversified their production processes but *not* their products. For example, the move to create 'world cars', the assembly of electronic equipment in Third World countries, the automation of mass production, have all led to greater concentration of power, deskilling of jobs and deindustrialization of vital industrial infrastructure without many of the benefits of diversity or multipurpose institutions.

Toffler seems to be relatively oblivious to the very contradictions within capitalist societies which have decimated traditional industries without bringing into being the benevolent corporation. Moreover, Toffler has little or nothing to say about the giant military-industrial complexes in North America, France, the USSR etc, which constitute a vital backbone of contemporary new technology, not to mention all the existing industries whose futures would indeed be bleak without such large government orders. While it is certainly true that a whole range of new, demassified products have come into being, Toffler appears to have an unreal analysis of transnational corporations – especially in relation to the so-called compatibility of these corporations with radical decentralization of power and the demarketization of economic life which will supposedly characterize Third Wave societies.

Given Toffler's belief in the desirability of using renewable energy sources, maximizing social equality, reducing the work week and so forth, it is inconceivable that transnational corporations and millions of small and medium-sized businesses could all profitably survive a transition to a Third Wave mixture of global integration and 'electronic cottages'.

In an attempt to evaluate what California – probably the world's most affluent and most consumerist Second Wave society – would look like in the year 2050, a group of analysts contrasted two alternative scenarios.[29] In Scenario One, it was assumed that Californians would like to maintain their existing lifestyle but increase consumption levels so that as many people as possible could enjoy the high consumption patterns of the upper middle class. In contrast, Scenario Two was based on a lifestyle very close to Toffler's ideal, for example, a preference for less consumption and more personal leisure and environmental sensitivity. Making allowances for the serious inadequacies of all long-term projections, it is nevertheless clear, that if Scenario Two were adopted, there would be a dramatic drop in several major indices connected with industrial production, consumption, energy usage, car travel, etc., compared with the increased levels of production and environmental problems in Scenario One.[30] Given the crisis in profitability of many existing enterprises, it is pure fantasy on Toffler's part to believe that such a massive drop in overall consumption would not result in the possible collapse of capitalist economies. Of course, Toffler and other post-industrial theorists could respond by pointing to the millions of new jobs and small enterprises in the non-market sector. But how millions of people would be sustained in welfare or generate income once there was a massive depression in the monopoly sector, a major depletion of government revenues and other stringent austerity measures, remains the great unanswered question.

Throughout *The Third Wave* it appears as if Toffler is writing two books in one. The first is an image of life in a capitalist society where all the capitalist enterprises are basically non-exploitative 'good guys', perfectly agreeable to increased equality, democracy, rational use of resources and possessing a deep concern for less fortunate nations and individuals. The second book is a catalogue of all that is irrational about capitalist societies, a recognition of the moral superiority of a non-market society based on greater participation, tolerance and mutual respect for nature and fellow human beings. Burdened with a schizophrenic understanding of capitalist societies, bereft of any plausible analysis of the relations between state institutions and social classes within capitalist societies (and why these relations are significantly different from those relations between state administrators and citizens in Communist countries), Toffler is quite unable to persuade his readers about the mutual viability of global Third Wave capitalist corporations and non-profit-making, decentralized communities. In calling for a drastic overhaul of NATO, COMECON, the IMF and other supranational institutions, Toffler wants a new, rational world free of war and power-bloc rivalry. The nation state, he says, is incapable of policing giant transnational corporations; Toffler's solution is larger and better supranational institutions to regulate global interactions.[31] Yet he calls for decentralization of government and other decision-making processes throughout his book! How these decentralized government institutions will be able to determine policy with the existence of even larger supranational institutions and the further development of global markets and enterprises, is beyond comprehension. It seems that Toffler espouses a naïve, small liberal belief in the mutual balance and coexistence of world institutions and local democracy. All the valid lessons learnt and criticisms which Toffler makes of Second Wave centralized bureaucracies, corporations, production processes and decision-making institutions are virtually ignored in his utopian world of Third Wave 'planetary consciousness' and local demarketized lifestyles. Somehow, transnational corporations blend and merge with demarketizing forces, capitalist and Communist countries develop a 'planetary consciousness', supranational institutional bureaucrats share power with local democrats (maybe it is because they all work from the 'electronic cottage'!), and scarcity, greed, war, unemployment, pollution, etc., are eventually, after much struggle, reduced to mere memories of what life was like in Second Wave societies.

## EVOLVING TO POST-INDUSTRIALISM: THE FABIAN WAY

Toffler's failure to probe the incompatible paths of global integration and local decentralization is not unique. It says something about André Gorz's own post-industrial vision that he could uncritically claim that 'Alvin Toffler, in the Third Wave has shown very clearly how the micro-electronic revolution can potentially lead to a civilization in which economic goals, market production, and money exchange, could become secondary.'[32] But while Toffler promotes a radical transcendence of the nation state (in the form of simultaneous decentralization and a new supranationalism), there are other post-industrial theorists who advocate global economic integration while adhering to most of the conventional political economic structures of existing nation states. This perspective is quite evident in the works of Barry Jones and Tom Stonier.[33]

One hundred years ago, the early Fabians believed that through a process of enlightened reforms, mass education and social planning, the irrational aspects of capitalist industrialism could be overcome in favour of a future society characterized by greater equality, culture, attractive urban environments and so forth. Today, this tradition lives on in the works of people such as Australian Labor Minister for Science, Barry Jones. Like the earlier Fabians, Jones is a social reformer who believes in working through the existing political economic structures. Other non-Fabians such as Stonier, various members of social democratic and centre parties in capitalist countries, 'Atari democrats', plus various advocates of more computers with more democracy,[34] all believe that the post-industrial economy will bring greater affluence provided we prepare for the necessary changes. Rejecting monetarist policies, Jones and Stonier champion post-industrialism as the antidote to contemporary deindustrialization, stagflation and social malaise. Pointing to the advances made by Japanese, American and other technological powers, Jones and Stonier believe that massive increases in higher education, research and development, government laws and incentives, etc., will make the transition to a post-industrial economy relatively smooth despite the closure of traditional industries and personal suffering.

In stressing the vital role of massive public education, research, job retraining and new forms of comprehensive social welfare, Jones has failed to take note of the lessons of the past one hundred years of Fabianism. Despite significant social reforms and improvements in the standard of living, the Fabians have been fundamentally mistaken about the strategy of greater education, social welfare and government intervention as the path to socialism. Anthony Crosland's claim that 'By 1951, Britain had, in all essentials ceased to be a capitalist country' (because economic power had supposedly moved to the government from the ruling class), is just as ludicrous 30 years later, as when this Fabian view was first asserted in the 1950s.[35] Similarly, in his belief that education and government intervention can transform capitalist industrial society into an egalitarian post-industrial society, Jones is naïve at best and utterly self-deluding at worst. In the next chapter I will discuss the fiscal and social possibilities of massive social welfare budgets and universal income programmes such as the guaranteed minimum income proposed by Jones and other post-industrial theorists. For the moment it is necessary to indicate why Jones, Stonier and others are mistaken about the policies needed to transform current capitalist societies.

If Jones et al. were merely theorizing the transformation of industries and occupations, then there would be less to disagree with when considering current restructuring policies. There is no doubt that there has been a major loss of jobs in manufacturing industries in leading capitalist countries. There has also been an increase in jobs in personal services, tourism, finance and public administration in various countries. But the belief that a massive infusion of funds into public education will provide the key to social mobility for the deindustrialized proletariat, is just as illusory as the earlier Fabian belief that education would overcome the inherent inequalities of capitalist social relations.

If we closely examine the prospects for new industries, sources of employment and so forth, we find little ground for future optimism that higher education will be the passport to high incomes for people who can find jobs only as waiters, janitors, guards, domestic cleaners, or other low-paying occupations in the post-service economy.[36] When we add to these bleak prospects the phenomenon of increasing numbers on low-paying, part-time work, the increasing concentration of productive forces in the hands of transnational, export-oriented firms, then the overall structure of the private sector in post-industrial economies looks quite unable to provide upward social mobility (for most low wage workers) through further education. This leaves the state or public sector. Like the Fabians before him, Jones fails to understand the severe limits on the expansion of the public sector in a capitalist industrial or post-industrial society. Many of the worthy jobs in education, community care and services, etc., which Jones, Toffler and others propose, are jobs which are actually incompatible with profitable capitalist production (save where they constitute a minor part of the overall economy as they do at the moment), and hence are unlikely to be increased in the coming decades.

Like Toffler, Jones creates an unreal feeling of technological optimism by focusing on abstract tendencies rather than upon concrete political economic realities. For example, it is true that many new jobs are being created in the areas of information technology, bio-technology, micro-electronics and so forth. But in the next few decades, these high technology jobs will only provide a small percentage of total employment in advanced countries such as the USA, for example, about 10 to 15 per cent. In contrast, Gorz rejects high tech as the panacea for mass employment and is highly critical of the French attempt to imitate the American New Right model.[37] Authors such as Etzioni, Jargowsky, Harrington and Levinson also argue that high technology jobs will account for less than 4 per cent of new jobs in the USA by 1995.[38] They cite Bureau of Labor Statistics to show that janitors or building custodians will account for more new jobs than the five fastest growing high tech jobs combined! While there were significant changes between 1950 and 1982 in the categories of professional workers, farm workers, clerical, service workers and machine operators, it is estimated that between 1982 and 1995 there will be very little variation in the total workforce in the categories of sales, clerical, service, professional and technical workers, managers, machine operators, labourers, craft workers and farm workers.[39] If these projections for 1995 become true, the occupational transformation predicted by many futurologists and post-industrial publicists will be much, much slower than imagined.

Many of the jobs in the 'post-industrial society' are in fact the same types of jobs found in industrial societies – sales in fast food outlets, domestic cleaning, clerical work and janitors in the old 'industrial society' vocabulary. In 1983, the USA had 69 per cent of its paid workforce in service industries, that is, banking, restaurants, sales, etc., compared with 54 per cent of the paid labour force in 1956.[40] It is clear that the growth of the post-industrial society in the largest and most technologically advanced capitalist country, has not been more than 15 per cent in the last three decades.

While there is still room for occupational changes within the USA, the largest percentage increases in service sector employment (in the past 30 years), were registered in countries such as Japan, West Germany, France and Italy. All these major capitalist countries started from lower levels of service sector employment in 1956 (about 28 to 38 per cent of overall employment), but have not reached much more than 50 to 58 per cent of their total paid labour force in services.[41] The USA also had 55 per cent of its 20 to 24 years old population in higher education, compared with only 20 to 37 per cent of similar age groups in Italy, Britain, West Germany, Japan, Canada, Sweden and France – the largest and most technologically advanced capitalist societies.[42] Despite such a high percentage of its workforce having higher education, the USA is characterized by widespread low-wage labour, a high percentage of semi-skilled and unskilled service jobs, a high number of part-time workers and lower levels of public sector employment in social welfare services compared with Sweden, Britain and other West European countries.[43] Equally important, the USA spends more than any other leading capitalist power on military expenditure – especially high technology research and development.[44]

Given the recent historical profile of advanced service sector societies, there would have to be a major defeat of

both the New Right and liberal Keynesians for public expenditure to explode to the extent necessary to employ fully the
post-industrial workforce in well-paid jobs (given recent
unemployment rates); moreover, there would have to be a
massive increase in world trade (an export-led recovery), to
counter further growth in unemployment, let alone generate
adequate revenue to expand the public sectors of national
economies.[45] This scenario is incompatible with the stated objectives of higher environmental harmony, demarketized use-
value services and other 'post-capitalist' goals. Either the
private sector grows, continues to shed labour, continues to
pollute, and continues to destroy traditional industrial and
craft bases at a national and local level, or the public sector
grows. If the growth in public sectors is mainly confined to
areas which assist in the accumulation of private capital, then
there will be little chance of achieving many of the egalitarian
and environmental objectives desired by the post-industrial
theorists. But if political forces manage to achieve public sector growth in badly needed social welfare services and other
goods and services which put people before profits, then
these improvements will not only threaten private profitability, but erode labour discipline and motivation. This is
because the desirable objectives of full-employment,
guaranteed incomes, booming cultural and educational
opportunities, will all provide social alternatives to working
as alienated serfs in traditional industries or new zombies
feeding health-hazardous computer and video terminals.

In short, Jones reveals his utopianism by default. Having
virtually no understanding of the political economy of state
and private sectors in capitalist societies, unable to indicate
which social forces in the private sector would endorse his
massive infusion of funds into non-profitable expenditure in
education and welfare, unable to show how a proliferation of
small enterprises could break the market dominance of the
IBMs of this world, the only course left for him is to place his
faith in the harmonious expansion of post-industrial pies
which can be distributed equitably to the deindustrialized
masses. Unintentionally, Jones, Stonier and others are supporting the very Rightwing policies of restructuring going on

at the moment. This Rightwing market model is also being pursued by socialist and social democratic governments. Every call for more high technology, less protection for existing industries, more integration into global networks, etc., is a recipe for loss of local and national democratic sovereignty, erosion of skills and services and weakening of labour organizations; this is because restructuring creates more unemployment, opens national markets to foreign imports, deregulates finance and capital movements, while capitalist forces oppose the implementation of the very social reforms (proposed by Jones et al.) which would supposedly make the post-industrial society a socialist heaven as opposed to a capitalist hell. Despite their belief in major social reforms when in government, many contemporary Fabians are loathe to upset capitalist interest groups. In the face of recession, the Fabians are content to rely on private sector profitable recovery and hope that the benefits 'trickle down' to the 'less fortunate'.

## THE THIRD SECTOR: PROGRESSIVE FORCE OR ROMANTICIZED DEFORMATION?

Although not all post-industrial society theorists believe in the compatibility of transnational corporations and small, decentralized production and democratic control, there is a wide consensus concerning the desirability of promoting more formal economic alternatives, for example, co-operatives, as well as less formal, cash-based and/or money-less transactions. Workers owning their own enterprises, being free of the worst aspects of large capitalist exploitation and monopoly, or being free of statist control and bureaucracy, have long been ideals promoted in both socialist and non-socialist programmes. In recent years, various Left activists have supplemented their belief in co-operatives with a positive endorsement of the informal, underground economy; all forms of do-it-yourself work, simple barter, or illegal part- and full-time paid work, have been seen as prefigurative forms of anti-capitalist organization which weaken mass commodity production and exchange, foster communal forms of lifestyle, erode the puritan work ethic as well as combat the worst excesses of consumerism and related environmental destruction.

The informal part of the Third Sector has boomed in the past decade with the related growth of underground economies in capitalist societies. Until recently, blackmarkets and illegal forms of work have been essential component elements of Communist countries, Third World societies and wartime economies – given shortage of goods and the undemocratic organization of production and exchange. But since the early 1970s, the widespread restructuring of capitalist industries and persistent stagflation in OECD countries have given rise to large but structurally essential underground economies – varying from between 5 and 30 per cent of individual nations' gross domestic products (accurate figures are impossible to collect). In extreme cases (such as Bolivia), the near collapse of the formal economy in the early 1980s has witnessed the move of over three-quarters of the paid workforce into the informal sector.[46] These informal sectors survive in the interstices of capitalist production processes and welfare state institutions. Simultaneously thriving on new forms of shady and semi-legal business opportunities, as well as disguising the personal and social costs of economic depression (as unemployed workers supplement low dole payments with illegal work, or underemployed and poorly paid workers also take on extra illegal work), informal sectors are closely tied to the very health and future prospects of money-based private production and state welfare income.

Within these informal sectors limited demonetarized exchanges survive in urban and rural environments (for example, certain repair networks and food producers). However, it would be romantic to believe that current informal practices constitute the basis of a massive demarketized sector along the lines envisaged by post-industrial theorists and members of environmental movements. Nearly all the current forms of cashless transactions depend directly or indirectly on income derived from the formal market or state sectors (that is, from individuals receiving all or part of their sustenance in money form).

Moreover, these alternative urban communes, craft centres, etc., have limited market and non-market viability; a proliferation of cafés, repair shops, craft centres and other alternative institutions would be very difficult to sustain in most capitalist cities. Most existing alternative enterprises barely survive; this very delicate informal economy could not possibly support a flood of new entrants. Without the fallback support mechanisms of welfare income, student allowances or paid jobs, most of these *cashless* enterprises would probably never have survived in the first place.

Studies of the cash-based, informal sector by Beverly Lozano, Priscilla Connolly and others, also reveal that a sizeable proportion of paid workers and self-employed are involuntary participants – remaining only until they can find better paying and more satisfying legal work.[47] But even assuming that most informal workers are happy, and that enterprises are providing useful alternatives to existing capitalist products, it is quite another thing to believe that these informal sectors are viable as future demarketized, post-industrial socialist economies. To move from the interstices of a capitalist mixed economy, to a position where demarketized goods and services become the major characteristic of a new post-industrial economy, would entail the transformation of large transnationals into small enterprises, an abolition of the capitalist market as the dominant mechanism of social and economic reproduction, and the abolition of income dependency on state welfare institutions – which in turn depend on the health of the private market sector for their revenue. Equally importantly, one cannot create a demarketized sector from an informal economy which is itself largely determined by market forces (even if they operate underground).

In short, an informal sector can only become a viable, *demarketized formal* sector of an alternative society if

(1) a radical self-sufficiency replaces capitalist production;
(2) a planned economy moves from monetarized transactions to payment-in-kind, i.e., 'social wage' goods and services;

(3) a minority market sector of the overall economy is some-
    how able to generate sufficient wealth to finance a
    guaranteed income for all citizens (a highly unlikely
    possibility); ·
(4) a mixture of planning and decentralized self-sufficiency
    replaces capitalist markets.

Implementation of radical self-sufficiency would severely
limit the viability of all market-oriented enterprises – whether
large or small, co-operatives or self-employed individuals –
simply because self-sufficiency as a principle conflicts with
constant growth and market expansion. A planned economy,
on the other hand, would involve a significant degree of
regulation and bureaucracy – the very elements which anti-
statist romantics believe they can survive without. Like most
post-industrial utopians, the advocates of an expanding, self-
managed informal sector would dearly like to believe that a
dominant demarketized economy could regulate itself
without socialist state institutional planning. And even those
who believe in the necessity of state institutions, would dearly
like to believe that non-market socialism was viable in a purely
radically decentralized form.

All the above comments relating to the illusions held by
supporters of informal sectors, are also relevant to advocates
of co-operatives. It is important to differentiate between the
several kinds of co-operatives, as well as to examine the compatibility of co-operatives with other post-industrial society
objectives such as quality and length of work, size of enterprise and demarketized sectors. Being in favour of co-
operatives is like being in favour of peace. Conservatives,
liberals, radicals, Communist and capitalist societies, all
openly endorse the operation of co-operatives. Somehow co-
operatives are compatible with free enterprise, market
socialism, central planning, self-management and anarchism.
The key question is whether co-operatives can form the basic
economic unit of a particular society, or whether they must
remain a secondary, minor form of organization. There is no
doubt that many thousands of co-operatives have flourished
in both capitalist and Communist countries. Where co-

operatives are governed by market mechanisms, it is clear that the successul co-operatives have managed to carve out a niche for themselves in particular local or national markets.[48] Others have survived by pooling limited resources, for example, many agricultural co-operatives, while a minority have even grown into multi-million dollar giants.[49] The least successful have been those newly formed co-operatives which have arisen out of capitalist business crises, that is, those co-operatives formed by workers as desperate measures to save jobs and industries. Instead of being islands of socialism, many of these co-operatives have survived only by workers accepting lower wages, working longer hours or introducing other negative measures imposed by market pressures. Just as piece-work is the highest form of exploitation (because the worker drives himself or herself without a boss), so too, co-operatives are equally capable of being transformed into bastions of self-exploitation rather than enterprises of enlightened solidarity and mutual self-help.

The relatively uncritical enthusiasm for co-operatives has given rise to a new sacred cow – Mondragon. Just as the alternative plan at Lucas Aerospace came to represent the model for all socialists believing in the smooth transition from capitalism to socialism, so too, the co-operatives in Mondragon have become the inspiration of many post-industrialists. I have already argued elsewhere that despite its many positive qualities, the Lucas Plan is inapplicable to most workers in private and state sector employment (especially those not directly involved in the production of commodities – which is in fact the majority of the working class in administrative, finance, retail, social welfare, transport and other service organizations).[50] Similarly, we must closely examine the suitability of co-operatives as alternatives to current economic organizations.

There is no questioning the relative success of Mondragon compared with non-co-operative enterprises in Spain. Over 18,000 people are employed in the various co-operatives – with over 3,500 people employed in the largest co-operative named ULGOR.[51] It is precisely the size of ULGOR, plus the nature of its products and place in the national market which

make Mondragon a poor example for post-industrial
theorists. If a post-industrial society is to be based on small
enterprises which eventually evolve into a demarketized
economy, Mondragon is not only too large, but also irrelevant
because of the dominant position which ULGOR has in the
production of stoves. It is clear that if many co-operatives
began to produce stoves, then ULGOR's hold of the Spanish
national market would suffer. This is true of any co-operative
whose life and health depend on market mechanisms. Many
seem to overlook the specific characteristics of particular co-
operatives, believing instead that they possess inherent
qualities because of their size and the fact that they are co-
operatives. But many co-operatives actually reduce employment by restricting entry of new workers and new firms,
consolidate the sovereignty of producers over the interests of
consumers, are anti-trade union and depend on raising productivity through work processes which hardly meet the
desired reduction of the work day as advocated by Bahro,
Gorz, Toffler and Jones.

   In a capitalist society, co-operatives are forced to accept
the prevailing logic of market forces. For example, Daniel
Zwerdling has shown that many food co-operatives in the
USA failed to survive in their original radical form because
they lacked store space compared with large supermarkets;
hence, in contrast to Ralf Nader's and Gorz's promotion of
consumer choice at co-operatives, they could not keep a wide
range of goods or match supermarket prices.[52] Workers' co-
operatives either counter prevailing rates of mass unemployment by sustaining labour-intensive production (thus
ultimately failing to hold costs down in comparison with
capital-intensive private enterprises, unless the co-operative
reduces members' wages), or implement high technology production processes, shed labour and confront the problems of
raising sufficient working capital. All proposals for a market
socialist economy based on workers' co-operatives assume
that central governments will have to play a vital role in the
provision of loan finance, tax policies, international trade
policies, planning structures and so forth.[53] But this reveals
one of the fundamental contradictions between small-scale

self-managed enterprises and socialist objectives such as equality and social welfare. If a post-industrial socialist society is characterized by a large market-oriented sector (that is, worker controlled or owned enterprises freely producing and selling their goods and services despite strong government regulations and investment policies), it would be extremely difficult to contain these economic practices within the boundaries of a democratically sovereign and self-sufficient nation state. All enterprises governed by market mechanisms (whether co-operatives, or publicly or privately owned), are pressured into competition and constant growth in order to sustain income, market share and hence survival. Only a planned economy can avoid the problems of overproduction, labour shedding, pursuit of international markets and crises in profitability which market mechanisms produce for both Eastern European market socialist firms and Western private capitalist businesses.

The problem for advocates of small-scale decentralized economies who also desire strong and supportive central governments, is that effective planning often negates local market mechanisms. Yet many advocates of self-sufficiency oppose the need for democratic central planning (because of the experiences of undemocratic planning in Eastern Europe), or decentralized market socialist practices (because they equate market mechanisms with only capitalist market practices). It is extremely difficult to imagine any self-sufficient socialist society operating according to simple barter or non-market exchanges between co-operatives. While I am a strong critic of market socialism, I do believe that those radicals or post-industrial theorists who believe that one can do without either market mechanisms or state planning are completely utopian. However, before one can construct a post-industrial socialism (based upon either radical decentralized self-sufficiency, market socialism or democratic central planning combined with increased self-management), all radicals have to deal with the enormity of existing social problems. As I will argue in a later chapter, any post-industrial society is going to fall far short of achieving greater equity, social justice and genuine popular sovereignty, without the construction of a democratic state structure together with a radical redistribution of privately owned wealth. Without the development of a centrally, but democratically planned economy (which also includes a small market-based sector), any post-industrial society operating along predominantly market socialist principles will have to be geared to permanent growth and all the environmental and unemployment problems associated with the expansion of markets. How are contemporary societies suffering from high unemployment, deindustrialization, fiscal crises and growing international competition going to achieve post-industrial goals and environmental balance, increased leisure, better social welfare and so forth, if they adopt market socialist mechanisms which continue to expose workers and environments to the pressures of domestic and international market pressures?

Equally important, small size is not in itself a guarantee of more humane work conditions. Most capitalist enterprises in the world (more than 95 per cent) employ less than a hundred people. These millions of capitalist enterprises are far from ideal – especially the small sweat-shops, typically employing cheap labour and violating workers' health, sexuality, safety and civil liberties. Co-operatives would have to compete in these capitalist markets if they were to replace private ownership. Yet the growth of co-operatives weakens trade unions as workers begin to own and run their own enterprises. Few trade unions are radical forces; nevertheless, in the slow transition to a post-industrial society, the erosion of trade-union power would hardly improve workers' conditions. More importantly, the widespread development of co-operatives would weaken political parties based on trade unions, which in a capitalist society would only bolster the forces of conservatism and reaction. While there are many co-operatives which have set concrete examples of non-exploitative alternatives to private enterprise, it is important not to overlook the negative aspects of co-operatives existing within capitalist societies.

All post-industrial advocates of small-sized co-operatives fail to tell us how such organizations will

(1) sustain themselves in the face of increasingly difficult market conditions;

(2) transform themselves into demarketized sectors if they are modelled on market successes such as Mondragon;

(3) self-manage local resources and remain viable, without central government support and regulatory structures;

(4) simultaneously maximize employment and reduce the length of the working week while operating within markets;

(5) increase democratic power, through the growth of co-operatives, 'electronic cottages', informal economic exchanges, etc., given the existence of giant anti-democratic transnational firms which are thriving on the weakening and fragmentation of labour and environmental forces;

(6) fail to explain how the Third Sector can sustain an adequate social welfare programme if the growth of this Sector means the decline and eventual withering away of both the state sector and the market.

Although I support local forms of 'popular planning', co-operative initiatives which provide employment and socially useful services, it is important to demystify co-operatives and not treat them as 'sacred cows'. It is also important to raise the above questions and problems because co-operatives operating in a non-market economy would be free of most of these dilemmas – provided there was an appropriate planning structure and institutionalization of national and grass-roots democracy. Some people may argue that my negative evaluation of the Third Sector in capitalist societies grossly underestimates the room for growth and transformation of existing capitalist and state sector practices. After all, one could point to all those arguments at the beginning of the twentieth century over whether small businesses and the petty bourgeoisie were going to disappear or expand into a new middle class. Yet both the revisionists and the revolutionaries were wrong. The orthodox Marxists were wrong in believing in the inevitability of class polarization; they grossly underestimated the durability of small business sectors, not to mention the transformative capacities of large capitalist enterprises. But the evolutionary revisionists were completely naïve in their belief that equality, social harmony, let alone socialism, could be legislated through parliamentary systems. Moreover, the durability of the petty bourgeoisie and the occupational transformation of the working class (from blue to white collar, etc.), has coexisted with a massive increase in monopoly capitalist power, the destruction of tens of millions of people in a century of endless imperialist wars, the maintenance by transnational corporations of dozens of brutal regimes in the Third World and other horrors.

As capitalist societies in the First World undergo large-scale restructuring, it is clear that major corporations, plus millions of small businesses, continue to oppose the extension of social welfare to increasing numbers of impoverished people. It is against this historical background that all post-industrial theorists who believe in the mutual growth and compatibility of monopoly, competitive and Third Sectors, must be able to explain to us how a post-industrial economy will be constructed, and how private business will come to abandon their current ruthless pursuits and anti-democratic practices. It is utterly utopian to believe that corporations based on continued growth, opposition to environmental controls, opposition to adequate social welfare for OECD citizens (let alone for hundreds of millions of the Third World), opposition to reductions in military-industrial complexes and so forth, could possibly be the crusaders who fight for a just and more egalitarian post-industrial future! In the past 20 years there has been a growing awareness that the development of new technologies – for example, cable television and various computerized equipment making small, decentralized and democratic lifestyles possible – have not in themselves been able to achieve the goals which radicals had earlier predicted. So too, in noting the vast proliferation of technological capacities, informal sectors and social variety, we must not lose sight of the deep-seated structure of private capitalist power relationships. In a later chapter I will discuss the gap between images of post-industrial lifestyles and the political forces necessary to bring these utopian practices into existence.

## POST-INDUSTRIAL SOCIALISM: SELF-SUFFICIENCY OR INTERNATIONAL INTEGRATION?

André Gorz and Rudolf Bahro are two of the leading advocates of post-industrial socialism. Yet both theorists have devoted more energy to criticizing existing industrial societies and traditional Left parties than to elaborating notions of how the post-industrial society will function. Since his conversion to Green politics, Bahro has seemingly rejected his own important observations on planning developed in *The Alternative*.[54] It is not clear how he believes a national network of basic self-sufficient communes will be able to meet the complex organizational problems which must be resolved in a post-capitalist society. If capitalist market mechanisms cease to be the predominant form of social co-ordination apart from state institutions, and Bahro also promotes the radical decentralization and withering away of state bureaucracies, then how is co-ordination to be achieved? Bahro himself had earlier argued that no information theory existed which could conceptualize a horizontal flow of information between thousands of institutions and communes without vertical structures of hierarchy.[55] If this is still true, then what kinds of hierarchical structures would be compatible with 'basic communes' and radical anti-industrial and anti-statist lifestyles? Furthermore, would a Green post-industrial society minimize or maximize social planning? If it minimized social planning and relied predominantly on market mechanisms, then all the major deficiencies of market socialism would appear. If the new society maximized planning, then how would this be possible without national state institutions?

It is one thing to draw up a transitional programme in a mixed economy (as the Green Party in West Germany has done), but this assumes the continuation of state welfare institutions and extensive capitalist production. (Bahro actually criticized the Green Party's economic programme as Left SPD reformism.) A close inspection of the Green Programme of 1983 reveals many fine suggestions, but just as many vague and politically unreal proposals.[56] Nowhere in the Green Programme, nor in Bahro's writings, is there any clear position on a post-industrial economy – other than general moral principles about the environment, civil liberties and technology along with vague calls for planning to be shared by both the state and grass-roots movements. But a *demonetarized*, self-sufficient economy presupposes a clear solution to the following major problems:

(1) co-ordination of social and natural resources *without* paid social planners in state institutions;
(2) institutional mechanisms to guarantee sustenance for millions of welfare dependants and residents in non-fertile, rural areas or poor urban regions;
(3) clear social standards and priorities at local and national levels relating to equitable standards of living, political mechanisms for the regulation of justice, education, defence, communication and so forth;
(4) mechanisms which either facilitate international trade and aid, or maintain autarkic isolation and low or no growth.

While Bahro is conscious of the need to answer all those eager to know what an alternative economy will look like, his reply falls far short of a satisfactory answer. 'We have in mind an economic order' says Bahro, 'of the greatest possible self-sufficiency at a local, regional, provincial and national level. We envisage markets for the exchange of activities between base communities and cooperation at levels above this, complementing each other to form a market-free economy for basic needs and built from the bottom up.'[57] I agree with Bahro's objective to maximize self-sufficiency at local, regional and national levels. But the notion of market-free co-operation without state planning mechanisms is highly unrealistic. Moreover, an elaborate network of market exchanges between thousands of 'basic communes' presupposes some form of regulatory mechanisms if these markets are not to grow into capitalist markets with all the inherent qualities of inequality, exploitation and so forth. Just how the market-free part of the economy will relate with the plethora of market exchanges – that is, will co-operation or market exchanges predominate – is entirely unclear from Bahro's utterly vague model.

There is no reason why a semi-autarky should not be based on moneyless exchanges or vague forms of co-operation. One can envisage a democratically centrally planned semi-autarky with complex socio-economic mechanisms and the maximization of decentralized decision-making and production – which to that extent is compatible with central planning and socialist pluralism. But it is not clear from various statements by Bahro and other members of the Green movement whether their goal is a demonetarized economy, or one which accords a decisive role to either state planning, market mechanisms or mixtures of both. Bahro calls for new social planning but does not specify whether this planning will be predominantly centralized or decentralized. So far, no advocate of completely decentralized planning has been able to show how material redistribution, domestic and international trade, etc., can be achieved without the existence of central state institutions.[58] In subsequent chapters I will try to show why market socialism is anti-feminist and anti-ecological. For the moment it is important to emphasize that socialist self-sufficiency without decentralized or centralized state planning (or mixtures of both), is not only utopian, but can only result in the inequalities of primitive barter or the selfish and negative aspects of market practices.

In his post-industrial utopia, Kirkpatrick Sale envisages thousands of small, decentralized communities, thriving in self-sufficiency and without the need of national state institutions.[59] Sale is a propagandist for small cities, small enterprises, a steady-state economy and the revival of the old New England style of local democracy. His book contains numerous persuasive examples of why small-scale cities, institutions and practices are healthier, more democratic and so forth. But he is also incredibly naïve in his belief that self-management works wonders in Yugoslavia, or that early pre-capitalist societies without states were better than contemporary welfare state societies. In Sale's post-industrial America, local towns will use the taxes they currently pay to

State and Federal governments for their own use. Somehow, the increasing widespread public debt of hundreds of American cities, the enormous ghettos and urban poverty will all be transformed by the creation of thousands of small-scale, self-financing towns. It is true that local residents could do a lot more with their own revenue. But the present level of public revenue would not be available if the post-industrial economy ceased to exist in its current military–industrial complex form, or if the high level of consumerism were not maintained. How would Sale's towns survive without current dependency on imported raw materials, national marketing chains, earnings from foreign exports, for example, agribusiness, as well as dividends from American multi-nationals earning fortunes abroad, or all the military contracts, government jobs and other forms of state support?

In other words, Sale wants a new, democratic America (with roughly the same standard of living and pattern of consumption of affluent Americans), but somehow free of all the worst forms of American capitalism (widespread squalor, poverty and inequality) which make this very affluence possible. His stateless society is a mish-mash version of democratic socialist moralism and utopian hopes, but based on the long tradition of American free enterprise. As such, Sale's self-sufficient post-industrial economy is riddled with contradictions – from the problem of how to maintain affluence without imported raw materials, to the fundamental issue of how a market-based order can afford to accept a no-growth, steady-state economy, if co-operatives and small business profits, jobs, community services all depend on constant growth and consumption – given the absence of state institutions (that is, the non-market allocation of goods and services).

Finally, we have André Gorz's mixture of local autonomy and international and national integration, high tech and environmental or convivial tools, state planning and local control, anti-market practices which yet allow room for non-state services. Of all the post-industrial theorists, Gorz is the most puzzling and paradoxical. On the one hand, Gorz recognizes that only new socialist state institutions have the capacity to reduce the necessary amount of labour time, or can co-ordinate and regulate a post-industrial economy. Yet, on the other hand, Gorz appears to believe that central planning is compatible with market forces and autonomous communal spheres of production. The basic premise of Gorz's post-industrial society is the division of social life into heteronomous and autonomous spheres. In the heteronomous sphere are to be found all the interpersonal and programmed necessities of life, centrally planned production of major industrial goods, unpleasant daily tasks and services, administration, specialized division of labour and other necessary forms of work and production. Gorz believes that heteronomous work can be reduced to a bare minimum, while efficient production and planning can provide the material conditions necessary for the conduct of autonomous, creative activity. The organization of the heteronomous sphere must be subordinate to the objectives of the autonomous sphere – that is, the sphere of individual freedom where non-necessary material goods, services and activities can be pursued. People will move between heteronomous wage-labour and autonomous, individual and communal activity which enables people to live and produce according to their fantasies and not just their needs.[60]

In contrast to Bahro, Gorz does not believe in the virtues of 'basic communes'. For Gorz, 'communal autarky always has an impoverishing effect: the more self-sufficient and numerically limited a community is, the smaller the range of activities and choices it can offer to its members. If it has no opening to an area of exogenous activity, knowledge and production, the community becomes a prison – exploitation by the family amounts to exploitation of the family. Only constantly renewed possibilities for discovery, insight, experiment and communication can prevent communal life from becoming impoverished and eventually suffocating.'[61] As Gorz does not believe that one can have full self-management in complex institutions, large cities, or with central planning of key industries (although he does advocate technical self-management of the labour processes in order to determine work conditions),[62] it is necessary to recognize the impossibility of abolishing heteronomous work. Hence, Gorz proposes three conditions in order that the heteronomous sphere not dominate autonomous life-activity:

> First, only the socialization of knowledge, and of its storage and transmission, allows a plentiful supply of technologically advanced tools. Second, the highly productive machinery capable of turning out such tools at low cost (whether they be cathode tubes or ball-bearings) is beyond the means of local communities or towns. Third, if the time spent on heteronomous work is to be reduced to a minimum, then everyone will have to do some work.[63]

Gorz's conception of a socialist society which utilizes the best of advanced high technology in combination with local autonomy, is very attractive, and yet fraught with economic and political inconsistencies. While Gorz recognizes that the post-industrial technical revolution must sweep away old social relations (especially work practices), if equality and democracy are to be maximized, his division of social life into two spheres is too schematic. For example, Johannes Berger and Norbert Kostede make the important criticism that Gorz's dual society of heteronomous and autonomous spheres is too neat and is based on *different* steering principles which are artificial and arbitrary. 'This rigid correspondence of social sectors and principles of organization is thus the weakest feature of Gorz's book. It would make more sense to ascribe a combination of organizing principles everywhere since no field (education, health, factory work etc.) can be reasonably organized according to any one principle.'[64] In trying to separate heteronomous and autonomous social relations and yet combine the notions of convivial tools (Illich), the 'withering away of the market' (Toffler) and democratic state planning, Gorz is also forced into an attempt to reconcile big technology with small-is-beautiful. His powerful critique of the suffocating limits of small, self-sufficient communes, is not matched by any adequate notion, let alone substantial analysis of alternative national and international economic relations. Gorz is at his best in recognizing that not all work will be enjoyable and that state planning will be necessary. One also can sympathize with Gorz's desire to utilize new technology in labour-saving devices (in order to maximize free time).

In his analysis of potential Rightwing technological totalitarianism,[65] Gorz is fully aware of the negative consequences of high technology. But where is Gorz's analysis of all those current developments of high tech by transnationals which are directly negating the possibility of establishing autonomous spheres at the international level? Like most post-industrial theorists, Gorz appears to be almost oblivious to the incompatible paths of current micro-electronic developments (at the supranational level) and the protection of jobs and industries which are necessary for any transition to independent socialist nation states. For example, a number of Western countries are losing (or have lost) vitally needed manufacturing enterprises as as result of transnational corporate restructuring, competition from cheaper imports and bankruptcies. If a region or nation depends far too heavily on the importation of basic goods and services, for example, steel, machine tools, then not only is the economy subjected to constant balance of payments and other fiscal problems, but the capacity to pursue independent political policies (whether on the domestic or foreign fronts) is severely constrained by foreign pressures. But then it is not clear whether Gorz believes in socialist nation states or in some other form of socialist territorial and political arrangements. While it is clear that Gorz is opposed to village or local autarky, it is not clear whether the necessary socialist state institutions which he advocates will be organized at national or global levels. It is hard to know what Gorz actually stands for. On the one hand, he recognizes the need for central planning of major industries and resources.[66] On the other hand, Gorz follows Toffler in believing that because of information and organizational complexity, 'our industrial system no longer can be centrally managed' – an ideological assertion which is portrayed as a common truth![67] Gorz's image of utopia (see Appendix 2 which first appeared in *Ecology as Politics*) is, in Murray Bookchin's scathing summation, 'a childish "libertarian" Disneyland'.[68] Presidential decrees, meetings in the morning, work in the afternoons, compulsory education mixed with 'anything goes' in the autonomous sphere, self-management of time but central planning – little wonder that Bookchin's patience ran out.

It is a pity that Gorz's failure to establish the political and economic framework of his utopia should negate many of his valuable suggestions concerning the need for individual communal autonomy within a broader institutional network of key state institutions and industries. Like other post-industrial theorists, Gorz seems to make the giant leap from current global concentrations of economic power (especially the concentration of telecommunications, electronic and machine patents), to the utopian future where high tech is democratized and dispersed to the masses. Gorz rejects communal autarky but wisely suggests that national self-sufficiency in food be aimed for on ecological grounds. His praise for Toffler, however, seems to indicate that Gorz believes in global industrial integration in the future. Yet national food self-sufficiency presupposes policies on chemicals, biogenetics, plant patents, energy sources and industrial food processes. How can autarky in this vital area be achieved without similar autarkic or semi-autarkic policies in other spheres of the post-industrial economy?

Nearly all the dominant economic theories of today – monetarism, Keynesianism, market socialism – are oriented to greater international integration and growth. Gorz cannot simply advocate state planning of new technology and yet not indicate whether this planning will be carried out at central, decentralized levels, or both. Also, he cannot afford to remain silent on how a centrally or decentrally planned society can establish national self-sufficiency of key areas (for example, food), without directly challenging the whole thrust of ever increasing global integration. In dividing society into spheres, Gorz valiantly tries to keep one foot in each of the opposing camps: small, autonomous and autarkic practice on the one hand, and large, technically integrated production, information and administration on the other. Gorz combines the detailed knowledge of specialized technique and organization (which he observed on numerous occasions as a journalist), with the optimistic superficiality of a futurologist unable to recognize the incompatibility of many forms of capitalist high technology with socialist social relations.

Like other post-industrial theorists, Gorz says little on social welfare funding, the revenue options of a steady-state or low-growth, centrally planned society, or an economy based on a mixture of planning and market mechanisms. Ironically, Gorz is the only post-industrial theorist who devotes space to the necessity of socialist state institutions – this is ironic, because he conceives of states in too narrow a political or administrative form and neglects the crucial issues of how radical post-industrialists can safeguard local and national state structures in the face of increasing supranational domination. In later chapters I will discuss some of the problems associated with alternative welfare, defence, educational, legal and political institutions. All our post-industrial theorists advocate a more tolerant, pluralistic and democratic future. Yet I have shown that they all either appear oblivious to the incompatibility of new global forms of economic integration and desirable forms of decentralization and small institutions, or, in the case of Bahro and others, fail to indicate how local communes will interact with the outside world. It is for these important reasons that the incompatible paths of more integration or more autarky have to be confronted and resolved.

The guarantee of an income independent of a job will be emancipatory or repressive, from the Left or the Right, according to whether it opens up new spaces for individual *and social* activity or whether, on the contrary, it is only the social wage for compulsory passivity.

André Gorz, *Paths to Paradise*

We should guarantee the right to work for those willing and able to do so, regardless of age. We should also decide that the right to work must also include the right *not* to work and that the compulsory work ethic is now irrelevant, obsolete and counter-productive. Many people may feel a temporary sense of moral outrage if work ceases to be compulsory, but it will not lead to social disintegration.

Barry Jones, *Sleepers, Wake!*

Under communism it is also to be expected that each of the local community bodies would have considerable freedom to determine the extent and form of welfare provisions in its locality, but that this freedom would operate within some centrally-but-democratically laid down guidelines to ensure a degree of territorial justice and ease of geographical mobility.

Bob Deacon, *Social Policy and Socialism*

# 2

# The Feasibility of Alternatives to Bureaucratic Welfare States

It is rare to find New Left or New Right activists defending what is called the 'Keynesian welfare state'. In recent years, the New Right have campaigned to good effect against the 'Welfare State'; despite the dubious performance of New Right politicians in OECD countries, many social democrats have been on the defensive for the past ten years. Simplistic slogans depicting the individual being repressed by the Therapeutic and Leviathan state, demands to restore greater self-reliance instead of mass mollycoddling by the 'welfare state', as well as calls for law and order, the traditional patriarchal family, the three Rs in education and other old and New Right values, have had widespread success at the ideological level.[1]

From an opposite perspective, many Left radicals and reformers have welcomed the trenchant criticisms of the 'Keynesian welfare state' made by such diverse writers as Marcuse, Illich, Lasch, Offe, Donzelot and others.[2] The pervasiveness of surveillance, discipline, abuse, arrogance, humiliation, technocratic irrationality and other negative qualities, are amply documented by critics and victims of contemporary health, education, social welfare and legal institutions. The net effect of both New Right and New Left assaults on the 'welfare state', has been twofold. First, there has been a widespread and justifiable disbelief in the 'welfare state' as the answer to problems of poverty, inequality and lack of civil rights. Second, there has emerged a widespread belief that some form of non-bureaucratic delivery and provision of services must replace centralized, large bureaucratic welfare institutions.

As usual, most authors are much clearer on what they do not like than on what kind of alternative practices they would like to see in the future. There is no clear perspective on whether existing social welfare services should exist, and who should perform these roles (for example, family members or paid workers or both); moreover, there is very little clarity in regard to the financing of alternative social welfare practices and how these alternative practices relate to the overall political and economic structures of society. In probing the views of the post-industrial utopians on social welfare, much is revealed about the general neglect of social welfare issues (which the post-industrial theorists share with many on the Left), but also much about the neglect of problems particularly affecting women. It is not enough to condemn existing bureaucratic practices and proclaim the virtues of decentralization, guaranteed minimum incomes, self-help, alternative educational and health practices or other such widely held notions. It is not that the latter proposals are intrinsically wrong or undesirable. Rather, the advocates of radical alternatives to the 'Keynesian welfare state' show, almost invariably (with the exception of writers in journals such as *Critical Social Policy*), deficient understanding of the political economy of existing welfare services, and no basic comprehension of the role of state institutions. Few of them choose to discuss whether the redistribution of wealth, or the general reproduction of social relations, can be accomplished without the existence of central state organizations.

If a post-industrial society is characterized by decentralization, small institutions and enterprises, 'prosuming', 'basic communes' or 'electronic cottages', then it is imperative that we have some idea of how people who are in paid or unpaid work obtain social or communal services, and how these self-help or paid services are financed or sustained. Will the new social welfare services complement the new post-industrial relations in 'the economy'? Or will the tension that exists between paid workers and welfare dependents in contemporary OECD countries (that is, the need to keep welfare payments below that point which would nullify the 'work ethic') continue in modified forms? If central state institutions are abolished, will social welfare vary in quantity and quality depending on the resources and social priorities of each individual community? Or will criteria of equity and civil liberties be upheld by some as yet unspecified set of decentralized institutional mechanisms? These and other vital questions are in urgent need of an answer if we are to transcend the glaring deficiencies and irrationality of existing 'Keynesian welfare states'.

## THE SEPARATION OF SOCIAL WELFARE FROM 'THE ECONOMY'

Until recently, most non-radical economists as well as radical political economists have concentrated on problems related to commodity production, fiscal policy or other aspects of the monetarized economy. While it is true that welfare has been part of specialized analyses (for example, welfare economics, human capital theories) or part of general analyses of public sector finances, nevertheless, the overwhelming attitude to social welfare is one of seeing it as having significant, but secondary importance.

As Orio Giarini notes, '"economics", for the last two centuries, has been the "economics of industrialization" and not of the economy, which includes all assets and efforts that contribute to welfare; . . . ecological and other current movements (e.g. women's lib., etc.) are all directed at the rehabilitation of non-monetarized assets and activities which contribute to wealth and welfare and which have been marginalized or left out of account in the traditional economic (and socioeconomic) system.'[3] For many years, a minority of critics have continually pointed out that general indices such as gross national production, which conventional economists and politicians worship, consistently fail to measure social and environmental damage or the non-improvement in human welfare.[4] In the last decade, millions of unemployed and poor people have felt no benefits from yearly increases in GNP, GDP and other conventional economic indices. Even if annual growth rates of 6 to 10 per cent were achieved in leading OECD countries, it is very unlikely that unemployment would be significantly reduced (as higher productivity can often be achieved without additional labour), and high growth rates would exacerbate environmental problems such as acid rain. Therefore, any conception of a non-polluting, post-industrial economy would not only have to resolve mass unemployment, but would also have to give far more priority to new forms of social welfare, educational and community leisure services and facilities.

The growing recognition that high levels of economic growth are less likely to bring about qualitative improvements in the lives of both marginalized people and well-paid workers is an ever present theme of books on contemporary poverty, mental illness, drug addiction, urban lifestyles and professional 'burnout'. In earlier years, many orthodox Marxists believed that socialism would build upon the forces of production developed under capitalism, thus increasing growth in a planned economy. Somehow, social welfare problems would be resolved simply by redistributing the products of increased economic growth to the poor and needy. Radicals placed nearly all their emphasis on paid workers in socialist enterprises and focused on worker democracy, unalienated labour and other aspects relevant to paid workers labouring within exploited capitalist enterprises. It was implied, but never spelt out, that social welfare, education, health, etc., would cease to be problems, simply because socialism was different to capitalism, or scarcity would cease to determine social existence. A variation of the latter image of socialism can also be found in many anarchist and syndicalist theories. The creation of a radical stateless society – free of welfare bureaucracies, prisons, mental institutions, repressive schools and disease-creating medical industries – appeared to flow from the mere fact that hierarchical, Western capitalist and Eastern 'state capitalist' enterprises would be overthrown. Both the orthodox Marxist vision of increased forces of production, and the anarchist and utopian Left image of radical stateless decentralization, rest upon an unproblematical relationship between the forces of production and the provision of social welfare. Only a minority of Marxist and socialist feminist theorists (for example, Corrigan, Deacon, Gough, Offe, Piven, Wainwright[5]) have confronted the hard issues of the political economy of welfare.

In the last chapter I showed that the post-industrial theorists were divided between those who envisaged greater global integration, and writers such as Bahro who advocated national self-sufficiency. Despite the contrasting and incompatible images of future economic developments, the post-industrial utopians share a belief in the need for greater decentralization of communal services and the abolition of existing bureaucratic institutions. Each theorist, regardless of other differences, is committed to greater democracy, the removal of alienating and impersonal administrative structures, the elimination of sexism, racism and other social forms of intolerance and parochialism. Yet no post-industrial theorist seems to have much understanding of the political economic conditions which would make possible their humane alternatives – let alone how these new social relations could reproduce themselves once established. For theorists who devote so much space to criticizing the irrationality of existing 'welfare states', it is incredible that so little space is allocated to analysing the institutional bases of post-industrial communal services. Bahro and Toffler say virtually nothing on social welfare (other than the odd comment or paragraph), while Gorz and Jones are much stronger on what they would like to see done rather than how to achieve their numerous recommendations. In the following pages I will discuss the problems associated with the scattered and undeveloped notions of social welfare contained in the writings of the post-industrial utopians. I will also indicate why many of their alternative notions (equally held by other radicals and reformers) rest upon an inadequate understanding of the interrelationship of social welfare and 'the economy'. In other words, it is the artificial division between 'the economy' and social welfare, which has helped to perpetuate such woolly and naïve images of the future.

## CONFRONTING THE NATURE OF EXISTING
## WELFARE STATES

In using the all-encompassing concepts of Second and Third Waves, Toffler is forced to emphasize the similarities between capitalist and Communist countries, rather than stressing the crucial differences in political and economic institutions. Not only are there major differences between capitalist and Communist countries in the relationship between paid and unpaid workers, the delivery and financing of social welfare, health and education, but there are also significant variations within capitalist societies. If the notion of a post-industrial society is to gain credibility, then the vital political economic differences between so-called emerging Third Wave societies (the USA, Japan, Sweden) should be given more attention. Similarly, if Bahro or Gorz wish to see the transformation of work, a new relationship between autonomous and heteronomous spheres, or the ability of local communities to sustain themselves, then far more attention has to be given to existing occupational relations, the proportion of the workforce in private or state employment, the source of local and national state revenue and so forth. It is not that Bahro and Gorz wish to retain existing relations – far from it – but they reject a violent revolutionary strategy thus basing their hopes for major social change on existing social movements experiencing existing social welfare structures and income. This means that post-industrial socialists have to confront the complex problems associated with dismantling existing bureaucratic welfare institutions while sustaining and increasing mass support for their radical alternative lifestyles. But what are the major aspects of existing welfare institutions which they cannot afford to ignore? How can the diversity of local control, which the post-industrial utopians favour, be reconciled with existing forms of social inequality and opposition to higher welfare taxes?

In contrast to Communist societies, the level of state involvement in 'social wage' goods and services (that is, all those goods and services which make up a standard of living, but are not necessarily earned or expressed in money terms) in OECD countries, has depended on a number of socio-historical variables. These variables include the length in office of social democratic or Labour governments in the past 80 years, the level of class struggle and social movement struggle resulting in specific improvements in welfare, education or health services, the pressure exerted by business groups and social reformers to gain particular housing, transport and urban renewal projects, the implementation of educational retraining schemes or immigration programmes, and the specific national need to reconstruct after war and natural disasters.[6] While Communist countries have large black markets and social inequality which affect the level of individual welfare,[7] there is little comparison with the clear and blatant division of education, health and other services (into private and public schemes) in capitalist countries. The fundamental division of 'social wage' goods and services along private and state provided lines, is further complicated by the great variety of funding schemes, tax policies, local, regional and national administrative structures to which the post-industrial theorists seem to give little attention. For example, Japan has a three-tiered social welfare system consisting of workers covered by better pensions schemes in large monopoly businesses or state institutions, compared with workers in small businesses and the rest of the population exposed to minimal income sustenance. In Western Europe and the USA a number of contributing pension schemes based on occupation and employment perpetuate inequality during working lives and in retirement. Other schemes where social welfare is paid for out of general taxation (in Australia) provide less welfare in retirement than occupational super-annuation and other joint employer–worker schemes. The importance of these various welfare systems, as well as private supplementary and discriminatory forms of income sustenance, become evident when we examine the possibilities of radical alternatives.

It is also important to note several other aspects of contemporary 'welfare states'. The fiscal crises experienced by so many OECD 'welfare states' are closely related to general problems experienced by capitalist businesses in the past decade. The significant growth in unemployment, the increase in people over the age of 55, and other recipients of welfare income, has severely strained the various social security and pension budgets of leading capitalist countries.[8] The future health of these welfare schemes is fraught with difficulty as populations age,[9] unemployment shows no sign of decreasing and public hostility to more taxes for social welfare remains. Add to this financial malaise the fact that many private and public sector pension fund investments are bound up with the continued profitability of the private sector, and one has a fundamental problem: how to provide millions of people with a minimum income. If the current financial situation of many government welfare budgets looks grim, think of the revenue crisis if all those eligible for welfare payments in capitalist countries (up to 50 per cent of particular social categories in some countries), actually claimed their legal entitlement to such things as unemployment relief.

Not only are there major problems in raising sufficient revenue for the various 'social wage' programmes, but there is also the equally important issue of employment in state institutions.[10] It is relatively well known that national and local state health systems, educational institutions, transport and urban management authorities are some of the largest employers of labour in capitalist societies. It is in this vital sense that social welfare is inextricably part of 'the economy'. Quite apart from the crucial role played by capital works for 'social wage' services (for example, buildings for hospitals or schools) or by transfer payments (for example, pensions) which sustain consumer spending, capitalist economies would be severely shaken, if not destroyed, if major cuts in state sector employment were implemented. On the one hand, the very size and nature of 'social wage' programmes threaten private profitability; on the other hand, the level of state employment and provision of services in health, education and general welfare, maintain profitable accumulation, reproduce labour power and prevent dangerous eruptions of social disorder. It is this very contradiction of contemporary 'welfare states' which leads people to demand more rational alternatives (because of their bureaucratic functionalism)', and yet the better aspects of 'social wage' programmes also lead citizens to demand more, rather than less, of these same services.

As capitalist societies began restructuring industries and employment in the 1970s, it was no surprise to see Rightwing parties lead the chorus of calls for cuts in 'social wage' goods and services. I have focused on the fiscal crises confronting welfare programmes at local and national levels, the variety of funding schemes, taxes, entitlements, as well as the very large percentage of workers who depend on employment in state institutions. Despite the massive growth in 'social wage' programmes during the twentieth century, one thing is abundantly clear – that is, these extensive services are still woefully inadequate in terms of income sustenance for the poor and the provision of socially useful services.[11] If we are to move into a post-industrial society which is characterized by the dismantling and decentralization of services which in themselves are grossly deficient, the onus is on post-industrial theorists to show how this social transformation can be achieved. Nearly all post-industrial theorists favour the very important objectives of reduced working hours, greater community services and more leisure activities. But if people are not to be shunted into millions of jobs for janitors, waiters or cleaners, if we reject short-term job retraining schemes (to keep the unemployment figures down), increasing educational credentialism for unsatisfying jobs, and other negative features of capitalist restructuring, then alternative 'social wage' programmes must be firmly and centrally integrated into an overall conception of the new post-industrial economy. Unfortunately, our utopian theorists have very little idea of what would make a post-industrial economy feasible, and even less idea of how to transcend the bureaucratic nature of existing 'social wage' programmes.

## GUARANTEED MINIMUM INCOMES: THE UNIVERSAL PANACEA?

Just as there are major differences between Toffler and Bahro in relation to the nature of the post-industrial economy, so there is no agreement about the desirability of guaranteed minimum income schemes. Yet, Jones, Toffler and other theorists are all in favour of such income schemes – and in this respect are representative of a growing international body of social reformers who all promote guaranteed minimum income schemes as alternatives to existing poverty and unemployment. There are two common types of guaranteed minimum income (GMI) schemes proposed. The first type is usually constructed in relation to existing pension payments and tax structures in particular OECD countries.[12] The second type of scheme is more generous and ambitious in that it generally aims to replace or transform existing labour patterns as well as welfare programmes.[13] Both types of GMI schemes are highly problematic in that they are either very austere (hence doing little to overcome poverty), or provide generous payments thus challenging the continuation of capitalist enterprises. Nearly all GMI schemes have been proposed without adequately grounding the feasibility of financing these schemes or analysing the implications of GMI programmes on existing social relations, labour markets, gender relations, welfare bureaucracies and rates of profit. A few schemes such as the Seattle-Denver experimental programmes, which took place between 1970 and 1976, showed the importance of such schemes on work motivation, marital stability, migration patterns, education, health and housing for males and females in different age groups.[14] But there have been no nationwide GMI schemes in capitalist countries providing adequate income for the poor and neglected.

Most post-industrial theorists are opponents of the Protestant work ethic and the amount of time which wage labour takes up in an individual's life. We have already seen that Toffler et al. favour the development of numerous forms of do-it-yourself practices, convivial tools, informal networks and self-help alternatives to rigid bureaucracies. Gorz not only favours the flexible self-management of working time, but also the possibility of having two or three part-time jobs, working in different seasons of the years and so forth.[15] Jones is in favour of altering the relationship between work and education so that people can drop in and out of work and education over the period of their adult lives. He is also in favour of establishing the 35 year working lifetime as the norm, thus freeing more time for leisure and personal development.[16] The West German Green Party favours the recognition of housework and childcare as full-time work with the same rights as other jobs.[17] These and other proposals sound very attractive compared with existing social relations. The problem is that they all rest indirectly and directly on some form of GMI which can guarantee two things: (a) the material basis of freedom and (b) the transcendence of the realm of necessity (in its present form as wage labour and the adherence to bureaucratic regulations). That is, a GMI scheme should not be a bare minimum – thus perpetuating or increasing poverty. And, it is to be hoped, the GMI would free individuals from the necessity of alienated labour and bureaucratic control.

Toffler supports a GMI because 'even prosumers need some money income'.[18] But, he argues, 'Such transfer payments don't have to come through the conventional channels. They can be handled as negative income taxes, or they can be decentralized, privatized, funnelled through families, churches, schools, businesses, local governments and a thousand other pipelines, so as to reduce the centralized bureaucracy and the accumulation of power in the hands of Big Brother.'[19] It is clear that Toffler has little idea of the complex moral and financial issues related to a GMI scheme. There are more than enough problems associated with a centrally administered GMI, let alone Toffler's pluralist utopia. If the GMI is a universal scheme (as all the proposed GMI schemes have been), then a negative income tax presupposes a nationwide tax structure with standardized rates of collection and exemption. Taxes could be collected at local level and GMI payments made at local level, but these would still presuppose some standardized central policy department, if not a large centralized tax department. If the GMI scheme is decentralized and privatized, however, it is highly likely that no universal standards of eligibility or income payment would be implementable. First, the controversial criteria of eligibility. There are several criteria of eligibility which constantly rear controversial heads whenever GMI schemes are discussed. These disputed categories include: whether the GMI should be given to an individual or to a family unit; what is classified as a family unit and should there be extra payments for each child; should the GMI be available to individuals and if so, should it be given to women, men or children regardless of the income levels of related spouse or parent; should the GMI begin at the age of 18 or earlier; if the person is still going to school and lives with his or her parent/s, should the GMI be equivalent to student allowances or should all other payments such as rent allowances, supplementary benefits, etc., be permitted or abolished regardful or regardless as to whether the individual lives in his or her own or rented accommodation; should the recipient of a GMI be permitted to earn extra income, and if so, at what point should the GMI be withdrawn, reduced or unaffected by any extra income earned.

Given the extremely controversial nature of the above criteria, it is almost absurd to believe that churches, businesses and a thousand other pipelines could possibly agree on universal criteria if a GMI scheme were to be privatized. The prevalence of conservative religious organizations (bitterly opposed to womens' rights, homosexual relationships, children's liberation from patriarchal bullying) would jeopardize entitlements to millions of people if left in local, privatized and decentralized hands. One already has the institutionalization of highly uneven and discriminatory welfare entitlements in the 50 United States as well as in other federal and unitary nation states. Why should one not fear an even greater degree of inequality and discrimination if income schemes are left to a thousand different organizations?!

Apart from this underdeveloped notion of a privatized GMI, Toffler also advocates the expansion and diversification of the education, health and social welfare services. 'This sector can be transformed from a bastion of governmental bureaucracy to a decentralized entrepreneurial sector based on small units serving micro-markets and consisting of small businesses, non-profits, co-ops, plus public agencies.'[20] Toffler appears to have fused various contemporary schools of thought – from Illich's ideas on deschooling to New Right notions of privatization and anarchist co-operatives – without fully appreciating their internal inconsistencies. If the Third Wave is going to be characterized by the growth of 'prosuming' (which eventually leads to a demarketized economy), then 'social wage' services can only be marketed so long as exchange relations and the market sector still exists. Whether a privatized 'social wage' market can improve upon non-marketed services, is highly controversial. But to posit an alternative to welfare bureaucracies without thinking through whether these decentralized services will be 'prosumer' or marketable, is myopic and unreal. Moreover, Toffler is merely articulating popular utopian notions of a society which provides a GMI on the one hand, and yet is characterized by economic arrangements which leave social welfare to the 'invisible hand' of the market. Many people yearn for a non-bureaucratized society which guarantees equality as well as the provision of a wide range of services. Somehow, little thought is given to the institutional mechanisms which make decentralization compatible with equality. Even less thought is given to the compatibility or incompatibility of GMI schemes and marketized or demarketized diversity and local autonomy. I will return to some of these issues when I discuss the problems in market socialism later on.

While Toffler's GMI scheme is riddled with contradictions and problems, Barry Jones is more conventional in his advocacy of a state-run GMI scheme. Like Gershuny and Miles,[21] Barry Jones differentiates between employment and 'social wage' programmes which are state organized or privately marketed.[22] Yet Gershuny and Miles are far from optimistic that the post-industrial society will witness a great surge of employment in state sector services – given the political economic crises affecting welfare budgets in the 1980s.[23] Jones, on the other hand, puts forward dozens of proposals for new services and jobs without adequately considering whether they are implementable in a capitalist society. Most of the new jobs and income programmes in Jones's scenario are to be found in the following areas:

(1) state sector services such as education, administration, welfare and environmental protection;
(2) domestic services, leisure and tourist activities which are either provided by private enterprises or made possible by GMI and other publicly organized forms of income sustenance.[24]

Being a Fabian evolutionist, Barry Jones's alternative 'social wage' society rests on the ability of new technology to generate sufficient revenue to pay for all the social welfare services. Like Toffler, Jones envisages OECD countries as oases of post-scarcity, as post-industrial societies where human welfare and leisure will take priority over profit and self-denying toil. Yet a closer examination of Jones's proposals reveals the following obstacles and problems. First, nearly all his positive ideas for a much expanded education, welfare and health system, depend on the very considerable growth of state employment or state subsidization of incomes and infrastructure. As a campaigning minister in a conservative, minor reformist government, Jones knows how difficult it is to maintain expenditure on 'social wage' programmes at current levels, let alone expand state sector growth to the very high levels he proposes.[25] Such massive growth of 'social wage' programmes is politically non-negotiable in capitalist societies where capitalist interest groups are bitterly opposed to even small increases in state employment. This is not to deny the possibility of various social reforms and the introduction of new tax schedules or revenue allocations. However, the scale of Jones's 'post-service society' programmes far outweighs the reality of piecemeal incrementalism – so typical of most OECD 'social wage' programmes.

Second, it is not uncommon to read post-industrial theorists (especially of the Right), constantly citing the historical transformation of agricultural labour as evidence of the difficulty those in earlier generations had in believing in the coming transformation of lifestyles.[26] Jones and Toffler share this post-industrial optimism in their attempt to equate the move from agriculture to industry with the move from industrial to post-industrial employment. Even if we suspended our disbelief and assumed that capitalist classes would find a massively expanded 'social wage' programme complementary to their profit needs, and even if we assumed that there was sufficient tax revenue generated from the Third Wave industries, we would still be left with some giant conceptual headaches. For example, Jones argues that much of the new employment within the private sector will be in those areas to do with domestic services and leisure activities. He proposes a GMI scheme, however, which is based on the Australian Poverty Commission recommendations formulated during the 1970s.[27] Such a scheme would be far from generous as it conceives a GMI as being equivalent to no more than 20 per cent above the poverty line (which is itself about 30 per cent of average weekly wages). If Jones assumes that private work can be found in the domestic sphere (for example, cleaning, gardening, etc.) plus increased tourism and leisure activities, who will be able to afford such services or consume such leisure activities on an austere GMI which barely enables the poor to survive in the first place?! As many of the traditional industries and employment will be eliminated by new developments, it appears as if Jones believes that the post-industrial society will be one characterized by a massive social-industrial complex (that is, state-run 'social wage' programmes), a small, but highly productive capital-intensive private sector and a labour-intensive, services sector based on both private and public criteria. How such a post-industrial economy could remain capitalist, or provide adequate state employment and an adequate GMI to sustain high technology consumerism, is beyond comprehension.

Third, one of the differences between Jones and Toffler is that Jones comes from a Labour movement tradition, whereas Toffler's ideas are infused with the values of American free enterprise. When Toffler addresses the questions of social welfare, he emphasizes anti-statist solutions, privatization, 'prosuming' and GMI schemes which are catch-all solutions. Jones, in contrast, recognizes the need for the employment of numerous people in state sector institutions – from public libraries to hospitals – because private market forces have neglected and opposed many of these socially useful services. While both Jones and Toffler favour a highly decentralized society, Toffler assumes that new employment will be more of the 'prosuming' type – backed up by a comprehensive and generous GMI. Jones recognizes that a GMI can not in itself be a substitute for labour-intensive 'social wage' services. The problem which both Toffler and Jones ignore, is how does a society finance a generous GMI, or a massive increase in state sector employment (even though these new state jobs will be decentralized). It would be extremely difficult to finance even Jones's austere and conservative GMI scheme (within capitalist countries) let alone one which provided more than 50 per cent of average weekly wages to all individuals regardless of relations to spouse or parent(s).

Nearly all the GMI schemes proposed in OECD countries have had to be sensitive to the cost of labour on the market and the need to avoid undermining the incentive to work for low wages. Jones and Toffler are representative of those who ignore the conditions of capitalist reproduction, who ignore the disciplining affect of high unemployment on the paid workforce, or who advocate extensive 'social wage' programmes without considering their compatibility with capitalist institutions. While it would be wrong to create a polarity between private enterprises and 'social wage' programmes (as many capitalist businesses benefit from existing state services and 'social wage' contracts), it is nevertheless utopian to believe that capitalist relations can survive the extensive demarketized social practices and income schemes proposed by Jones and Toffler.

Although Jones and Toffler are not committed to the perpetuation of capitalist social systems, many of their utopian visions are infused with concepts and practices first developed and maintained by capitalist businesses. In a later chapter I will discuss the cultural and political implications of home-based work and 'prosuming' activities. For the moment, let me pursue a few other problems related to Toffler's and Jones's images of alternative 'social wage' programmes. Both Jones and Toffler criticize the waste and irrationality resulting from mass unemployment, drug dependency, poverty, urban squalor and social alienation. Toffler is a strong advocate of the 'new family' – of multiple combinations and forms of co-habitation –of wages for housework, of job sharing within the 'electronic cottage', of child labour which is non-exploitative but allows children to relate to parents and new technology in a more holistic form, of the deinstitutionalization of social services and education and so forth.[28] Jones and Toffler share a refreshing belief in the emergence of varied work patterns, lifestyles, new mixtures of private and public employment, services and values. Much of their analysis rests on the assumption that a 'new class' of 'mind workers' will replace traditional First and Second Wave classes.[29] These new workers will be well paid, highly educated and communally active. The problem is that most of these 'new class' workers are to be found in state sector employment rather than in the private sector. While it is true that millions of new jobs have been created by the micro-chip revolution, many of these jobs are not high-salary jobs (for example, process work assembling new technology) which can be shared by couples in the 'electronic cottage'. Toffler argues that affluence makes the non-nuclear Third Wave 'new family' possible. A return to pre-1955 standards of living in the USA would prevent the Third Wave from emerging.[30] Toffler does not show how the Third Wave can create enough well-paid 'mind-worker' jobs to sustain the new independent lifestyles.

The historical record of OECD countries has been one characterized by private enterprises shedding labour, avoiding social responsibilities for damage caused to humans and natural habitats, etc., and expecting state institutions to look after the mess left behind. As Toffler and Jones cannot indicate which private industries will create sufficient numbers of new jobs, it is most likely that the 'social wage' burden will fall even more heavily upon the shoulders of the government – or wage workers paying the bulk of taxes used to keep governments. Moreover, Toffler and Jones say little or nothing about the voluntary and paid sector of contemporary social welfare industries. Idealized images of community residents caring for the old, sick, young, lonely or unemployed fill the pages of many books by reformers and revolutionaries. These ideals are to be applauded providing that such alternative services are properly grounded and avoid the exploitative qualities of contemporary voluntarism. If one cannot establish the economic viability of adequate GMI schemes, or how local communities can generate sufficient revenue and resources for non-bureaucratic welfare services, then the deinstitutionalization of existing 'social wage' programmes will be in danger of degenerating into new realms of charity, voluntary aid by the minority of affluent, or increased workloads for overworked and underpaid community workers.

The close relationship between low wages and long hours for community workers, negligent or inadequate social welfare budgets, and business opposition to more 'social wage' programmes, has long been a feature of most capitalist societies. Opposition to existing welfare bureaucracies should be based on a greater appreciation of the role and nature of existing state institutions. In many OECD countries, money derived from state sources accounts for about 28 to 30 per cent of household income. If 'the state is to wither away', then utopians (of the Left or the Right) will have to account for the new sources of income sustenance, wage rates, working conditions, the relationship between paid and unpaid labour, and the type of social and individual problems that may still require institutions whether they be prisons, hospitals or schools. If post-industrial societies are to avoid repeating existing 'social wage' inequalities (where middle and upper income people benefit from state subsidies, services and well-paid professional jobs in health, housing, transport, law and education), then far greater redistribution of wealth, reallocation of resources, rectification of gender and race discrimination will have to be implemented. But these very drastic reforms challenge the continued growth of highly paid 'mind workers' as well as requiring greater, not lesser state intervention in the market place.

If elaborate GMI schemes and decentralized 'social wage' programmes are incompatible with the long-term survival of capitalist relations, are they possible or compatible with socialist relations? André Gorz is in two minds about the desirability of GMI schemes. In *Farewell to the Working Class*, Gorz argues that

> the right to a 'social income' (or 'social wage') for life in part abolishes 'forced wage labour' only in favour of a wage system without work. It replaces or complements, as the case may be, exploitation with welfare, while perpetuating the dependence, impotence and subordination of individuals to centralized authority. This subordination will be overcome only if the autonomous production of use-values becomes a real possibility for everyone.[31]

There are several major weaknesses in Gorz's abstract critique of GMI schemes. Because Gorz divides life into heteronomous and autonomous spheres, and yet also retains the Marxian distinction between use-value and exchange value, he appears to be caught within a productivist framework. Yet millions of citizens do not work for wages (for example, the aged or dependent), and are not able to engage in the production of use-values regardless of whether the society is capitalist or socialist. Either one maintains all the current welfare categories, eligibility tests and means tests – with their associated stigma and discrimination – or one adopts a universal income support system.

Second, unless Gorz envisages a moneyless society, the charge that 'forced wage labour' is replaced by impotence and the subordination of individuals to centralized authority is not only evasive rhetoric, but is also wrong. It is evasive because Gorz would have to show how millions of people in unpaid work would derive their sustenance and support their leisure activity. It is wrong because a GMI scheme (free of existing welfare policies) would give recipients much more dignity, and more importantly, lessen the power of centralized control which currently exists in the form of numerous eligibility tests and constant policing.

Third, Gorz confuses a 'social income' with the 'social wage'. In capitalist societies, the concept 'social wage' is generally used when referring to all those services such as education, health and social welfare which constitute a vital *non-monetary* part of an individual's standard of living. These state provided services tend to be predominantly use-values as opposed to the exchange-value commodities obtainable with money. A society may be characterized by greater or lesser reliance upon wages or 'social wage' goods and services. But it is difficult to imagine how a complex socialist society could ever operate without some form of monetary or social income system – even though there could be a dramatic increase in the provision of 'social wage' goods and services. For example, Gorz favours the self-management of time which would permit a worker to change jobs and length of hours over a working lifetime. How this could be implemented for all citizens without the back-up support system of a GMI – given that people are frequently changing residence or are in-between jobs – remains a mystery.

While I believe that some form of GMI scheme will be necessary in a socialist society, I am critical of many contemporary advocates of GMI schemes because they often propose these schemes in a political vacuum or else underestimate the socio-economic consequences of such proposals. This is also true of Gorz who changes his argument in *Paths to Paradise* by coming out openly in favour of a GMI scheme. The problem with Gorz is that he fluctuates between imagining that a GMI can abolish wage labour, while believing in an equally utopian exercise of the imagination, that a GMI can be financed within a capitalist society by taxing automated production. Let me examine the reasons why both proposals are highly improbable or unrealistic. In breaking the existing connection between labour and wages, Gorz hopes that a more automated society will meet the needs of a *citizen* as opposed to a wage slave.[32] The drastic reduction in work time could liberate citizens for autonomous production. At the moment, a section of the population has to produce inessentials in order to be able to earn wages to buy necessities.[33] But, Gorz warns, 'freeing time will create new spaces of autonomy only if the time released does not have to be spent in the autoproduction of some of those necessities which previously could be bought.'[34] If Gorz is opposed to the pre-industrial toil and drudgery which women were subjected to in producing and servicing their families, he either presupposes sharing these necessary but unpleasant domestic tasks, automating them, or having outsiders do them in return for money or exchanged services. Gorz does not really tell us how domestic labour will be freed of its heteronomous quality. Nor does he tell us how a continuation of the production of many existing labour-saving chemicals, packaging and so forth, will prevent ecological destruction while also avoiding a return to simple, labour-intensive domestic labour. However, Gorz does favour the implementation of local co-operatives (following Nordal Akerman) where members provide services and goods in exchange for a given number of hours they can labour.[35] Instead of being paid wages, members receive vouchers which they can exchange for painting, holiday accommodation, etc. Gorz thinks that this system of barter abolishes monetary relations and assumes a non-market form.[36] In this belief he is either naïve or just plain wrong.

First of all, an elaborate form of bartered exchange of goods and services between members of co-operatives is not planned allocation; hence the transactions must be governed by supply and demand – even though this market is not the same as existing profit-oriented markets. Second, the voucher system does not abolish wage labour. It merely replaces money as each voucher is worth a number of hours labour, which in turn is valued by the number of hours of labour embodied in a particular service, material good or other communal need. Third, and most importantly, if most people conducted their heteronomous and autonomous labour in vouchers, how would tax revenue be collected in order to pay citizens the GMI? I am all in favour of increasing co-operative schemes, but we have to be quite clear about the extent of these schemes, and whether they are compatible with a GMI based on monetary exchange. Moreover, I am not optimistic that wage labour will ever be abolished in complex societies – although the highly exploitative *quality* of current wage labour certainly can be abolished by radical transformation of property and power relations.

Gorz is just as unreal when proposing a tax on automated production to finance GMI schemes in capitalist societies.[37] It is certainly possible to impose new taxes on each unit of automated production (given political support for these measures). But taxing automated production is not equivalent to taxing alcohol, tobacco and other commodities. Gorz desires political pricing mechanisms (to replace capitalist market prices) so that all new labour-replacing production can be controlled and used to pay for GMI schemes and other community needs. While I endorse his strategy of increasing political price mechanisms (which currently determine the cost of alcohol, etc.), it is stretching the imagination to believe that sufficient revenue could be raised for a nation-wide GMI scheme if taxes were imposed on automated production. If such a large amount of revenue were collected, capitalist firms would most likely cease to be profitable. Furthermore, many of the profit-making businesses using automated equipment do not produce units which are equivalent to a packet of cigarettes or a bottle of whisky. Information processing, automated services and other non-labour intensive production would require new forms of taxation calculation if Gorz's proposals are to be even considered as viable, let alone sufficient.

Many radicals believe that GMI schemes as well as widespread poverty can be solved by simply increasing taxes on the rich or on new forms of production. Certainly there is ample room for capitalist classes bearing a larger tax burden. The major problems of poverty and exploitation, however, can only be resolved by a transformation in the use of privately and publicly controlled wealth and resources, rather than in a purely income distributing strategy. Consequently, redistributing profits will not in itself provide sustainable funds for GMI schemes (after the initial expropriation); what is needed is a more radical transformation of material and immaterial resources so that new social priorities are not constrained by existing patterns of private production and consumption. Gorz does recognize the need for this revolution. Yet his GMI proposals and moneyless utopia fly in the face of his own perceptive critique of existing capitalist relations.

## POST-SCARCITY WELFARE OR SELF-SUFFICIENT ENVIRONMENTAL HARMONY?

Whereas Toffler and Jones envisage new 'social wage' programmes within a context of high technology, continued high consumption levels and even more affluence (despite their desire to see less environmental damage and healthier lifestyles), Bahro rejects the fundamental bases of industrialism.[38] Rejecting the occupational division of labour in developed industrial societies, the implementation of high technology (which he sees as leading to Big Brother), and the continued affluence of Western consumerist materialism, Bahro posits an image of post-industrial socialism very different from Toffler, Jones and Gorz. But like most anarchists, self-management socialists or fundamentalist members of the Green movement, Bahro has an idealized image of communal life where there is little need for extensive government-run 'social wage' programmes as these jobs and roles will be performed by mutual self-help within the confines of 'basic communes'.

Nearly all the references to social welfare made by Bahro are couched in negative terms. Criticizing the 1983 Green Party Programme, Bahro notes that of the 21 pages of the immediate programme, 19 and a half 'deal with piecemeal repairs to the system'.[39] This 'eco-reformist' and 'left social democratic programme' cannot be the main concern of the Green Party, claims Bahro. 'Our main concerns cannot be the old questions of capitalist politics: whether pensions are adequate, whether mothers should draw a child allowance and so on . . . We must use our strength for something else: to be the instrument of a new orientation beyond the conflicts of supply-and-demand politics.'[40] Yet Bahro is against the immediate dismantling of the 'welfare state'. 'Doing away with the Welfare State is not, of course, the *first* task. Unemployment can only be an opportunity if you don't have to go begging the next day, if you can devote your time over the next six months to thinking about fundamental questions.'[41] Strategically, Bahro wants the Green Party to be different from trade unions or conventional reform parties. But his whole attitude to existing social welfare programmes seems to be one of using them as vehicles for transition to a post-industrial utopia.

In so far as welfare income subsidizes the creation of the new Green society, Bahro is happy for welfare bureaucracies to continue to exist. This strategy is based on the creation of alternative 'basic communes' in the womb of capitalist society. As more and more people opt for non-industrial lifestyles outside of conventional patterns of employment and consumption, the problem (which Bahro does not discuss) becomes one of fiscal crisis as welfare budgets are forced to pay for that increasing percentage of the population which 'drops out'. Either this 'bleeding' of the welfare structure will be bitterly resented by all those workers and capitalist businesses remaining within the system, or the new 'basic communes' will become self-sufficient and not require outside welfare income. However, to become self-sufficient within a capitalist society would require a much more detailed plan as well as more extensive social resources than those Bahro and his supporters have intimated. Not only is this strategy highly dubious in relation to the future sustenance of all those millions currently dependent on state welfare income and services, but it tells us precious little about the care and sustenance provided for all those able to live in 'basic communes'. Would the new communards use money? Would all those not working in food production or crafts (for example, teachers, doctors, childcare workers, etc.) be paid wages or food and goods? Would the 'basic communes' only provide that level of social welfare which each commune could sustain, or would income supplement for poor communes be provided by other organizations or communes?

If Bahro's alternative society requires much less in the way of consumer goods and services, then income earned, or a GMI scheme, could be based on much lower thresholds. Nevertheless, any such comprehensive income scheme would have to overcome all the eligibility criteria, organizational problems, relations between paid rates and unpaid labour conditions, which I outlined in criticizing Toffler and Jones. Failure to do so would doom Bahro's society to primitive and unequal barter, parochial inequalities or demands for reinstituting industrial production in order to emerge from self-imposed austerity. While there is no question that many present levels and forms of consumption and waste could be significantly reduced or abolished, it is still unclear how Bahro thinks his post-industrial society would work. How is it possible to reduce the amount of daily toil if industrial production in its present form is abolished? Bahro does not answer this vital question as his 'basic communes' are inadequately differentiated concepts resting upon a more simple lifestyle. However, many pre-industrial societies were characterized by high degrees of toil and scarcity. If the pre-industrial patterns of the past are not to be repeated, then the relationship between leisure, consumption, wealth creation, environmental care and hours of labour must all be substantially clarified and articulated.

As for Gorz, we have seen that his solution to the question of alternative work and leisure arrangements is to divide society and activity into heteronomous and autonomous spheres. This division is far from satisfactory when it comes to alternatives to existing social welfare services. The reason for this is that Gorz has failed to spell out the nature of housework, childcare, care for the aged, sick, etc., and in what way these tasks will be part of either autonomous or heteronomous spheres. In his image of utopia, Gorz sees students being required to do compulsory work for 20 hours a week in the areas of public hygiene, care for the sick and aged.[42] He also believed that nobody should do dirty and unpleasant jobs such as cleaning garbage on a permanent basis. These jobs should be rotated and involve as many people as possible.[43] In contrast to Toffler, Gorz opposes wages for housework. According to Gorz, if housework were renumerated at the marginal price of an hour's work – so that the performance of an hour's housework entitled the person in question to receive the quantity of goods and services that could be produced in one hour in the commodity sector – the cost of domestic payments would be so high as to exceed the capacities of even the most opulent society.[44] In addition to pointing out the prohibitive cost of housework, Gorz also opposes the reduction of housework to exchange relations. He fears that making housework equivalent to other forms of wage labour would result in the search for higher productivity and would lead to

> the standardization and industrialization of such activities, particularly those involving the feeding, minding, raising and education of children. The last enclave of individual or communal autonomy would disappear; socialization, 'commodification' and pre-programming would be extended to the last vestiges of self-determined and self-regulated life. The industrialization, through home computers, of physical and psychical care and hygiene, children's education, cooking and sexual technique is precisely designed to generate capitalist profits from activities still left to individual fantasy.[45]

In opposing the 'computerized socialization of autonomous activities' and wages for housework, Gorz is clearly at odds with Toffler,[46] Jones and various feminists who advocate the socialization of domestic labour. The interesting point here is how can Gorz be so attracted to Toffler's vision of the Third Wave, when this new society is based on computerized 'electronic cottages' if not the computerization of sex and child rearing? Moreover, how does Gorz think that individual parents learn child rearing and other domestic roles? In what sense can these practices ever be truly individual and autonomous practices – given that all individuals are socialized into particular ways of family interactions, gender and sexual relations and so forth? Gorz is correct in objecting to the various forms of commodification which make parents depend on particular packaged models of the 'good housewife' or 'caring father'. But the issue is not so simple. If an alternative society is to be characterized by a plurality of family forms, people living alone, etc., then greater recognition has to be made of the vital 'social wage' services (such as health care) which have to be provided regardless of the transformation, or perhaps, precisely because of the transformation in gender relations. It is perfectly legitimate to ask of Gorz: what is wrong with socialized laundries, childcare, domestic cleaning services, health care, etc.? If these domestic tasks are servile (to use Gorz's term), then why should these 'heteronomous' tasks not be paid for just like other forms of heteronomous labour?

What is apparent about Gorz's work is that he is far more familiar with wage labour processes than with contemporary 'social wage' programmes and unpaid domestic labour. Consequently, his division of life into heteronomous and autonomous spheres of activity falls down badly when it comes to all those forms of labour which defy the strict division between wage work and leisure. Like Bahro, Gorz would like to see a society which is characterized by communal solidarity, convivial tools, non-industrialized health and education services and so forth. Yet Gorz is not an advocate of self-sufficient communes and recognizes the vital roles that will still have to be performed by state institutions. But can one have a socialist society which is not based on communes and still have a fully individualized sphere of non-heteronomous labour? If local communities are to be larger than a few thousand people (as Gorz believes they will be), then it is impossible to avoid a certain degree of standardization of 'social wage' programmes. Either one favours a radical self-sufficiency along Bahro's lines, or one has to spell out the relationship between state planning, local autonomy, eligibility criteria for 'social wage' services, values to be cultivated in educational institutions, responsibility for the provision of income sustenance and institutional mechanisms which permit an individual to receive comparable 'social wage' services if he or she moves to another city – in other words, all those issues and problems which cannot be covered by Gorz's generalized images of presidential decrees or vague notions of local autonomy.

## TAKING FEMINISM SERIOUSLY OR POST-INDUSTRIAL PATRIARCHIES?

No group in society has more at stake when alternatives to existing welfare bureaucracies are proposed, than women. It is therefore crucial that any notion of a post-industrial society which claims to be pro-feminist is able to demonstrate how alternative social relations overcome existing forms of inequality and discrimination. While it is clear that Toffler, Jones, Bahro and Gorz are all in favour of eliminating the major forms of existing gender inequalities, it is important to ask whether their proposed alternative institutional arrangements promote or negate these moral objectives. If the overcoming of women's oppression could be achieved merely by getting men to do their share of domestic labour, passing laws against discrimination in public institutions and employment, then our post-industrial utopians could feel pleased about their pro-feminist ideas. However, women should not only feel upset over the neglect of issues important to them, but also demand much more clarification of how the vague proposals for decentralized, small-scale institutions would actually improve conditions for women.

Because all the theorists discussed appear to be either ignorant or relatively oblivious of 'social wage' problems, it is not surprising that they have also neglected issues of great importance to women. In a world which is characterized by high levels of poverty amongst women (especially women raising children on their own), low levels of pay and low status jobs for women, minimal urban and rural support networks and facilities and so forth, a literal revolution in conditions is necessary if feminist criticisms of existing conditions are taken seriously.[47] But let us look at the proposals for women put forward by our post-industrial theorists. Toffler paints an optimistic picture of Third Wave transnational corporations and local 'prosuming'. How women will benefit from these developments is unclear because Toffler says little or nothing about new jobs for women, wage rates, social services and so forth. Will millions of existing low-paid female jobs be converted into well-paid 'electronic cottage' work? Will the restructuring of industries, welfare bureaucracies, privatization of education, etc., mean that women's wages are raised or that male wages are reduced to existing low-paid female rates? Where are the new private sector industries that Toffler hopes will emerge? Will these industries also be based on cheap female labour as in Third World countries (for example, existing micro-electronic process work), or well-paid jobs for women in OECD countries? Similarly, Jones lists numerous new jobs and 'social wage' programmes that could directly benefit women and children providing that such incremental reforms are implementable within capitalist societies. The old Fabian belief in social mobility via higher education has failed to overcome major differences in wealth and privilege. Why should women believe that 'post-industrial Fabianism' is any more feasible or achievable? I will discuss the issues of new technology, domestic labour and women's social conditions in chapter 4. But it is worth mentioning here that both Jones and Toffler are uncritical champions of new reproductive technology – which is rightly feared by many women as being detrimental to their welfare in its present form and application.[48]

As for Bahro and other advocates of 'basic communes', how can women be confident that this alternative is not going to be a new form of primitive, 'earth mother' drudgery? It is bad enough that Bahro cannot even tell us how these communes will achieve self sufficiency, let alone whether women will be better or worse off than before. On the other hand, even Ivan Illich, who has made a self-critique of how his earlier work (for example, *Medical Nemesis*) overlooked gender issues, has criticized Gorz for neglecting the international economic implications of gender discrimination and exploitation.[49] Equally important, Alec Nove criticizes Gorz for failing to indicate how his non-self-sufficient but small-is-beautiful institutions will work.[50] Nove is in favour of small-scale institutions but sees these working according to a mixture of market mechanisms and state planning. Gorz is opposed to market socialism but provides no analysis of how such an alternative heteronomous and autonomous set of practices will be reproduced. These questions are extremely important for all socialists, especially women. Toffler, Jones, Gorz, Sale and others openly advocate a non-bureaucratic form of small-scale decentralization. Either these local communities and small enterprises conform to non-market criteria of administrative self-sufficiency, or their interdependence with other communities and institutions are determined by market mechanisms, central planning, mixtures of market and planning mechanisms or mixtures of central planning, semi-autarky and a very small market sector.

All those images of post-industrial socialism which are based on high technology innovation, increased global integration through export-oriented industries and supranational administrative institutions, implicitly favour market mechanisms playing a prominent role. If post-industrial societies are going to become market socialist societies, we have to ask Toffler, Jones and Gorz, as well as Nove, Hodgson and other advocates of market socialism or post-capitalist democratic economies,[51] whether market mechanisms will perpetuate or overcome the oppression currently suffered by women. Will a market socialist society be able to function, let alone provide the massive amounts of finance and non-market resources if post-industrial societies are characterized by large 'social wage' programmes and environmental protection?

It is no accident that most male political economists have neglected the central issue of social welfare in their various proposals of 'feasible socialism', alternative economic programmes or post-industrial socialism. In raising the vital issue of paid and unpaid services, we should be aware that any party or movement claiming to be socialist in the 1980s will become irrelevant to more than half the population if it fails to address the crucial issues of widespread gender discrimination in the quantity and quality of 'social wage' programmes. It is revealing to note that while Toffler, Jones, Gorz and Sale put forward many utopian proposals (affecting market and non-market practices) but have little understanding of political economy, Nove, Hodgson and other political economists are more sensitive to the conventional problems ignored by our post-industrial theorists, but say virtually nothing about all those 'social wage' programmes which would precisely be one of the distinguishing hallmarks of a post-capitalist egalitarian and caring society. The gender-blind nature of most market socialist proposals is equally evident when it comes to the issue of labour processes, occupational divisions, wage rates and conditions. Let me elaborate on why market socialism is at best unable to satisfy major feminist concerns, and at worst is indifferent to women's oppression by way of neglect and adherence to traditional male-oriented economic problems.

Market socialists are opponents of both central planning (along Soviet lines) and stateless forms of local self-sufficiency. Their concern is to have a democratic society which permits a maximum amount of self-regulation and interaction between local institutions, while still having a strong central state which can plan key industries (for example, steel or rail transport) and also iron out social inequalities created by market mechanisms. No contemporary society has ever had a totally planned set of social relations or one which has been left completely to market forces. The point of dispute is over the possibility of democratic central planning, how much of society's material and human resources should be left to market mechanisms or state planning, and the desirability of planning at local, regional, national or supra-national levels. Although I share most of the criticism made by market socialists of Soviet planning, anarchist scenarios as well as the Yugoslav version of market socialism, I regard the views of Nove et al. as historically obsolete.[52] The major weakness of market socialists is not their attempt to avoid the worst aspects of capitalist and Communist inequalities and dictatorship, but their neglect of issues central to women, ecologists and anti-militarists. Most of their market socialist or 'feasible socialist' scenarios are premised on the continuation of high levels of contemporary forms of economic growth and consumption and the continued integration of national production and credit and food production processes with global processes.

If a society is divided between a small number of key industries which are centrally planned, and a vast number of small and medium-sized publicly owned enterprises, workers' co-operatives or individually run crafts and services which operate according to market mechanisms, the goal of greater self-regulation must be balanced against the social objectives of greater equality and the overcoming of widespread poverty and oppression. In a world characterized by intense national trade rivalry, constant technological retooling and labour shedding, widespread local and regional material inequalities, massive unemployment and poverty, seriously deficient 'social wage' programmes and so forth, it is utopian to believe that socialist enterprises governed by national and international market forces would be able to rise above the cumulative practices of inbuilt inequalities and discrimination unleashed by the forces of competition. A socialist society which comes into being against a general background a widespread sexism, racism and other social discrimination, would have to make a major effort to overcome or drastically minimize these inequalities in the first ten years of radical restructuring. But if we look at Nove's five-tiered 'feasible socialism', it can be seen that most enterprises in the non-centrally planned sectors would have autonomy over labour processes as they would operate according to market mechanisms with central controls remaining only over certain things such as taxes and income policies.[53]

Now imagine that all existing transnational enterprises, medium and small businesses are converted into 'socialist enterprises', co-operatives, etc. It is possible that the new socialist government may institute an egalitarian incomes policy for all workers. But this is most unlikely as it would undermine the so-called benefits of a free labour market which Nove and other market socialists advocate. On the other hand, tax policies and other central state incentives or penalties could be implemented in order to see that more women are hired or given job equality with males. These central policies could achieve a certain degree of social improvement for women. But how much interference could the labour market tolerate before it ceased to have autonomy and local enterprises lost control? After all, we are not talking about discrimination in a few enterprises, but right across the whole society! Imagine that you are working in an enterprise which has to function according to market mechanisms; would you hire extra women, pay equal wages to women, retrain women for jobs currently dominated by males? Remember that all these proposals would cost more, perhaps reduce or seriously disrupt production, threaten enterprise profitability, threaten existing bonus rates, wages and so forth. In so far as workers in each enterprise have to weigh up the cost of each extra wage or production change against central government incentives or penalties, I believe that market socialism has an in-built structural sexism and racism which only greater control over the labour process could remedy. Just as advocates of free enterprise overlook the inequalities of actual capitalist market places, so too, market socialists tend to work with a model of minimal social inequality which thus enables socialist enterprises and co-operatives, etc., to satisfy the needs of local democracy and central state planning. But if the major historical task is *first* to achieve material and income redistribution, eliminate poverty and overcome gender and racial oppression, then market mechanisms leave a lot to be desired. Any woman who does not demand from Nove, Hodgson and other market socialists a satisfactory account of how market mechanisms will overcome institutionalized discrimination, is surrendering to vague proposals which 'feasible socialism' is unlikely to be able to deliver.

But could a democratic society based on centralized or decentralized planning (with only a small sector determined by market mechanisms) be less sexist than a market socialist society? Assuming that the level of consciousness was the same in both the market socialist scenario and mine, I would argue that a society which was predominantly planned, would be much freer of precisely those structural features (for example, the institutional pressures of market competition) which would determine general conditions of work in enterprises left operating according to their own devices and standards. If enterprises were not threatened by bankruptcy or less profits, a society committed to gender equality could pursue this objective in a manner which was free of the conflicting interests of market viability as opposed to central directives, or of enterprise autonomy as opposed to national egalitarian values. It would be utopian to believe that serious obstacles to full gender equality would not exist under democratic centralized or decentralized planning. But the whole relationship between paid and unpaid services, labour process conditions, etc., would not be circumscribed by market mechanisms

having to be constantly policed and curbed by central administration (simply because market socialists themselves admit
that market mechanisms will give rise to a range of socialist
inequalities!).

A society which is predominantly determined by the profitability of enterprises in national and international markets
(even if these enterprises and co-operatives are controlled by
workers and there is significant state planning), will be in
constant conflict with all those social forces demanding more
revenue and resources for unprofitable 'social wage' goods
and services. I have argued elsewhere that market socialism
will perpetuate social and regional inequalities, create
political conflicts between those workers able to have enterprise autonomy and those working in centrally planned
industries, lock new socialist societies into the worst features
of global integration and so forth.[54] When it comes to alternatives to existing bureaucratic welfare states, there is
madness in advocating market socialist alternatives – precisely
because a socialist society needs to be committed to a significant increase in all those jobs, services and practices which are
incompatible with market mechanisms and market criteria.

## CONCLUSION

There are several important lessons which the post-industrial
utopians have not learnt from the debates over planning and
market mechanisms. If a new society is to be more democratic,
less oriented to the work ethic, based on small rather than large
bureaucratic institutions, etc., then either this society is based
upon a mixture of state and extensive market-oriented institutions, is democratically planned at central and decentralized
levels, or radically self-sufficient. It is clear that Jones's and
Toffler's theories are far too integrated with existing capitalist
technological developments on a global scale to be free of the
disastrous effects of capitalist market forces. Their future
societies will almost certainly be unable to deliver vastly
improved, 'social wage' programmes combined with continued private profitability. When we look at the self-
sufficiency scenarios of Bahro and Sale, two contrasting alter-

native social orders are advocated. Bahro opts for a radical deindustrialization which is not matched by any clear notion of the geo-political scale of urban centres, labour processes, the funding of 'social wage' programmes or the means by which interaction between 'basic communes' can be free of hierarchical administration. Sale, on the other hand, correctly shows the advantages of small cities over large megalopoles in the areas of health, transport and other 'social wage' services. The problem is that Sale fails to show how a self-sufficient market-oriented network of small communities can sustain high standards of affluence and yet provide vastly improved 'social wage' programmes without a non-market state sector. Whereas Bahro wishes to reduce the length of the working week and radically change the nature of production and consumption without adequate consideration of demographic and planning problems, Sale's utopia is based on the naïve belief in stateless market mechanisms – the continuation of many of the very businesses which Bahro correctly sees as preventing a qualitative improvement in work conditions or alternative forms of consumption.

In stressing the alternative options of more global integration or more autarky, I have attempted to show that no significant improvement in 'social wage' programmes (whether locally organized or centrally administered) can be conceptualized if 'the economy' is seen to be separate from social welfare. Many radicals, such as those in the West German Green Party, are opposed to existing hierarchies without any clear notion as to whether greater consultation at local level, more social planning, decentralized delivery and control over 'social wage' programmes, etc., are compatible with particular tax and fiscal strategies, or will result in greater inequalities rather than more equality. Gorz is also a good example of those radicals who oppose capitalist social relations without recognizing the incompatible tensions within his own post-industrial socialist scenario. If one is a supporter of small-scale institutions, but is opposed to both capitalist and socialist market mechanisms as the dominant form of social mediation, then it is imperative that co-ordinating and reproducing structures be established if one also opposes central planning. However, if socialism presupposes some form of general citizen participation and planning (in contrast to the secrecy and privatization of power under capitalist orders), then ritual endorsements of decentralization, small-is-beautiful and anti-bureaucracy will hardly be an adequate substitute for detailed considerations of what planning mechanisms are necessary.

I have not said anything in detail about the specific nature of alternative education, health, housing and other services. Space does not permit an extensive discussion of these matters. It is important to emphasize, however, that as the post-industrial theorists are conscious of the finite nature of environmental and social resources, the mechanisms whereby 'social wage' goods and services are provided and reproduced will be of critical importance. In so far as money will still be used, and social inequalities are not eradicated overnight, an alternative society will have to price and ration all goods and services in accordance with their abundance or scarcity and the relationship between paid labour and guaranteed social income, and decide upon short and longer term social priorities, for example, whether to provide adequate housing before more hospitals. The interrelation of social welfare and 'the economy' means that any future society will also have to decide whether it provides wage security as opposed to social security, or both. For example, until recently, the Soviet system has provided wage security for all those in paid jobs (provided one was not sacked for various dissident or illegal activities), but very poor social security for those not in the paid labour force. Similarly, the issue of democratic participation and organization has given rise to a small body of literature which has tried to learn from the experiences of alternative co-operatives, self-help organizations and other prefigurative radical collectives in North America and Europe.[55] Just as 'social wage' goods and services will not grow on trees, the very struggle to replace bureaucratic 'experts' will not come easily simply because people believe in self-management. I believe these problems are surmountable if citizens are given the political opportunity and social resources to construct alternative welfare services. But if socialists wish to come to terms with how to optimize a set of social priorities (for example, how do we improve 'social wage' programmes and urban centres which have hitherto been provided or designed without any major consideration for women, children and the disabled), then the incompatibility between a society based largely upon market mechanisms or simple barter and one based on greater equality, reduced working hours, extensive unprofitable services, etc., will have to be recognized.

Despite the defects in his analysis, Nove does recognize some of the vital issues at stake. Discussing Gorz's writing, he argues that technological economies of scale differ widely in different activities.

> Everyone benefits from large-scale generation of electricity, it would be idiotic to decree that every household fetch water from wells, or that pipelines be condemned as inappropriate labour-saving technology, when the only alternative is little men with buckets running across the desert. Gorz is right in his formulation: if large scale offers only a modest saving in costs, one's predisposition should be to opt for small scale, on just the grounds that he advances . . . But be it noted that 'small' means a small number of workers, which may not imply labour-intensive techniques. Sometimes a small number can do the job only if highly labour-saving technology is used. The choice must depend on whether shortage of labour or unemployment is the main problem, and whether the labour that is saved is agreeable or disagreeable, skilled or repetitively boring.[56]

It is the same in the vital area of alternative 'social wage' goods and services, economies of scale, the ability of local communities to provide an adequate variety of services and income sustenance, the advantages of decentralized or centralized administration, the preference for paid or unpaid labour, the level of affluence which is compatible with local, national or imported materials and natural resources – all require far more analysis than that provided by the post-industrial utopians.

If Bahro's 'basic communes' are incompatible with Gorz's, Toffler's and Jones's technological pluralism (that is, mixtures of large and small-scale industry), and if a decentralized society cannot function without market forces (which in turn will fail to eradicate existing social inequalities), is it better to have more local democracy and less equality in living standards, or more central planning and more 'social wage' programmes, greater control over environmental resources but less autonomy for individual enterprises? Can one have more leisure and less damage to the environment as well as existing OECD standards of affluence if imperialist exploitation of Third World countries ceases? These and other questions can only be answered after further consideration is made of the post-industrial theorists' analyses of ecological, military and cultural issues.

Whilst the independent, alienated Megamachine is preparing to collide against the bounds of the Earth, pressing us – its original creators – up against the wall and crushing us, it is already destroying untold millions of human lives in the Third World each year, where we have for a while diverted war, unemployment, hunger and misery of all kinds. To stop the industrial system – and first of all the military machine it has created – in its tracks, here in the metropolises where it started, is just as much the first command of solidarity with the most wretched of this Earth as it is the requirement of a reasonable self-interest. For we shall not be able to bear the backlash of either the social crises or the ecological catastrophes which our way of work and life leads to on a world scale.

Rudolf Bahro, Building the Green Movement

There is a reciprocal relation between arms and democracy. The more of one, the less of the other. Ideology has it that arms are there to defend democracy. But reason tells us that when arms cease to be defensive and become extensions of an aggressive technocracy, then they are destroyers of the democracy they were supposed to protect; they feed upon the very flesh of democracy. It follows that we fight arms by building true democracy, which spontaneously wants to lay down such arms as are not really defensive.

Joel Kovel, Against the State of Nuclear Terror

# 3

# Eco-Pacifism or Post-Industrial Militarism and Exploitative North–South Relations

It is supremely ironic that most of the post-industrial writers, who devote so much energy to analysing and outlining the future, should say so little about the immediate catastrophes facing the world today. With the exception of Bahro, post-industrial theorists either are glaringly inconsistent on major questions of nuclear weapons, high tech, environmental problems and the future of people in the Third World, or else they say little or nothing on these vital issues. While it is true that Bahro and Gorz have been at the forefront of debates over the peace movement, there is much of importance which both authors have glossed over or ignored. It is therefore crucially important to examine whether the post-industrial utopians' views on military policy, North–South relations and ecology, complement or contradict their views on small-scale, democratically decentralized societies. In earlier chapters I have tried to show how the character of any future post-industrial society will be predetermined by its degree of global integration – or, to phrase it differently, by the level of self-sufficiency the dominant political forces implement. The less the self-sufficiency developed in any particular society, the less likelihood of maximizing grass-roots decentralized control and national sovereignty over key socio-economic policy options. Similarly, I have stressed the vital role which new state institutions will have to play in the development of an adequate 'social wage' programme; the more this role goes unrecognized, the higher the probability that social inequality and discrimination will continue to flourish.

Given the perennial conflict over more guns or more bread, it is extremely important to ask the post-industrial theorists the following questions: Will the post-industrial society emerge independently of, or uncontaminated by, the existing military-industrial complexes? Is it possible to be logically consistent in opposing nuclear energy and yet supporting nuclear weapons? Can a radically decentralized society implement an adequate alternative defence system? Can the existing exploitative relations between the North and the South be eliminated without reversing the growth of military exterminism? Is the image of a post-industrial society global, or merely confined to the leading OECD countries? These and other questions will be discussed in relation to the overall conceptions of post-industrialism put forward by the utopian theorists. In this chapter I will first discuss the differences between the post-industrial theorists on the issues of nuclear weapons, defence policy and alternative strategies. I will then proceed to discuss the relevance of post-industrial theories to all those countries still characterized by pre-industrialism.

## SMALL BOMBS ARE NOT BEAUTIFUL

It is important to note at the outset that there are two main types of theoretical post-industrial responses to nuclear weapons. The first group, consisting of Bahro, members of the Green movement and others, is hostile to nuclear energy, as well as to existing military strategies, policies and alliances which involve nuclear weapons. The second group, comprising Jones, Toffler and many small-is-beautiful liberals and reformers, opposes nuclear power but explicitly or otherwise supports NATO, ANZUS and other nuclear-based alliances and policies. The first group faces the problem of developing an alternative defence policy as well as policies on international trade and international relations which are compatible with a Green post-industrial society. The second group either suffers from a fundamental inability to recognize the inseparable connections between the nuclear fuel cycle and the nuclear arms race, or supports nuclear weapons on so-called Realpolitik grounds. In this section I will focus on the inconsistencies and problems inherent in the post-industrial utopia advocated by Toffler, Jones and other supporters of nuclear armed military policies.

Nearly all the post-industrial theorists are united in their opposition to the development of nuclear power stations as a prime source of energy.[1] The main reasons for opposing nuclear energy include the form of technology involved and the social and environmental consequences resulting from a heavy reliance upon such energy. Given the nature of nuclear technology – its giant, centralized, capital-intensive and massively expensive form – supporters of small-is-beautiful and 'appropriate' technology argue that nuclear power is fundamentally at odds with the needs of a post-industrial society. Environmentally, it is argued that not only is uranium a finite raw material (and it is preferable to have renewable energy sources such as solar power), but, equally importantly, the enormous hazards associated with nuclear waste disposal are more than sufficient grounds upon which to oppose the spread of nuclear stations. Finally, the social costs resulting from the implementation of nuclear technology are the massive increase in the surveillance and bureaucratization of civilian life – all necessary measures to counter the permanent threat of terrorist sabotage of power stations, theft of nuclear fuel and the increasing risk of nuclear war.[2] Therefore, on the basis of a commitment to grass-roots democratization, 'appropriate' levels of technology, opposition to environmental pollution and bureaucratic domination, the post-industrial theorists reject the desirability as well as the necessity of having nuclear energy in a post-industrial society.

But if we examine the overall connection between post-industrial economic development, energy usage and defence policies advocated by writers such as Jones and Toffler, it becomes apparent that technological advances are conceived in almost total isolation from current military and energy policies. To be consistent on the vital issue of nuclear energy, Jones, Toffler and other advocates of 'mixed economies' would have to show how current trends in energy consumption could be significantly altered without deleterious affects upon private corporate profit levels, national and international foreign policies and so forth. While Jones and Toffler are supporters of soft energy developments, their actual record of support for hard energy and conservative foreign military policies far outweighs any flirtation with environmentalists and members of the peace movement. For example, Barry Jones, as a minister in the Hawke Labor government, has failed to disassociate himself from the mining and export of uranium – a major issue in the Australian labour, environment and peace movements.[3] He has also failed to attack the presence of American military bases on Australian soil (which are key component elements of American nuclear policy). He has not opposed the visit of American, nuclear-armed warships to Australian ports, and has tacitly supported the whole Australian–American foreign and military interconnections.

In response to questions concerning American–Japanese relations, Toffler also revealed his preferences for existing military relations. While opposing Japanese rearmament, Toffler conceded that he would change his mind very quickly if he saw signs of a Chinese–Soviet *rapprochement* – thus subscribing to the traditional 'world communist plot' to attack the 'free world'.[4] Furthermore, according to Toffler, the Japanese 'peace clause' was 'premised on US economic dominance and the presence of an American military umbrella over Japan. To the degree that the US military presence is weakened and US–Japanese economic rivalry intensifies, it becomes harder and harder to maintain Article Nine.'[5] While rejecting the prospect of history repeating itself in the Pacific area, Toffler not only accepts the continued need for an American nuclear umbrella over Japan, but appears virtually to ignore the American and Japanese military–industrial complexes and their continued co-operation as well as economic rivalry. Despite intense business rivalry, the current complementary developments and interests of Japanese and American corporations and governments will crucially predetermine the possibility of any non-nuclear post-industrial future. Toffler concedes that economic rivalry will be intense, that the coming decades in the Pacific–Asian area will be characterized by extreme instability, but he somehow sees the dynamo fuelling the post-industrial economy as immunized or divorced from current military–industrial complexes. In fact, the glaring absence of any substantial discussion of military technology or research and development in writings such as *The Third Wave* lends Toffler an air of utopian disregard for the crucial engines of economic production and consumption in his emerging 'post-industrial' nations.

The downturn in the fortunes of the American and other nuclear construction industries is due not only to the political and economic costs stemming from mass resistance to nuclear power stations (the higher the resistance, the higher the costs due to delays), but also to the failure of economic forecasts concerning projected consumption levels, the price of oil, synthetic fuels, availability of electricity, plus the high cost of financing new stations; these problems were related to the lack of sustained economic growth in OECD countries. Any projection of post-industrial economic and energy trends must be able to show whether the future society is going to be based on similar forms of transportation, levels of industrial output and energy consumption, or radically different forms and levels of production and energy usage. Apart from vague statements of support for renewable energy sources, Jones and Toffler give no indication of how existing key dynamos of industrial capitalist development, for example, the car, oil, steel, aluminium, aircraft, chemical, construction and other industries, are to be affected if energy policies and military policies are changed. Given the fact that over half a million research scientists and engineers in leading industrial countries work in areas relating to military defence, that the research and development budgets of countries such as the USA, France, the UK and West Germany are heavily slanted towards military technology,[6] that the electronics, cybernetic and aero-space industries are all key component elements of existing military–industrial complexes, how can Toffler possibly imagine that a nuclear-free, post-industrial society (using soft energy) could possibly ever emerge from existing trends and forms of production? For example, in the USA, which is the largest economic power in the world and also the country with the largest R & D budget, three out of every five federal dollars spent on research and development go directly to defence related projects.[7]

In other words, how can Jones, Toffler and others who are uncritical admirers of transnational corporate giants, naïvely believe that these major contemporary users of non-renewable energy and major beneficiaries of existing military policies will construct a post-industrially peaceful and ecologically harmonious future? How can these post-industrial theorists so readily close their eyes to the dynamic interconnection between the massive military budgets and the post-Vietnam conservative offensive of Reagan's administration? The restructuring of American business investment in the past decade, trade rivalry between the USA, Japan and the EEC (especially in the high technology industries connected to military R & D) are either ignored by Toffler and Jones, or given minimal weight in their theories of the historical transition from industrial to post-industrial society. While it is perfectly legitimate to analyse developments in new industries and technologies without explaining all in terms of military and foreign policies, it is a utopian leap into fantasy to pretend that the fortunes of many large computer companies, electronic and engineering firms, service industries, etc., are not tied to the general economic health resulting from military and foreign relations with rival socio-economic powers. In this respect, any fundamental changes, in military expenditure, energy policy, trade and foreign alliances, directly affect the success or failure of many, but not all key industries, and more importantly, the future of all post-industrial scenarios.

The crucial role of military expenditure is further complicated by the disagreement amongst analysts over the affect of military production on the rest of the civilian economy. Critics of military expenditure, such as Seymour Melman, argue that defence industries sap a nation's investment funds as well as its talent. According to Melman, the sluggish performance of the US, Soviet, British and French economies is due to the burden of large military industries. For every $100 of new capital invested in the civilian economy in 1980, the USA put $38 into the military economy, compared with less

than $4 in Japan. By 1988, Melman predicts, the military side
in the USA will be claiming $87.[8] If Melman proves to be
correct, the implications for leading industrial powers other
than Japan will be potentially disastrous. For if the USA is
currently the leading service sector economy in the world –
and post-industrial scenarios depend on the rapid growth of
all these new high technology and service industries – how
will Toffler's, Jones's and other predictions materialize? On
the other hand, if all those economists who believe that
military spending has been beneficial to major high technology and other civilian industries are also correct, how can
the future post-industrial society emerge free of increasingly
militarized or military-dependent industries? The glaring
inconsistency of Jones and Toffler on military and foreign
policy reveals how shallow are their analyses of the connection between industrial and post-industrial societies. The talk
of small-scale enterprises, 'appropriate technology', decentralized social and political institutions, etc., can have no
credibility, as long as General Dynamics, IBM, General
Motors, Exxon, General Electric and their equivalents in
Japan, Europe and other countries continue to lead us into
the 'post-industrial' world.

That the world of finance, technology, and commodity
production is currently being restructured by giant corporations and their political–administrative allies is the major
obstacle which small-is-beautiful advocates have to confront.
But to believe that Western Europe, Australia and Asia will
become nuclear-free post-industrial societies or zones while
massive American bases continue to protect Western economic and political interests, is ludicrous. As for Eastern
European countries, Toffler's comparative sociology, which
reduces Eastern European countries to the common denom-
inator of Second Wave industrial societies, founders on the
rocks of Realpolitik analysis – the Realpolitik of which he
himself claims to be aware. Not only are the Western capitalist military–industrial complexes going to fight every inch
of the way for a growing slice of new markets, technologies,
budgetary allocations, etc., but any Communist transformations from Second Wave to Third Wave societies are

inconceivable while NATO and Cold War policies are matched by their own military–industrial complexes, internal repression and authoritarian disregard for pluralist decentralization. In Eastern Europe the nuclear power station programme – with its disasters (Chernobyl) and construction defaults – is being extended under dictatorial control, thus making the foundations for Third Wave 'soft energy' paths even more remote.[9] In Japan, most non-military high-technology industries are highly profitable, but heavily dependent on the very standardized and hierarchical social relations and work patterns which Toffler sees as the hallmark of Second Wave societies. In Western Europe, President Mitterand has promoted the 'Eureka' programme as a rival plan to Reagan's 'Star Wars'. The need to prevent a European high-technology 'brain drain', and to match US and Japanese new technology, is widely recognized as being inseparably related to military programmes. Leaving aside the 'Eureka' programme, many European corporations are worried about participating in 'Star Wars' research; for it is not clear whether the US government will share the commercial benefits of new R & D. In short, it is beyond belief how Toffler, Jones or other advocates of 'post-industrial mixed economies' can believe that one can achieve a peaceful, environmentally safe world without a dramatic process of disarmament, reduction in military budgets and radical changes in transport and energy policies.

## POST-INDUSTRIAL THEORISTS AND THE PEACE MOVEMENT

In contrast to Jones and Toffler who say little or nothing about military–industrial complexes and the arms race, Bahro and Gorz have been representative of a major debate within the European Left over the role and policies of the peace movement.[10] Although they do not articulate the complexity and variety of positions to be found in the various peace movements, their conflict over key issues provides a valuable insight into areas that transcend the immediate strategic issues of Cruise missiles in Europe and East–West relations. In a later chapter I will discuss the strategies proposed by post-industrial theorists which are necessary to achieve their social objectives. But in the meantime, it is worth looking at the Bahro–Gorz debate as an example of the varying responses to nuclear power and industrialism and of the Left-wing dilemma in choosing an appropriate form a defence.

The opposition between Bahro and Gorz is simultaneously surprising and yet predictable. Both advocate a radically democratic, egalitarian and environmentally conscious society, both criticize the limits of orthodox Marxism. Yet their shared concerns are mediated and influenced by their presence in quite different political cultures. Bahro reflects the anxiety of Germans living on the front line of the East–West conflict. Gorz responds to the peace movement from within the French political culture with all its insularity and chauvinism – traits no less evident in the French Left under Mitterand's government than in its traditional home on the French Right. Whereas the French Right arrogantly proclaim their national chauvinistic values, the majority of the French Left (there is still a minority of non-chauvinistic French Leftists) endorses the near-identical foreign and military policies of the Right, but under the banner of Realpolitik or universal freedom.[11] Thus, much of the critique that Gorz and the French Left level at the West German peace movement could be endorsed by the Pentagon, but the French couch their arguments in the abstract language of universal ideals over which the French Left has always imagined itself to be the sole guardians. However, when Gorz and other French Leftists attack the West German peace movement for promoting allegedly inferior values (for example, the West Germans allegedly support the fatherland rather than freedom), one can hardly avoid the suspicion of racism; the British, Dutch, Belgian and other countries also have strong peace movements, but do not incur the same degree of open French hostility as does the 'German Culture'.[12] Yet, ironically, Bahro's overall theory of the relationship between nuclear disarmament and industrial disarmament is no more convincing than Gorz's attempt to defend nuclear deterrence strategy. Gorz's critique of the West German peace movement's failure to oppose repression in Eastern Europe cannot be ignored, however, if the peace movement wishes to remain independent. Bahro's political practice (that is, his active involvement in the peace movement) as opposed to his global post-industrial theory, is much more radical and constructive than Gorz's political conservatism-cum-quietism which leads him to endorse the *force de frappé* and a high defence profile in response to an alleged Soviet threat to Western Europe.

In Western Europe and Australia it is possible to place most social democratic and Labour politicians unambiguously, since they divide into Left and Right camps over socioeconomic and foreign policies. It is no accident that most social democrats of the centre Right are supporters of the American alliance, strong defenders of the 'mixed economy', and opponents of more radical social-welfare policies. Gorz is unusual because while he rejects pedestrian social democracy in favour of utopian solutions, he also advocates a *de facto* Atlanticism (that is, support for NATO or some other version of an Atlantic alliance). According to Gorz, for Western Europe

> it is necessary to break up the bipolarization of world politics in favour of multi-polar relations in order to create room for its autonomous appearance as a subject in world history. To achieve this goal, Europe certainly needs to end American guardianship or tutelage, but not the alliance. It certainly needs the capacity to defend itself independently, and a strategy of deterrence (even if also supported by the United States), but it does not need (at least in the present stage) the total renunciation of its own nuclear weapons. Without these weapons, Western Europe would still be subordinate to the strategy of the two world-powers; it would remain dependent on their reciprocal relations.[13]

There are several glaring contradictions in Gorz's project for a Europe 'born again' as an autonomous subject in world history. First, when Gorz speaks of a European nuclear deterrent, he really means the French and British nuclear capacity.

But would the rest of Western Europe be content to be protected by French and British 'tutelage' rather than American 'tutelage'? Would the other European nation states be prepared to subordinate their economic interests, and their research and development objectives, to programmes and policies largely beneficial to the French or British military–industrial complexes? Second, does Gorz believe that an independent European deterrent is technically feasible without French violation and abuse of the Pacific islands and their peoples? Where in Europe would the new independent nuclear weapons be tested without the danger of nuclear fallout? After all, the British left a trail of nuclear damage in Australia (with their early tests), and now depend on the American government to permit testing of new weapons on American territory (thus losing their military independence). Does the new 'European subject' depend on the old French colonialism, or risk American blackmail and control over Europe's new weapons systems? Third, Gorz concedes that the USSR 'would gain nothing through an atomic destruction or military occupation of Western Europe'.[14] Yet he still believes that the Soviets can threaten Western Europe's economic and social relations by the use of nuclear blackmail. Apparently Gorz still believes in the possibility of limited nuclear wars. Yet, even if the American 'nuclear umbrella' were removed from Western Europe, how any nuclear power could believe that a limited first strike attack on a European nation (if that nation resisted Soviet blackmail) would not escalate into full-scale nuclear war – given the highly precarious nature of East–West relations, the fault-ridden nature of military command systems and so forth – is difficult to comprehend. Moreover, the high potential of even a so-called 'small' nuclear war to bring down a nuclear winter on us all renders Gorz's position on a independent European nuclear deterrent fatally myopic and counter-productive.

Like many other French theorists, Gorz has not come to terms with the fundamental difference between nuclear weapons and conventional defence. His nuclear 'Maginot line' depends on the illusion that a new 'European subject' can be immune to a confrontation between the two super-powers, and furthermore, defend itself in a manner only applicable to non-nuclear defence systems. More importantly, Gorz locks Europe into the arms race, since a 'genuine' independent deterrent (assuming one believes in this nonsense) would entail constant technical innovation and the upgrading of weapons of mass destruction.[15] The very future of Western Europe's military–industrial complexes depends on whether Gorz's preferred option is developed, or whether Europeans pursue a strategy of nuclear disarmament and disengagement from Bloc politics. Moreover, the possession of an independent nuclear force and large conventional military–industrial machine is not just related to extricating a nation from superpower rivalry and conflict. With military and technological strength comes the power to interfere in other nation's affairs, for example, French intervention in African countries. A post-industrial world which included an independent, but nuclear-armed Western European bloc, would not necessarily be any less dangerous, nor free of exploitation of Third World countries by Western European nation states.

Gorz is on more solid ground when he criticizes the peace movement for failing to be adequately concerned about Soviet repression in Eastern Europe.[16] There are many people in the peace movement who have naïve ideas about the USSR as an innocent victim of American militarism. Gorz's evenhandedness (that is, he protests against Soviet repression as well as against American imperialism), is to be applauded – but not if Leftists go on to support NATO or ANZUS. It is essential that solidarity with dissidents in Eastern Europe be given without reference to nuclear or non-nuclear weapons; but the dissidents can not justify support for Mitterand's or any other leaders' nuclear weapons policy. In equating the contemporary Soviet regime with the Nazi threat of the 1930s, Gorz not only makes a serious error, but also overlooks the fundamental historical differences between the outcome of conventional arms rivalry before 1939 and the catastrophic consequences of persisting with policies based on nuclear weapons. The absence of a large, independent peace movement in France (as opposed to the pro-Soviet peace movement supported by the French Communist Party), the belated awakening of many French Leftists to the Soviet

'Gulag', and the failure of the French Left to counter the conservative domestic policies of the Mitterand government, have all provided the context in which Gorz and other French Leftists adopt *de facto* Right-wing policies towards the peace movement in Europe.

More important, Gorz's attack upon Bahro and the peace movement reveals the abstract utopianism of his post-industrial alternative. Isolating alternative economic and social welfare projects from the current fight against the threat of nuclear war, as do other abstract Leftists, Gorz cannot explain how there can be a struggle against unemployment, poverty and environmental abuse, without challenging existing military–industrial complexes and their disproportionate claim on fiscal and social resources. Like Toffler and Jones, Gorz cannot show how his post-industrial socialism will emerge in its nuclear-free form. It is nonsensical to advocate small-is-beautiful technology, while approving the French nuclear military apparatus. This is particularly true when we examine the French military–industrial complex (exceeded in size only by the US and Soviet complexes) whose promotion by French Socialists and Communists has made arms one of the most lucrative of France's export commodities. To imagine that the French post-industrial socialist society is going to be shaped by giant electronic, computer, engineering and other military contractors is to believe in fairy tales. There can be no development of 'appropriate technology', no guaranteed minimum income, no transformations in the centralized state and corporate structure, so long as the existing military arms race continues. Gorz has opposed the 'techno-fascism' of nuclear power station progammes, yet he seems somehow to believe that the continued growth of the French military–industrial complex – which demands large budgetary allocations, makes people dependent upon higher export sales in order to maintain up to one million jobs and a healthy balance of trade figures, etc. – can be countered without seriously rethinking NATO and policies of so-called independent nuclear deterrence.

The failure to reject an independent European nuclear deterrent (which is a most dubious strategic objective in the first place – given the 'Star Wars' project and other alarming new phases of the arms race) is the Achilles heel of Gorz and other anti-Stalinist Leftists. In order to move beyond the dead-end policies of Mitterand, Craxi, Gonzalez and other European Socialists, the Left has to develop an alternative vision of a socialist post-industrial society. But it cannot do this while key military–industrial policies and practices are based on variations of existing Atlanticist political–economic frameworks. Gorz makes the fantastic leap into utopia while leaving the masses with no option but to support the construction of a post-industrial society with a nuclear-based, military–industrial complex. How this defence of an 'independent civil society' against the 'Soviet Bear' can avoid the militarized features Gorz himself warned against in relation to nuclear power stations remains a mystery. In fact it is extremely difficult to comprehend how so strong a critic of technical rationality, so strong a supporter of eco-socialism, can accept so many dubious arguments about nuclear weapons (put forward by the very people Gorz opposes in other parts of his writings). The one-sided opposition of many peace activists to nuclear weapons – without linking these weapons to existing capitalist and Soviet political economies – is mirrored in Gorz's one-sided image of utopia which lacks an adequate consideration of defence policies, industrial trends, the connection between welfare-warfare budgets and so forth.

Turning to Bahro, he exhibits two main theoretical differences from Gorz on the issues of nuclear defence and the peace movement. The first difference affects the whole issue of East–West relations. The second theoretical difference revolves around the role of technological and industrial development. In contrast to Gorz, Rudolph Bahro has been one of the leading figures in the European peace movement. Championing the West German Green movement's demand for disarmament in both the East and the West, Bahro stands in diametrical opposition to European social democrats who support Atlanticist defence policies. According to Bahro, the future of all natural species is at stake if citizens do not make a unilateral renunciation of nuclear weapons. Rejecting all theoretical defences of nuclear deterrence as simply variations on the theme of a necessary arms race, Bahro argues that any form of nuclear defence (whether it be independent or part of NATO), is inevitably promoting the logic of exterminism.[17] In opposition to Gorz, Bahro defends the move to extricate the two Germanies from the NATO and Warsaw Pacts.[18] While agreeing with Gorz that the peace movement has to be a vigorous opponent of Soviet repression and colonialism in Eastern Europe, Bahro explicitly rejects the use of anti-Sovietism as a justification for European solidarity with American militarism. Queried whether Cold War politics may be in the interest of both Eastern and Western elites (as a method of social control over dissenters), Bahro comes close to agreeing with Toffler's conception of converging or similar industrial systems in capitalist and Communist countries. As Bahro puts it,

> from the economic point of view the West no longer has any need to change the political structure of the Soviet Union. The world market has been re-created. The autonomy of the socialist system is very relative. The material structures, at the technological level, are generally the same. The technological inferiority of the socialist countries forces them on to the world market, subordinating them to the rules of that market which works against their interests, as in the case of the pipeline. There is no longer any political or military reason to change the regimes in Eastern Europe for the sake of profit.[19]

Rejecting the argument put forward by the New Left Review editors that the Soviet economy is autonomous of the West, Bahro states that the 'mechanisms of arms competition and technological dependence are so powerful that the Soviet Union is more or less a periphery of the world market'.[20] While allowing for the growing marketization of Eastern economies, Bahro's thesis of subordination and integration into the 'world capitalist market' is a gross oversimplification. The view that East and West have a common industrial structure and that the Soviets are agents of an industrial monoculture,[21] is used by Bahro to support his demand for disarmament. According to Bahro, militarism and its ultimate logic of exterminism is linked to anthropological, psychological and structural conditions. In various disjointed observations, Bahro conveys the thesis that militarism is a natural consequence of the dependence on raw materials;[22] he also explains militarism and aggressiveness by attempting to synthesize a strange mixture of theorists such as E. P. Thompson, Reich, Galtung and religious and spiritualist traditions together with child psychologists and cultural anthropologists.[23] Bahro's sources are very similar to those schools of thought which animated the counter culture in the 1960s – a mixture of valuable insights and speculative pop psychology. Elaborating on these anthropological and psychological attributes, Bahro claims that

> there was an aggressive Indo–Germanic disposition inherent in our European civilisation which was already displayed by the Hittites in Asia Minor, the Greeks at Troy, and the Germanic tribes in their struggle against Rome. Galtung refers to this character-type as *homo occidentalis*, further defining the Nazi *homo conquistador* as an extreme variant of this. The necessity of a profound transformation in European civilization implies that this *homo occidentalis* or *homo conquistador* must be spiritually exorcised.[24]

Like many other recent critics of the negative characteristics of 'Western Man', Bahro sees the salvation of the human species, in an almost quasi-religious or spiritual sense, as necessitating a conversion away from aggression, competition and the desire to accumulate goods and power.[25] The positive qualities which could be brought about by cultural revolution, for example, overcoming competitive violence and greed, must not, however, be confused with Galtung's and Bahro's simplistic cultural anthropology and social psychology, or based upon sexist and highly dubious categories such as *homo occidentalis*. Bahro contends that 'without a cultural revolution we have no chance against the arms race'.[26] But the struggle against exterminism is not necessarily reducible to the struggle against industrial civilization. It is possible to conceive of industrial society without nuclear weapons, large military–industrial complexes or *homo conquistador*.

In blurring the fundamental differences between particular historical societies, for example, their varying political economies, Bahro can only sustain his fundamental opposition to industrial society by relying upon a speculative anthropology and psychologism. As the New Left Review editors comment, Bahro has taken E. P. Thompson's concept of 'exterminism' and confused it by adding on the problems of mass starvation in the Third World, the destruction of nature through continued industrialization, and the psychological origins of *homo occidentalis*.[27] Each of these latter problems is related to the arms race, but not reducible to this logic of exterminism.[28] The distinction is crucial. For if Bahro is correct about the inseparable connection between the threat of nuclear war and industrialism, then the future of the human race in a non-nuclear world would indeed be bleak. The reason for this pessimism is that Bahro's advocacy of industrial disarmament remains a set of slogans without even the barest details concerning the nature of production and existence in a non-industrial future. A cultural revolution at the psychological level will be futile if Bahro cannot even specify how the elementary forms of human life could be sustained (not a life of luxuries, but the mere minimum required to reproduce life free from malnutrition, homelessness, cold and darkness).

But in fairness to Bahro it should be said that he also gives the impression that his advocacy of industrial disarmament is essentially a critique of existing forms of production and consumption rather than a sweeping attack on industry *per se*. I agree with Bahro that 'the earth will not yield the material consumption of the North American middle class for the 10 or 15 billion people of the next century'.[29] I also endorse his outright opposition to the expansion and growth of polluting industries such as the car, chemical and nuclear power industries. The burning question is: How much, and what sort of industry is compatible with a life-reproducing environment and an egalitarian and democratic set of new social orders?

It appears that Bahro has moved from a position of critizing the worst aspects of industrial growth and gigantic projects and waste production, to one which virtually requires the opting out of any sort of industry as we know it today. Bahro approaches the problem of industrial production – and nearly all other political and socio-cultural issues – from the single-minded perspective of ecological fundamentalism. That is, Bahro's increasingly extreme opposition to anything which he believes is continuing the 'industrial system', invariably distances him and other 'fundamentalist Greens' from the momentous tasks of constructing alternative defence strategies, jobs, and intermediate or transitional strategies – short of the ultimate ecotopia. I will return to some of the problems inherent in the advocacy of industrial disarmament when I discuss the post-industrialist's analysis of the Third World, and also when discussing the issue of political strategy in chapter 5.

In aiming his critical missiles at the most dangerous and destructive elements of the consumer and militarized industrial structure in contemporary nation states, Bahro displays a close affinity with Marcuse's notion of the 'logic of domination'. 'Today', says Marcuse, 'domination perpetuates and extends itself not only through technology but *as* technology, and the latter provides the great legitimation of the expanding political power, which absorbs all spheres of culture.'[30] While there is a great deal of truth in Marcuse's and Bahro's critique of the inherent destructiveness of Western science, the problem for socialists remains one of how to break with this 'logic of domination'. I do not believe that one can develop a totally new science – even though one can certainly reject many of the worst aspects of past and present technological rationality, institutionalized science and so forth. In equating industrial society with a deeply entrenched historical tradition of violence and psychology, Bahro succumbs to a one-dimensional reading of science and reason. Like the Frankfurt School and Foucault – who overstressed the reifying and dehumanizing aspects of the Enlightenment – Bahro's psychologism severely limits his ability to explain how an eco-pacifist alternative can be constructed without utilizing certain achievements in science, industry and organization which are themselves contaminated by the 'logic of domination'. If 'industrial disarmament' means a radical disengagement from the worst aspects of capitalist industrial growth and Communist productivism, then the critique by Bahro and

Marcuse deserves the fullest support possible. But if Bahro's break with the present entails a total rejection of industrial activity, then the onus is on Bahro to provide a much more detailed explanation of the feasibility or logical possibility of this new world.

Not only does Bahro say little or nothing about the acceptable levels of non-aggressive and non-destructive production and consumption, but this simplistic explanation of the connection between militarism and the dependence on raw materials overlooks the historical complexity of past, present and future international relations and causes of conflict. For example, it is possible to envisage a situation where nations have become independent of raw materials such as oil, coal, etc., by creating renewable energy sources such as solar power or synthetic substances. Such independent self-sufficiency will not necessarily lead to peaceful relations, because the causes of war are not reducible to Bahro's simplistic psychologism and its industrialization thesis. On the other hand, Bahro is highly sensitive to the dangers inherent in genetic technology – which is in marked contrast to the uncritical support of bio-technology to be found in the writings of Toffler and other post-industrial theorists. Bahro argues that 'it is even more essential to ban genetic technology than nuclear'.[31] Even if we share Bahro's deep concern over bio-technology, we can still believe that certain developments in this area (for example, the creation of plant species which can grow in difficult climates without chemical fertilizers) may be compatible with safe environmental criteria. Bahro is perfectly correct, however, to warn us against much that is being developed by industrial capitalist geneticists.

It is a pity that Bahro's vigorous opposition to the military–industrial complexes in the world is not grounded in a more plausible theory of the historical development of the current arms race. It is also unfortunate that he links nuclear disarmament and industrial disarmament so inextricably that it must leave people confused and sceptical. Until Bahro outlines in detail the type of production and technology which would be compatible with his socialist post-industrial society, serious reservations and doubts must surround his whole alternative strategy. The difficulty of accepting Bahro's analysis *in toto* should not blind us to the many valuable contributions he makes. But when Bahro writes of the all-embracing logic of exterminism, of the capitalist industrial project in East and West alike, it is both necessary to agree with many of the examples Bahro points to, and yet reject the overall picture as being seriously flawed and apocalyptic. In the following sections I hope to show in more detail why the thesis of industrial disarmament put forward by Bahro leaves socialists and post-industrialists with major problems.

## DEFENSIVE DEFENCE SYSTEMS AND POST-INDUSTRIAL SOCIETY

Even if we put aside the serious differences between Bahro and Gorz, and other post-industrial theorists, over the role and objectives of the peace movement, we are still left with the long-term problems of defence in a non-nuclear world (assuming that elimination of nuclear weapons has been achieved, or is well on the way to being achieved). A number of prominent opponents of nuclear weapons, such as Galtung, have advocated the creation of defensive defence systems as opposed to offensive military systems. Bahro is a reluctant supporter of alternative defence systems. According to Bahro,

> even the so-called alternative defence policy ultimately forms part of the exterminist context. It is a response at the level of practical politics, so to speak, but in the end we must develop a radical eco-pacifist alternative, of the kind that certain circles in the Protestant Church represent. However, since there is a general obsession for defence of one kind or another, I simply speculated that it might be possible to develop an indisputably defensive system with weapons demonstrably incapable of launching an attack.[32]

While it is clear that Bahro prefers no defence system at all, and believes that only a transformation of Galtung's *homo occidentalis* into an eco-pacifist will remove the causes of war, it is still necessary to discuss the problems and social conditions associated with the development of alternative defence systems. As Bahro admires Johan Galtung's work, it is perhaps easier to approach the matter by examining the latter's writings on defence, given the absence of any detailed analysis by Bahro or the other post-industrial theorists.

In writings such as 'Transarmament: From Offensive to Defensive Defence',[33] Galtung develops some of the key aspects of an alternative defence strategy. According to Galtung, the main difference is not between weapons of mass destruction and conventional defence, nor between military and non-military defence, but between offensive and defensive means of defence. Defensive weapons are defined by Galtung as those weapons systems which have limited range and destruction area, and for that reason can be used essentially only on one's own territory. Offensive systems are all others. He does acknowledge that there are grey areas (for example, anti-aircraft guns which can be converted into offensive weapons), but these grey areas can be minimized if seen as part of a total national form of defensive defence. Furthermore, Galtung recommends three types of defensive defence in order to construct a good, non-provocative or inoffensive defence system. These three types or component elements are: (a) conventional military defence; (b) paramilitary defence and (c) non-military defence. A defensive defence system also presupposes a high level of national self-reliance in defence rather than military alliances. It also presupposes a high level of local self-reliance, which in turn means a move away from centralized and hierarchical economic and political structures in society. Finally, Galtung warns that a defensive defence system would be vulnerable to an enemy who attacks the system with offensive arms from his own country, that the system is not offensive to outside adversaries, but could be highly offensive against an inside adversary, and that this alternative system presupposes a higher level of readiness for defence in the population. Despite these risks, Galtung argues that the move from offensive weapons systems to non-military defence would be unacceptable to the masses at the moment and hence it is better to eliminate national offensive weapons, and adopt a defensive defence system, rather than risk nuclear destruction.[34]

Two things stand out in Galtung's proposal which have immediate relevance for the post-industrial theorists. First, a defensive defence system would be incompatible with the military alliances advocated by Jones and Toffler or the independent European nuclear system advocated by Gorz. Second, a defensive defence system presupposes a level of industrial development which is (as I will show later on) incompatible with Bahro's fundamentalist call for industrial disarmament. Thus, without a clear analysis of the relationship between technology, political and economic structures and international relations, no adequate response to the current interconnection between military and industrial structures can be developed. It is particularly important to recognize the problems associated with any significant move away from highly centralized economic and political systems.

As most post-industrial theorists call for small, decentralized institutions, it is necessary to consider how feasible defensive defence systems might be within societies adhering to Galtung's plan for a high level of local and national self-reliance. If we examine the various conditions necessary for national self-reliance in defence, it can be acknowledged that it is well within the capacity of most nations to organize their own para-military and non-military defence structures. The main problem with para-military defence organizations is how effectively they can be mobilized, without nurturing a militaristic culture within the society as a whole. There is also the problem of co-ordination, as Galtung points out – the level of communication and co-ordination between the military, para-military and non-military components of a defensive defence system. A society which depends on the *voluntary* commitment of the civilian population for its national defence must have a much closer and more open relationship between government and citizens than exists at the moment. This openness of government presupposes that state institutions are not organized as repressive apparatuses – that is, apparatuses which maintain dominant classes or elites via coercive and bureaucratic methods.

While there have been numerous examples of nationalist mobilizations of soldiers within offensive defence systems, it is quite another matter to believe that dominant classes would trust millions of citizens with arms in a society promoting self-reliance, yet still characterized by major inequalities. Even Yugoslavia has a conscript army, despite its emphasis on non-offensive weapons. In order to avoid the re-feudalization of society (for example, a society divided by local fiefdoms, selfish parochialism or aggressive warlords), a strong universalistic ethic promoting social equality, rights for women, ethnic minorities, etc., would have to link local communities across a national territory. All these preconditions for national self-reliance fly in the face of those existing notions of post-industrialism which are based on the expansion of private enterprise, but with little transformation in the ownership of wealth, the nature of existing military complexes, or the distribution of power and privilege.

At the technical level, national self-reliance in defence presupposes a level of industry capable of producing the (non-mass destructive) weapons systems. One of the weapon types approved by alternative defence advocates is precision-guided munitions. These weapons can be used in anti-tank, anti-aircraft, anti-missile and anti-ship systems. The problem is that these precision weapons necessitate an elaborate high-technology infrastructure, which, according the William Agrell,[35] is almost exclusively possessed by the Americans. While it is possible that a few small, non-aligned industrialized states, for example, Sweden or Austria, could co-operate in the construction of these high technology weapons, the possible effects of any such technological infrastructure force us to demand a more precise account of the type of post-industrial society to be constructed. In Bahro's industrial disarmament scenario, any such 'practical political' strategy of defensive defence would contradict his strong opposition to many aspects of technological innovation. For example, it is not clear where Bahro and other advocates of the Green movement stand on the development of information technology, electronics, computer networking, and other component elements necessary for the inoffensive defence of nations – other than non-violent resistance. Bahro wants to have it both ways. On the one hand he opposes high technology and the industrial system. On the other hand, he believes that 'Microchips can serve complex reproduction in a relatively small commune of several hundred people . . .'[36] But Bahro ignores Gorz's important point: the need for national or regional industries which are beyond the technical resources of local communities. As for Gorz, it is far from clear how an independent nuclear-armed Europe could match American high tech without also promoting large European capitalist transnationals – unless this technological development was undertaken by state sector enterprises. Because Gorz favours mass destruction weapons in the form of nuclear deterrents, his advocacy of non-capitalist local and national industrial infrastructure is sadly at odds with his subscription to the continuation of the arms race.

For a more plausible theory of non-offensive national self-reliance, it would be necessary to combine Gorz's advocacy of a mixture of local and national industries with Galtung's model of locally decentralized civilian and military initiatives. It is difficult, however, to conceive of a decentralized defensive defence force being effective without a modern communications system. It is plausible enough to rely on an army of local guerilla or partisan forces, but the prevention (as opposed to the harassment) of an invading force depends on the rapid mobilization of the numerous local defence groups. Clearly, too much decentralization would make any defence system ineffective. But how much central control do people like Galtung favour? This is the difficult issue which advocates of decentralization do not resolve. Moreover, the notion of local self-reliance does not solve the problem of major disparities in the size of decentralized forces – for example, the differences between cities with millions of people compared to villages and small towns. Would defence be concentrated in regional headquarters? Would industrial infrastructure be organized along regional or local lines? None of these problems is insurmountable, but they require far greater recognition of the complex relations between central and decentralized power centres than our post-industrial theorists have offered.

Advocates of defensive defence systems are ultimately caught on the horns of a dilemma. The first problem is not to concede too much ground to existing advocates of the politics of fear, and to demands for increases in non-nuclear offensive defence systems.[37] It is very difficult for any defensive system to prevent a foreign power from attacking with weapons of mass destruction – if that foreign power is absolutely determined to destroy the inoffensive society. Consequently, a defensive defence system will always appear to be relatively weak militarily when compared with existing offensive defence systems. The future success of a defensive defence system depends just as much on the promotion of an international peace culture, nuclear-free zones, etc., as it does on the three component elements of national and local self-reliance. But while the first tendency of alternative-defence advocates is, perhaps, to over-reassure those used to existing offensive military systems, the opposing tendency is to construct models of alternative societies which require no defence system at all. This is certainly true of Bahro's model, which at times reads as if it is not only completely at odds with the nation state (in its advocacy of 'basic communes'), but is also at odds with the most elementary level of industrial technology necessary for a defensive defence system.

Interestingly enough, Marxists such as Mandel also argue in fundamentalist terms when they continue to believe that only the end of the capitalist system will prevent nuclear war.[38] While many peace activists ignore the vital role of capitalist class rule, or divorce military questions from socio-economic structures, Mandel and other Marxists brush over non-capitalist conflicts (for example, between China and Vietnam), and take comfort in the panacea of 'world revolution'.[39] Although Mandel has never had a great interest in environmental issues shown by Bahro and Gorz, all three share a profoundly a-political notion of alternative societies. Mandel and Bahro ultimately see everything being resolved by workers' councils and 'basic communes' (even though they are poles apart on the questions of technology, consumption and production). Gorz stands between Bahro and Mandel on issues such as the level of technology, but his political conservatism on nuclear weapons is mirrored by his utopian disregard for defence in the future. If Bahro and Mandel are more appreciative of the present dangers, despite their simplistic scenarios of the future, Gorz makes the fantastic leap from supporting weapons of mass destruction to the pacifism of post-industrial society.

The transition from industrial to post-industrial society is generally conceptualized as the transition from centralization to greater decentralization. Not only do Bahro and Gorz envisage life being centred in 'basic communes' or in local communities, but both make much of the obsolescence of the nation state. Many other writers have commented upon the obsolescence of the nation state when discussing the causes of international conflict and the need to prevent war. Within Europe, the European Nuclear Disarmament Movement has fostered transnational links from Poland to Portugal as a solution to East–West conflict, as have Asian–Pacific peace and independence movements in the Southern hemisphere. While such movements are to be applauded, the concept of a defensive defence system still presupposes the continued existence of the nation state, despite a significant increase in peaceful co-operation between governments and social movements at a bilateral or multilateral level. The desire to build a 'global community' has long been a desire of socialists, peace activists and all other critics of parochial, chauvinistic attitudes and policies. But it is also very important to recognize that the desire for world revolution, one world government and other such universal solutions (advocated by many Marxists, liberals, Christians and others), sets up a profound conflict of interests between local and supranational institutions and movements. If the nation state is flawed and is also the cause of many conflicts, we still await alternative models, either of decentralized localism or global supranationalism, which do not promote intolerance, self-interest, indifference and hyper-centralization, or suffocate democratic control, pluralism, equality and freedom. I have already argued that it is one thing to promote greater economic, social and political co-operation between local and national institutions and social forces, but it is quite another to believe that the erosion of national institutions – leaving just local bodies relating to giant supranational government structures – will not erode democratic sovereignty or create bureaucratic nightmares.

Toffler argues that we need alternative supranational agencies to the IMF, NATO, COMECON, etc., in order to regulate the oceans, outer space, the bad effects of technology and other problems beyond the capacity of individual nation states.[40] There is great merit in his advocacy of agencies to relieve the overburdened national bureaucracies. I also agree with his observation that 'decentralization is no guarantee of democracy – quite vicious localist tyrannies are possible. Local politics are frequently even more corrupt than national politics. Moreover, much that passes for decentralization – Nixon's government reorganization, for example – is a kind of pseudo-decentralization for the benefit of the centralizers.'[41] Nevertheless, the major problems confronting humanity at the military and socio-economic levels are not organizational problems *per se*. For all the organizational improvements that one could suggest for the United Nations, the EEC and other supranational bodies, we are still left with the fundamentally incompatible political and economic interests of the various national members. For example, Bahro and others recognize that prevention of war is not possible unless one also changes the relationships between the North and the South (a matter I will discuss later on). It is possible to imagine a great variety of new supranational relations between social forces and institutions existing in territories adjacent to one another (let alone the need to overcome the basic divisions between the North and the South). In fact, it is futile to believe that any defensive defence system will prove to be enduring until and unless far greater transnational co-operation is implemented. But ultimately the role and status of the nation state has certain similarities to the role of the family. One can have a whole range of historical types of families. For example, we know that the struggle to create non-patriarchal families, free from violence and the abuse of women and children, necessitates a profound change of existing family roles and structures, as well as changes in the way members of families relate to other individuals and institutions. But, like the nation state, it is difficult to replace the family (although one can envisage new communal units, structures and quasi-families) and yet achieve essential qualities needed for the reproduction of universal values.

While nationalism has certainly been responsible for violent and irrational behaviour, the transformation of the nation state to a condition of defensive self-reliance holds out greater hope of a peaceful future than the mere creation of alternative supranational institutions. The reason for this lies in the need to revolutionize domestic class and social relations within nation states, whereas supranational agencies can be founded with minimal changes in the participating member states. Bahro partially recognizes this in his advocacy of a reunited Germany disengaged from the destructiveness of East–West Bloc politics.[42] In contrast, a post-industrial world (along Toffler's lines) where global corporations coexist with local 'prosumers', has (for deeply vested economic and political interests) minimal chance of reversing the power of military–industrial complexes. On the other hand, a consistent strategy of promoting international disarmament, while transforming the political-economic structures necessary for national defensive defence systems, makes a new supranationalism dependent on a new type of nation state. This does not mean that the territorial boundaries of existing nation states will all remain unchanged; but even the development of greater regional autonomy would (out of economic and political necessity) develop quasi-national features as a form of sovereign self-identity. The point is not to defend the irrational and negative characteristics of the modern nation state or nuclear family. Rather, it is to recognize that a post-industrial socialist society requires mediating state institutions which stand between a plethora of local communities and the gigantism of supranational agencies.

In recent decades, the prime movers behind greater supranational institutions and social relations have not had the protection of local, decentralized communities as a high priority. At a socio-economic level, the spread of large transnational corporations have had a highly negative effect on local self-sufficiency, cultural autonomy and political sovereignty. Most of the large, transnational co-ordinating institutions such as the EEC Commission, the International Monetary Fund and other economic structures, have tended to represent the interests of large corporations and national governments at the expense of workers, small farmers, local businesses and welfare-dependent populations. At a military level, the emergence of NATO, ANZUS, Warsaw Pact and other strategic alliances, have not only tied member countries to power bloc rivalry, but also helped militarize societies, influence the size and nature of economic developments, research and development, and restricted or perverted the nature of political representation. At an ecological level, transnational economic and military projects, installations and trade have done far more damage to local environments (air, water, forest and urban pollution or destruction) than the very limited, but beneficial regulatory and cleansing operations of transnational environmental protection authorities.

While it would be silly to argue that all supranational developments have been negative, one can not be optimistic that local democracy and natural habitats will survive even greater and more extensive forms of supranational relations – if these global connections are qualitatively and quantitatively similar to past and present economic and military practices. The difficult issue is to recognize when internationalism, or localism and nationalism serve either progressive or reactionary political economic and cultural interests. I believe that apart from transnational movements and activities which foster greater democracy, peace, cultural pluralism and economic and social equality, for example, peace and liberation movements, etc., the struggle for local and national democracy and socio-economic autonomy is more likely to achieve universal values (equality and democracy) than most contemporary capitalist and Communist champions of existing forms of supranationalism. I will discuss these issues in relation to semi-autarkic strategies in a later chapter.

### FROM NORTH TO SOUTH: CONFRONTING
### POST-INDUSTRIALISM WITH PRE-INDUSTRIALISM

It is easy to understand why so many environmentalists and peace activists devote so much attention to bread and guns. The manner in which human beings produce their food is, as Marx noted long ago, 'a definite form of their activity, a definite way of expressing their life, a definite *mode of life*'.[43] The industrialization of food production in the past one hundred years is a vital issue which post-industrial theorists cannot ignore. If the whole world is to become post-industrial, does this mean that meat eating will be drastically reduced or abandoned altogether? Can the Third World be fed by using the energy-intensive and chemically polluting methods of First World food production? Similarly, can the post-industrial society disarm nuclear weapons but tolerate chemical weapons and potentially disastrous monstrosities emerging from uncontrolled research in the field of genetic engineering? Many of the large chemical corporations engaged in military production are the same businesses who produce chemicals for agribusiness or support genetic engineering, plant patents (which restrict non-agribusiness food production) and other negative practices which especially exploit people in the Third World.[44]

While most post-industrial theorists make some analysis of the South, Bahro is the only one who radically pursues the whole relationship of the North to the South in his general thesis on the causes of militarism and the need for a post-industrial eco-socialism. Gorz is also concerned to establish the link between capitalist consumption in the North and poverty in the South, but his position on military questions compromises his consistency, as do the unconvincing analyses offered by Toffler and Jones. All three are certainly worried by the extreme suffering to be found in the South. But their preoccupation with post-industrial developments in the North means that change in the South gets low priority or is seen mainly as a by-product of technological and social changes in the North. It is only fair to note, however, that no post-industrial theorist advocates a model for the Third

World which adds up to a carbon copy of the old industrial modernization theories that were so popular amongst scholars in recent decades. In contrast, they all advocate social developments in the South which, it is hoped, will avoid or skip the 'industrial stage' or Second Wave.

The brief analyses of problems in the South given by the post-industrial theorists are clearly influenced by writers such as Illich, Schumacher, Gandhi, Galtung and the recent wave of environmentalists and other critics of large-scale industrialization. Toffler, however, rejects many of the 'appropriate technology' solutions as being obsolete. His utopian solution to the Third World is summarized in the title of his chapter: 'Gandhi with Satellites'.[45] According to Toffler, both the Second Wave and First Wave strategies have failed to resolve deep-seated social problems in the South. The Second Wave strategy of rapid industrialization has been a political, economic and cultural disaster. While Toffler cites Iran under the Shah as an example of corruption, disregard for indigenous culture, a haven for Western corporate investment, etc., he places the blame on his vague general concept of 'Second Wave industrialism', rather than on advanced capitalist exploitative development of Third World nations.[46] Similarly, Toffler criticizes all those First Wave (that is, reverting to pre-industrial society) proposals which advocate alternatives to heavy, large-scale industrialization in the form of labour-intensive, small-scale, 'appropriate technology' which maximizes food self-sufficiency and development suitable for village life. While he acknowledges that there is much about these First Wave alternatives which make excellent sense, Toffler is nevertheless scathing in his rejection of labour-intensive techniques as Band-Aiding and, quoting Samir Amin, as a 'return to the myth of the golden age and the noble savage' made popular by 'hippie ideology'.[47] Worst yet, for Toffler the First Wave strategy 'dangerously de-emphasizes the role of advanced science and technology. Many of the technologies now being promoted as "appropriate" are even more primitive than those available to the American farmer of 1776 – closer by far to the sickle than to the harvester.'[48]

Toffler uncritically accepts Amin's analysis,[49] and is also too hasty and dismissive of the diverse 'appropriate technology' movement which he lumps together under the heading 'First Wave' – a strategy he regards as 'a recipe for stagnation'.[50] Not surprisingly, he advocates a Third Wave solution. Yet, in Toffler's imagination, the 'developing world' already has features which resemble the emerging Third Wave civilization – 'decentralized production, appropriate scale, renewable energy, de-urbanization, work in the home, high levels of prosumption, to name just a few'.[51] Consequently, Toffler's solution of 'Gandhi with Satellites' boils down to an amalgam of First Wave 'prosumption' with Third Wave high tech. Toffler's strategy of getting rich countries to provide 'capital tools for prosumption' has much to recommend it.[52] The imaginative blend of specific forms of advanced science and technology which could improve the standard of living of the peoples in the South, without the negative features of current forms of gigantism and imperialist exploitation, sounds attractive and rational. The problem is that Toffler's depiction of the South as having many features of the future Third Wave is far too superficial and abstract. A closer examination of work in the home in Third World countries reveals an entirely different scenario from the affluent 'prosumption' and 'electronic cottages' that Toffler envisages for First World citizens. The South or Third World, is too diverse – ranging from impoverished pre-industrial countries such as Chad, Haiti or Bangledesh, to heavily industrialized South Korea and partially industrialized Brazil and Argentine. Moreover, the so-called decentralization and de-urbanization of Third World countries either ignores or minimizes the widespread reality of highly centralized, military and dictatorial regimes in dozens of countries, the growth of the largest industrialized and polluted megalopoles in the world (teeming with slum dwellers in their millions), and the destruction of rural self-sufficiency by luxury cash crops promoted by agribusiness. All these urban and rural developments make Toffler's idyllic 'prosumption' either impracticable or irrelevant without a major wave of social revolutions.

Once again, Toffler's blend of journalistic pop sociology and serious studies of the South accounts for his ability to be simultaneously illuminating and myopic. If Toffler devoted as much energy to analysing how to move from First Wave social forms to Third Wave technological innovation, his prescription would have a great deal more credibility. As it stands, Toffler's solution is no solution other than an indirect exercise in smoothing over all those atrocities and exploitative developments which conservative governments and trans-national companies perpetrate in the South. For the failure to indicate how Third World countries can develop Third Wave forms of 'prosumption' and political and cultural diversity and freedom, in the face of the coercive institutionalization of so many socio-economic practices which are incompatible with the Third Wave, leaves Toffler at best utopian, and at worst inhumane and indifferent to oppression. In advocating non-market forms of 'prosumption', Toffler posits an ideal which is unrelated to the oppression of existing market forces. How can 'Gandhi with satellites' overcome the terrible poverty of home weavers (the Gandhian economic ideal in its actual oppressive form), or the foreign domination of satellites and high technology? What does Toffler propose to do about the massive Third World debt crisis, the imposi-tion of austerity and starvation wages by the IMF and other agents of OECD market forces? Toffler's silence on all these vital problems is in marked contrast to his voluble promotion of a fusion of the First and Third Waves. (If Toffler sees the First Wave strategy as having been made popular in the West by 'hippie ideology', can it be that his own model is in reality an ideological rationalization for all those ex-hippies who have now become 'yuppies'?)

While Toffler represents the optimistic belief in the inte-gration of high technology and pre-industrial First Wave features, Gorz is to be located midway between Toffler's Third Wave and Bahro's radical environmentalism. In his critique of capitalist agribusiness, the petro-chemical industry and the exploitation of Third World countries, Gorz openly supports Bahro's critique of capitalist waste and ecologically destructive production.[53] Yet Gorz is also uncritical of

Toffler's book *The Third Wave* which indicates a tendency
on Gorz's part to fall for the superficial analysis provided by
Toffler. In an earlier piece on 'The Continuing American
Revolution', Gorz was equally uncritical in his account of
Californians such as ex-Governor Jerry Brown's adherence to
the principles of Gandhi and Schumacher.[54] On the one hand
Gorz points to the incompatibility of capitalist profits with
ecological goals, yet on the other hand he displays a naïve
acceptance of the soft sell ecology promoted by defenders of
private corporate America such as Brown and Toffler. Given
his endorsement of Toffler, as well as his open defence of
Atlanticism and the military technology needed for nuclear
weapons systems, it is difficult to accept that Gorz's concern
with ecological goals and the abolition of imperialism in the
Third World goes any deeper than a generalized moral
critique of Western affluence and wasteful consumption.

There is no doubt that Gorz, as a former Marxist, approves
much of the radical critique of capitalist exploitation of Third
World peoples. Yet like Toffler's, his recent works are con-
spicuous for their silence on post-industrialism (let alone
post-industrial socialism) in the South. If Gorz has bade
farewell to the proletariat in the advanced capitalist countries, which sections of the population does he see as the
agents of radical change in Third World countries? As a
socialist, Gorz opposes both socialist industrialism and
capitalist industrialism as solutions to Third World poverty
and hunger.[55] He also opposes the food chain established between the South and the North by giant agribusiness.[56] But he
says little about how the transformation of work and leisure
in the North will create equally well-fed and free populations
in the South. (I will return to the issues related to strategy and
change in a later chapter.) In a few brief sentences, Gorz calls
upon international aid and development organizations (for
example, the UN, World Bank, etc.) to promote self-
production and access to the means of self-production (land)
for the widest possible sections of Third World populations.
These measures, together with the development of 'appropriate' technologies in the industrial countries will, he asserts
'be of greater help to the people of the Third World than the
sale on credit of cement works and nuclear reactors'.[57]

What Gorz does not tell us is in what way his proposals differ from the calls for self-reliance made by World Bank ideologists such as Robert McNamara.[58] That is, at what level of society is Gorz recommending self-sufficiency – at village, regional or national level? Furthermore, Gorz's advocacy of 'appropriate technology' for the Third World is sadly at odds with his defence of nuclear deterrence – and hence high technology, military–industrial complexes – in Western Europe. The French and other European powers thrive on arms exports to Third World countries. By the end of the 1970s, military imports accounted for up to 30 per cent of total Third World debt.[59] Of the 125 or more conflicts which have occurred since 1945, 95 per cent have taken place in Third World countries with approximately 11 million people dying from weapons largely produced in the First and Second Worlds.[60] The militarization of the Third World is inseparably related to the global arms race fueled by the superpowers and their allies. In 1984 alone, world governments spent an incredible 800 thousand million US dollars on military-related items![61] Although there are dozens of Third World countries, a mere seven (Israel, India, Brazil, Taiwan, Argentine, South Africa and South Korea)[62] accounted for the vast majority of indigenously produced weapons in the whole of the Third World. Yet, when it comes to arms exports, these major Third World arms producers only accounted for a tiny 4 per cent of the total world arms trade.[63] In other words, Gorz's advocacy of 'appropriate technology' in the South is pretty meaningless without the conversion of military–industrial complexes to 'appropriate' or peaceful technology in the North. Yet this is most unlikely to happen if Gorz and others continue to attack the very movement trying to bring disarmament into being – namely, the peace movement.

Bahro is also a very strong opponent of agribusiness. But unlike Gorz, Bahro calls for a ban on the importation of luxury cash crops from the South and links this to a parallel call for radical industrial disarmament in the North. In contrast to the Brandt Commission and others, who favour increased aid to the South without radically changing the socio-economic relations in countries of the North, Bahro rejects all North–South conferences as essentially useless – given the failure of industrialized countries to reconcile their differences and their continued promotion of industrial aggression against the South.[64] According to Bahro, a new economic world order based on non-exploitative relations between the North and the South will be possible only if there is military disarmament, based on industrial disarmament in both the West and East, as well as the attainment of social justice and the prevention of ecological crisis. A resolution of ecological damage is impossible so long as the existing world capitalist market continues.[65]

Consequently, Bahro advocates the self-production of food – liberation not only from nuclear weapons, but also from supermarkets.[66] According to Bahro, the 'real alternative, which at the same time would begin to reconcile us with the peoples of the Third World, can only be the building of basic communities (of – it is suggested – a maximum of 3,000 people), which would agree on a mode of simple, non-expanded reproduction of their material basis.'[67] This ecologically based model is not only utopian, but most likely destructive of the very environment which Bahro wishes to preserve. For example, Bahro argues that investments in the economy are only permissible 'if they do not require a single square metre of land not previously built on. If however there has to be new building, then at least the equivalent area must be balanced against it for recultivation.'[68]

Given the highly concentrated nature of urban populations since the historical depopulation of the countryside in capitalist societies, how does Bahro believe that millions of basic communities of no more than 3,000 people, will not eat up every available square metre of land currently not used! Not only is this model of solidarity with Third World peoples a potential ecological disaster, but it is insensitive to the shocking poverty in dozens of countries such as Sudan, Pakistan or Angola, where some form of industrialization (to provide basic necessities, not luxuries) is imperative. Moreover, the important ideals of preserving the environment, ending exploitative businesses and the incredible waste of resources on military production, is nullified by Bahro's simplistic fundamentalism. One does not have to be a champion of capitalist industrial growth in order to recognize that millions of Third World people would reject the idea of leaving even those shocking shanty towns and slums in megalopoles such as Cairo or Bombay for the starvation of communal life in arid countrysides.

When he is not talking about 'basic communes', Bahro has many valid and sensible things to say about North–South relations. On the issue of local and national self-sufficiency, Bahro favours many of Galtung's recommendations.[69] Galtung's scenario of self-sufficiency for countries in the South is not, strictly speaking, compatible with Bahro's call for industrial disarmament. While it is true that Galtung also favours radical measures in both the North and South to prevent poverty, ecological catastrophe and nuclear devastation, his writings vary from sympathetic accounts of Maoist programmes to new global orders based on a contradictory mixture of non-market and market forces.[70] Although this is not the place to make a detailed evaluation of the positive and negative features in Galtung's highly eclectic works on nearly every topic under the sun,[71] it is worth mentioning his analysis of 'appropriate' technology to see how it compares with Bahro's position.

In works such as 'Towards a New International Technological Order',[72] Galtung rejects the existing forms of socio-economic relations between the North and the South. In this respect, Galtung shares with Bahro a radical critique of the exploitative nature of Western technology based on capital-intensive, profit-seeking principles which are environmentally, culturally, economically and politically disastrous for peoples in the South. Yet Galtung does not call for industrial disarmament. Instead, he develops a set of criteria which should be used to evaluate existing or new technology. Included in this elaborate set of criteria are questions such as whether the technology is culturally compatible, humanly enriching and environmentally safe.[73] In other words, Galtung asks: Does new or existing technology promote dependence or self-reliance, does it liberate human beings from boring degrading work or impoverish increasing numbers; does it use less or more raw materials, local or foreign resources and cultural inputs, does it satisfy basic needs for shelter, clothing, health and so forth – or does it simply make profits for companies? This standpoint does not in itself favour industrial disarmament, as there are a number of conventional and high technology developments which could possibly meet these criteria, if isolated from the way capitalist firms at present implement them. Galtung's position on technology could possibly be made compatible with Gorz's environmentalism mixed with use-value technology (minus his position on nuclear weapons), or with Toffler's 'Gandhi with satellites' (minus Toffler's support for transnational corporations, military-industrial complexes and global trade). However, it is unlikely that Galtung's call for local and national self-reliance would be able to accommodate Toffler's rejection of nation states for high tech and highly integrated globalism, despite the elements in Toffler's scenario (for example, 'prosuming') which also stress decentralized, use-value production of basic needs and services.

The point which I am trying to make is that a position which advocates greater self-reliance in food production, or which follows Galtung's guidelines on technology, does not have to envisage a world which is industrially disarmed in Bahro's sense. Once again, Bahro's radical solutions, linking military disarmament with industrial disarmament and new North–South relations, has the virtue of being consistent, but non-viable as a practical radical alternative scenario. To break existing North–South relations is highly desirable. But just as Bahro fails to indicate how a defensive defence system can be developed if industrial disarmament is pursued, so too his solutions for the South are partial at best, and non-achievable at worst – if Third World countries are to be told that even limited industrialization is regressive. Yet what does limited industrialization mean? Bahro is in favour of locally controlled production, electricity, drainage, transport, water supply and other goods and services needed for a self-sufficient economy.[74] He is also in favour of a new science and technology which is oriented away from 'industrialism'.

If billions of people can not enjoy the affluent standard of living of Americans, West Germans and East Germans, without an ecological crisis destroying the world's limited resources, what standard of living does Bahro believe is possible for the majority of the world's population? Technically speaking, the turn to renewable energy sources such as solar power requires levels of industrialization and high technology which may be at odds with Bahro's new science and industrial disarmament. The achievement of improved standards of living for Soviet citizens, which are still well below OECD standards of consumption, is already giving rise to the disastrous environmental abuse of Siberia.[75] A certain proportion of this Soviet quest for raw materials would be unnecessary, if energy conservation was pursued and the giant military apparatus was rendered obsolete due to world disarmament.

Bahro argues, however, that without industrial disarmament, 'that is, an absolute reduction in global demand for raw materials and energy, and a corresponding technological transformation – it will be possible neither to attain a genuine military disarmament nor to restore the ability of the South to provide itself with adequate means of subsistence'.[76] Yet, even a 100 per cent improvement in the standard of living of Third World peoples (which would still be well below most OECD living standards) would probably still require an absolute increase in energy usage and industrial activity, even after allowing for a massive decrease in OECD mass consumption and world-wide military disarmament. I am not arguing that the elimination of poverty and hunger in the South is impossible without causing an ecological crisis. Rather, I am concerned to show that either Bahro's best intentions have become subordinated to his slogan of industrial disarmament, or else his vision of a post-industrial eco-socialism is meaningful only to affluent Europeans (who can enjoy their life in 'basic communes' with the benefits of existing industrial infrastructure), rather than to many nations in the South who cannot afford the luxury to disarm industrially that which they have not yet developed.

In conclusion, it is clear that none of the post-industrial utopians has any real idea of how to resolve the enormous poverty and exploitation in the South. Certainly, Bahro comes closest with his radical advocacy of new relations between the North and South, his eco-pacificism and strong critique of the worst aspects of capitalist industrialization and agribusiness. It is a pity that his whole scenario has to rest on the untenable thesis of industrial disarmament in its fundamentalist form. Similarly, the positive suggestions made by Gorz and Toffler, to improve the life chances of people in the South, are unfortunately negated by their uncritical adherence to the worst aspects of militarism or transnational corporate domination (Toffler). For all his weaknesses, Bahro's advocacy of maximum self-sufficiency has more to recommend it than Toffler's or Jones's belief in the new post-industrial globalism currently being promoted by a mixture of corporations and conservative governments. Yet Bahro would do well to learn from the as yet ambiguous tendencies in high tech – which are balanced between more horrific anti-human developments and a minority current of potentially liberating technological developments. One thing is clear: Bahro is correct in launching the strongest possible attack upon the continuation of the politics and technology of mass destruction. If the South is to be liberated from hunger and oppression, it will not be thanks to Toffler, Jones, Gorz and the other post-industrial theorists who continue to support existing military alliances, technology and culture. As I will argue later on, we cannot pursue Bahro's solutions of industrial disarmament (or what Toffler calls the First Wave strategy), any more than we can afford to pursue Toffler's Third Wave scenario. But it is possible to advocate an anti-militarist, semi-autarkic strategy combined with some of the more enlightened aspects advocated by Gorz and Toffler (but minus their overall problematical baggage). In short, it is not necessary to adopt Bahro's take-it-or-leave-it attitude to industrialization, nor is it necessary to accept the pop sociological and journalistic impressionism of Toffler and Gorz.

In this chapter I have tried to show why military questions are connected to the future of post-industrialism in both the

North and the South. If many environmentalists are guilty of ignoring the importance of political economy and the need to understand the role of state institutions, it is equally evident that most post-industrial theorists give little attention to environmental issues, let alone the political economy of militarism and Third World exploitation. The feasibility of an eco-pacifist society will depend crucially on how well post-industrial socialists tackle the problems of constructing alternative defence systems, new political structures at local, national and supranational levels, and resolve the manner in which well-endowed nations relate with those suffering from centuries of unequal exchange and human degradation.

I believe that home will assume a startling new importance in Third Wave civilization. The rise of the prosumer, the spread of the electronic cottage, the invention of new organizational structures in business, the automation and demassification of production, all point to the home's re-emergence as a central unit in the society of tomorrow – a unit with enhanced rather than diminished economic, medical, educational, and social functions. Yet it is unlikely that *any* institution – not even the home – will play as central a role as the cathedral or the factory did in the past. For the society is likely to be built around a network rather than a hierarchy of new institutions.

Alvin Toffler, *The Third Wave*

To many critics of modernity who seek to defend family, tradition, authority and religion as the sole sources of ethical interaction, the new movements might appear as one more example of unbridled individualism, narcissism, and voluntarism. From this standpoint it is not the alleged anti-modernism of the movements that is alarming, but their cultural modernism. The movements might be interpreted as part of the cultural contradictions of capitalism, stressing gratification, immediacy, and self-expression against the work ethic required by the political/economic system. Both unfettered critical rationalism and self-indulgent egoism seem to destroy the social ties and foundations essential for the maintenance of morality. Yet one might note that resources for meaning, authority, and social integration are not threatened by the presence of social movements, but rather by the expansion of an increasingly illiberal corporate and an administered political system. The core institutions of the political system – parties, parliaments, elections and unions – have lost the capacity to provide collective identities and solidarities. The political system excludes the expression of concerns that are not amenable to strategic calculation while political parties have become severed from any connection with movements for the democratization of society.

Jean L. Cohen, 'Rethinking Social Movements' in
*Berkeley Journal of Sociology*, 1983

# 4

# Redefining Public and Private Spheres
## *The Cultural Contradictions of Post-Industrial Society*

Despite their major differences on technology, nuclear weapons and the 'mixed economy', post-industrial theorists, in the main, adopt rather optimistic outlooks on the future. They recognize, it is true, the enormous problems that confront existing capitalist and Communist societies, and vividly describe a host of socio-economic ills afflicting both types of societies and their respective citizens; nevertheless, they show no lack of optimism in their belief that their respective versions of post-industrial society will be largely free of contemporary social problems.

The gap between the identification of existing crises, and the resolution of these crises, is a matter dealt with in the next chapter. But before discussing the strategies of social change advocated by the post-industrial utopians, I will first examine some of the larger questions raised by their images of alternative domestic relations, education, law, media, and the cultural and political consequences of new public and private spheres. The themes pursued by the post-industrial theorists have also been addressed in contrasting ways by New Right theorists, feminists, and participants in debates over modernity. Capitalist societies have been conflict ridden for most of their existence. In recent decades, the public and private disputes over education, law, gender relations, family forms, gay rights, religion, the role of the media, have resulted in new splits within traditional Left and Right parties; the 'cultural contradictions of capitalism' (Bell) have also polarized new social movements such as the Moral Majority and feminists, as each side puts forward irreconcilable views on public and private life. In so far as Toffler, Bahro and Gorz articulate a range of alternative views, popular since the 1960s, on sexual, religious and other cultural and political relations, their views have a political immediacy (as opponents of the New Right) and are not mere speculative ravings in futurology.

Yet for all the conflict between local and national socio-economic and cultural forces, these 'contradictions of capitalism' take place within the boundaries of nation states (with their centralized state institutions), and against the background of centuries-old religious and cultural traditions. If such enormous cultural and socio-political conflicts can rage despite the unifying presence of nation states and hierarchial and monolithic institutions, what are we to expect in a post-industrial society to be based on highly decentralized community institutions, home-centred economic practices, and even the dissolution of the nation state? Will cultural contradictions and conflict significantly decrease when centralized, hierarchical and nationally based institutional values and practices decline, or will the proposed new social relations give rise to even greater conflict and contradiction?

Of the post-industrial utopians, it is only Toffler who devotes space to analysing alternative family forms and cultural relations. The other theorists make passing comments on a number of issues such as education and culture; but like many other people of the Left, they say little about the 'cultural contradictions of socialism'. It is one thing to analyse the 'cultural contradictions of capitalism'; it is another matter to think that a post-industrial socialist society will be free of major cultural contradictions simply because it is socialist rather than capitalist! Just as many of the alternative economic, social welfare and defence proposals are riddled with major contradictions, so too there are weighty grounds on which to question various post-industrial images of alternative public or private socio-cultural relations. Accordingly, in this chapter I will discuss domestic labour, family relations, law and education, as well as post-modernist and post-industrial views of culture, religion and new public and private spheres.

## THE 'ELECTRONIC COTTAGE', GENDER ROLES AND THE LABOUR PROCESS

Much has been said in the mass media and specialized journals about the growth of home-centred work. It is important here to distinguish between likely developments in the next 20 years, and the more futuristic images and predictions. Given the rapid developments in communication and information technology, one cannot doubt that fundamental changes are occurring in existing labour processes. With videotex, teletex, word processor, facsimile and other machines, information networks, micro-electronic processors, and the current development of voice-sensitive computers, it is not only tele-communications that have undergone a technical revolution. Newspaper articles and television programmes constantly inform us of innovations in the banking, health, social services, education, entertainment, retailing and other industries, which are changing before our eyes. In France, the government has a plan to provide the country's 30 million telephone subscribers with video display units and information terminals by the 1990s.[1] In other OECD countries the race is well under way to implement fibre-optical technology, to multiply cable networks, to extend and refine existing communications with satellite networks and elaborate private and public data bases. These technical and social developments progress at a rate which is much faster than any perceived change in Left or Right party policies, social policy initiatives or social movement responses to the 'new technology'.

In chapter 1 I cited various studies which argued that the growth of new jobs in high technology professions and areas would be nowhere near as high as the growth in jobs for janitors, hospital orderlies, fast-food servers and other unskilled occupations. Nevertheless, other analysts estimate that a minimum of 10 per cent of the labour force (and as much as 30 per cent) will work from home in the future. Toffler cites *Business Week* reports (in 1982) that, by the mid-1990s, 15 million people will be working at home in the USA.[2] Whether these predictions will come true is highly debatable. But as Toffler argues:

> We cannot today know if, in fact, the electronic cottage will become the norm of the future. Nevertheless, it is worth recognizing that if as few as 10 to 20 per cent of the work force as presently defined were to make this historic transfer over the next 20 to 30 years, our entire economy, our cities, our ecology, our family structure, our values, and even our politics would be altered almost beyond our recognition.[3]

Leaving aside the implications of home work for our values, our politics and our cities, I would like to discuss contemporary feminist concerns about the nature of labour within the new 'electronic cottage'. Toffler and other advocates of the 'electronic cottage' are aware of the completion of the historical circle – from cottage industries at the beginning of capitalist industrialization, to the return to the home from the factory in post-industrial society. Now, we have been well aware, since Marx's work, that the factory system refined the logic of control and exploitation, compared to the semi-autonomous nature of traditional cottage industry.[4] Two questions should therefore be posed to advocates of the 'electronic cottage'. First, is the paid work performed in the new 'electronic cottage' a return to the old form of self-exploitative piece-work? Second, in what way will the work in 'electronic cottages' be an improvement over existing labour relations and conditions of employment?

Electronic home work is a relatively recent arrival, and little research has been done to ascertain the likely nature and conditions of labour. We do know, however that the bulk of existing domestic work (using micro-electronics) can be divided into basic data processing and typing (nearly all of which is performed by women), and professional and business work, for example, that of architects, accountants, brokers (mainly performed by males). While women can also be found within the ranks of business and professional service workers, the gender division within the new communications and information industries largely reflects the discrimination against women in other industries.[5]

Responding to fears about the new electronic piece-work, Toffler argues that

> these aren't illiterate workers just off some feudal manor. They are sophisticated workers, and they may, in fact, be able to use their home computers, video and telecommunications links to organize new networks, 'electronic guilds', new professional associations, and other forms of self-managed or self-protective groups. New forms of collective action will be possible too. Some day we may see 'electronic strikes'. I'd worry more about the conditions of workers left behind in the offices and factories. Instead of resisting home-work, as unions typically do, the unions ought to be thinking imaginatively about how to set humane standards and how to help home-workers self-organize.[6]

However, Toffler's sanguine attitude ignores a number of crucial factors.

First, it is true that the conditions of electronic 'outworkers' will vary according to the specific social conditions and laws in various countries. For example, in Baden-Württemberg, West Germany, there is a pilot scheme for female workers using visual display units at home, combining piece-work payments with full employees' rights to holidays and social security entitlements.[7] But in countries such as the USA, where the union movement is weak, many women work for low piece-work rates without holiday and social security benefits. Even in West Germany, it is freely acknowledged by managers that the electronic home workers must forget about building a career and that, as more workers stay at home, the demands made by all workers will become less militant.

Second, Toffler is optimistic about the emergence of new self-organized networks and associations. But organizing home workers has never been very easy. Home workers, the unemployed or recipients of social welfare, have suffered from isolation and apathy. While 'electronic strikes' may eventuate, one has no grounds to expect any social organization of the electronic home worker that would go beyond a low level of militancy, historically typical of isolated, unpaid domestic labourers and welfare recipients.

Third, Toffler envisages that millions of professionals and business people will work in 'electronic cottages' at the same time as society moves towards a demarketized future.[8] But these two developments are incompatible. Either there is a proliferation of small businesses and marketed services from home, or there is a growth of non-marketed electronic home work free from the constraints of profit-making activity. It is clear that those workers governed by piece-work or wage rates face a future in the 'electronic cottage' quite different from that likely for fee-for-service business people.

While there are many danger signals warning us about the new pitfalls associated with electronic home work, perhaps the most significant arise when we consider gender roles. Building upon the work of Richard Gordon, Donna Haraway draws attention to the way the new home-centred work is becoming feminized.

> Work is being redefined as both literally female and feminized, whether performed by men or women. To be feminized means to be made extremely vulnerable; able to be disassembled, reassembled, exploited as a reserve labor force; seen less as workers than as servers; subjected to time arrangements on and off the paid job that make a mockery of a limited work day; leading an existence that always borders on being obscene, out of place, and reducible to sex.[9]

This prospect of deskilling, disassembly and servility is actually being realized for thousands of women in high-technology and information-processing industries. It is not accidental that employees in the computer industry generally regard work at word processors and other terminals (mainly performed by women) as low status, compared to the skilled and well-paid jobs in engineering, administration, electronics and so forth. If millions of existing jobs in high-technology industries are allocated largely on gender lines, then there is much to fear from a major synthesis of female domestic labour and electronic home work.

Toffler answers this feminist critique by claiming that the associated shift, from an economy based on muscle-power to one based heavily on mind-power, eliminates a crucial disadvantage for women.[10] Moreover, working from home will allegedly lead to much more sharing of paid and unpaid domestic labour as men and women spend more time together.[11] Toffler argues that women should welcome the Third Wave in general, as this new historical period will spell the end of the dominance of the nuclear family, the end of traditional gender roles, and the liberation of workers from lengthy hours of commuting – thus enabling them to devote more time to personal and communal relations.[12] One would have to agree with Toffler that the 'electronic cottage' holds a potential for more liberated and egalitarian relations between the genders. But the obstacles to be overcome – especially those deeply entrenched inequalities based on gender, class, income levels, and market relations – all make the future seem less liberating than Toffler's utopian scenario.

It appears to me that Toffler's image of work in the 'electronic cottage' is based upon a vision of highly paid professional or business types, earning enough to job share, free of piece-work and other exploitative conditions, and able to design their work – rather than that of a worker tied to a terminal (and left with all the domestic labour) with unemployment benefits often being the only real alternative to repetitive data processing. One thing is certain: electronic home work is increasing, and it is far from clear (depending on the level of social struggle), whether Toffler or feminist critics will be proved right about the labour process and gender relations. Defending the 'electronic cottage', Toffler argues that factory work destroyed rather than enriched human relations. 'Now, just when an alternative suddenly becomes historically possible, the factory is held up as an ideal! It's absurd.'[13] True enough. But if the 'electronic cottage' becomes an extension of the factory, if relations between labour and capital do not change, if home workers are burdened with double work, and if communities are starved of social welfare, entertainment and other vitally needed resources and services, why should we welcome this potential centre of enslavement? Moreover, if the factory, office and other outside work spheres all become debased (through electronic home work lowering wage rates, and increasing domestic exploitation of women), then this will hardly constitute a positive alternative to existing alienated wage labour.

One of the key questions about the 'electronic cottage' has to do with the intended and unintended consequences when large numbers work in physical (if not electronical) isolation. We know that the development of the factory and office resulted in new political organizations of solidarity, new divisions between work and leisure, new relations within family structures and a dramatic transformation of the relation between town and country. Given the unplanned nature of existing developments in new technology, electronic home work and so forth, it remains to be seen whether urban life will be as heavily disrupted as was rural life during the development of industrial capitalism. But family relations, educational values and cultural life are not redefined simply because utopian theorists proclaim the virtues of the new over the old. We have also to ask whether particular cultural changes are compatible with the new material means of production, whether new lifestyles assist or run counter to the consolidation of greater equity, democracy and environmental harmony.

## NEW FAMILY RELATIONS OR A PATRIARCHAL PRIVATE SPHERE?

There is no shortage of material on 'the decline of the family'. But historically, there has never been a single type of family to rise and decline. The debate or 'war over the family' is in fact a war over the male-dominated, nuclear family.[14] Bahro attacks the domination of patriarchy without indicating what kind of family relations will exist in 'basic communes'. Gorz does not state what kind of families he favours, except by implication perhaps when he attacks conventional gender roles or endorses Toffler's vision of new Third Wave families and cultural relations. It is clear that Jones favours males doing domestic labour and regards feminist values as life enhancing. But it is not clear whether Jones favours a radical alteration in family forms, or merely a radical alteration in the status and performance of domestic labour. However, Toffler makes no secret of his opposition to the dominance of the nuclear family and his opposition to Moral Majority values. He applauds the fact that

> technologically advanced nations today are honeycombed with a bewildering array of family forms: Homosexual marriages, communes, groups of elderly people banding together to share expenses (and sometimes sex), tribal groupings among certain ethnic minorities, and many other forms coexist as never before. There are contract marriages, serial marriages, family clusters, and a variety of intimate networks with or without shared sex, as well as families in which mother and father live and work in two different cities.[15]

Toffler promotes pluralistic family forms, which embrace the values of the gay movement along with the aspirations of individual heterosexual and celibate adults, desiring new living arrangements which are not necessarily child centred, let alone modelled on the nuclear family. The nuclear family will not disappear in the post-industrial society, says Toffler, but the Third Wave is based on socio-economic relations which are not conducive to the health of the nuclear family. According to Toffler, supporters of the nuclear family are pro-mass production or factory, and anti-computer because white collar, professional and technical workers are less traditional, more psychologically and intellectually mobile than blue collar workers and more prone to get divorced. A computer-based, demassified production system, a decentralized non-nuclear energy system, a demassified media and political, cultural and educational system, all weaken the bases of nuclear families – as the latter flourish in highly centralized socio-economic conditions. Moreover, attempts to drive women back into the home, cut youth wages, lower standards of living to pre-1955 conditions (in the USA) and ban all research into contraception and reproductive technology, would positively enhance the nuclear family.

This is because a nuclear family depends on adults who are in the home full-time, income levels which are too low to permit social mobility and more culturally diverse lifestyles, and restrictions on extra-marital sex due to lack of contraception.[16]

While the one-to-one parallels which Toffler draws between massified, centralized conditions and family forms are rather simplistic, there are also important socio-economic connections which are not easily dismissed. It is easier to criticize Toffler for overlooking all those pro-nuclear family supporters who also love computers, than it is to evaluate the consequences of radical diversity and decentralization on family forms and relations. On the other hand, it is difficult to see the direct connection which Toffler makes between the nuclear family and centralized energy production. After all, Toffler himself cites the multiplicity of existing family forms in technologically advanced nations – which all have highly centralized energy systems. Of course, the development of Bahro's 'basic communes' could herald new family relations, if existing consumption of renewable energy was drastically reduced or new energy forms required heavy labour-intensive production. Furthermore, the process of 'industrial disarmament' implies a return to pre-1955 standards of living – exactly those levels of consumption and income which, Toffler argues, mitigate against pluralistic and diverse family forms. This immediately raises the basic question: Does the variety and nature of families depend directly on the economic independence of individual adults, or are new family forms based upon the sharing of values and practices regardless of the level of material assets?

If Toffler is correct in claiming that the nuclear family 'has no nucleus when there are no adults left at home',[17] and that the nuclear family 'is further denuclearized when the young leave parental control to go to work',[18] what are we to expect of the 'electronic cottage'? On the surface it would appear that the nuclear family might be strengthened by electronic home work if the principal requirement is at least one adult working in the home. While Toffler believes that domestic labour will be equitably shared between men and women, he also believes that children will be able to engage in electronic home work, thus reducing the current high levels of youth unemployment.[19] If this new form of integrated paid and unpaid domestic labour becomes common in the 'electronic cottage', it is extremely difficult to see how the prolonged psychological and financial dependence of youth on their parents (reinforced by low youth wages and high unemployment) will in any way be improved by increasing labour in the home! Furthermore, Toffler appears to want it both ways. On the one hand, Toffler would like a society where the strict divisions between children and adults, school and work, leisure and work, individual and community, etc., are replaced by more integrated and holistic structures. Yet on the other hand, Toffler fails to analyse the fundamental bases of reproduction – that is, those factors, of income, socialization, division of labour and conditions within family structures, which either enhance individual autonomy or inhibit individual capacities and create deep-seated dependencies. For example, those children working with their parents at home would have to be earning enough to have a choice: whether to live with their parents, to live away from their parents, to gain an education and thus entry to occupations other than electronic home work, or to share income and authority with their parents.

Toffler's image of life in the 'electronic cottage' tries to include simultaneously an extension of existing individualism and pluralistic family forms, along with the new, non-alienated and co-operative 'prosumer' and locally or globally conscious citizen. But the varieties of family forms and individual lifestyles are not all products of choice. It is common for children to leave home because their parents deny them sexual and other rights. It is common for women to be deserted by men, or to seek refuge from violent men not because they value single-parent households, but out of necessity. If the Third Wave is to cure the current epidemic ills of addiction, alienation, violence and isolation, this cannot be done by simply changing the dynamics of familial socialization and domestic labour, without also changing those relations which reproduce dependency, repression, alienation and lack of material autonomy. It is a favourite and quite unjustifiable ploy of conservatives to place *all* the blame for societies' ills on the family, or on the school or on the media. Nevertheless, we cannot avoid asking whether there is a discernible relationship between diverse family forms and widespread social and interpersonal alienation and conflict. Can a post-industrial socialist society afford the price of post-modern relativism – the absence of any hierarchy of human values and practices? Are there particular forms of families and individual lifestyles which negate co-operative, egalitarian social values? Conservatives have always been clear about the 'traditional' values which need to be protected. But socialists have either imitated and promoted puritanical authoritarianism, or opted for a pseudo tolerance of all styles and forms while at the same time proclaiming the need for equality, democracy and co-operative solidarity.

Discussing the issue of autonomy, Gorz puts forward a rebellious anarchistic view of family relations which is also highly pessimistic in regard to social alienation. According to Gorz,

> autonomous persons, particularly creators, artists, intellectuals and others, often come from families lacking or without paternal authority, and where someone else (of influence) had a taste for ideas, books, art or simply an open curious mind. In short, autonomous individuals are those in whom the process of socialization failed to work: the part of them that is not socialized wins over the one that is. Society, all societies, are to them a contingency, somewhat haphazard and more or less absurd, from which they feel removed. They are forever conscious that the norms and laws of society do not correspond to the very needs, morality and aesthetics, of people, and of relations between people. The alienation is insurmountable in any type of society.[20]

While Gorz believes that alienation can be reduced in a socialist society, his conception of the relationship between autonomous individuals and 'partially socialized children' poses an alarming problem for socialists. Is there an alternative form of family relations which positively cultivates autonomous and creative individuals, or is autonomy a condition which must be acquired in opposition to parental influence – no matter how tolerant and enlightened? Furthermore, if the norms and laws of a post-industrial socialist society do not correspond to the individual's needs, is Gorz merely succumbing to the old existentialist dictum that life is absurd? Or is Gorz merely criticizing the repression of autonomy in most existing forms of familial socialization? More importantly, why does Gorz place so much emphasis on autonomy? What about co-operation, solidarity and a sense of autonomy balanced by responsibility?

Neither Toffler nor Gorz appears able to reconcile the processes of individual and familial reproduction with their visions of a dynamically decentralized and actively autonomous citizenry. Yet this problem is crucial not only for the future health of a socialist society, but also in relation to contemporary polemics over 'the family'. Conservatives and cultural critics such as Lasch,[21] have all attacked feminists and gays for postulating alternative relations to existing nuclear families. Rightwing post-industrialists such as Kahn have criticized the de-emphasis 'on traditional roles and values such as being a man or woman, religion, patriotism';[22] and have sought to show how more emphasis on personal happiness leads to loss of job-oriented skills, honor, duty, and other 'square hangups'. Brigette and Peter Berger are more sophisticated defenders of the bourgeois family. In a well-written and serious polemic against feminists and the Left, the Bergers call for the restoration of parental rights against the 'welfare state', and generally see the future of Western parliamentary democracies as being based on the defence of those familial relations which feminists and many gays see as being the cause of contemporary problems. Their thesis is that 'the family, and specifically the bourgeois family, is the necessary social context for the emergence of the autonomous individuals who are the empirical foundation of political democracy.'[23]

In an equally nostalgic defence of the patriarchal bourgeois family (but using quite a different methodological approach),

Christopher Lasch also attacks feminists for undermining 'the family' which, he claims, functions as a 'haven in a heartless world'.[24] Apart from criticizing the all-intruding 'welfare state' experts and capitalist consumerism, Lasch's thesis on private and public narcissism, loss of authority, the 'flight from feeling', the preoccupation with self as opposed to community, and other destructive developments, rests to a large degree on what he sees as the new relations between child and father – that is, children no longer experiencing the formative tensions of the Oedipal crisis. In other words, Lasch links the changing interpersonal relations within families to the changing social conditions within public institutions – both feeding off one another to produce narcissism. But no critique of narcissism is as effective as Stephanie Engel's excellent probing of the conceptual origins of Lasch's key category.[25] Engel shows how 'Freud's exposition of the term narcissism was framed by his general theory's assumption of the primacy and normality of male development, with respect to which female development was necessarily deviant . . . The concept of narcissism associated effeminacy, androgyny, and homosexuality with the instinct, not for generativity or creativity, but for self-destruction.'[26] Hence, the phenomenon of narcissism as described by Lasch actually originates in the disappearance of those very male–female relations which made the oppression of women possible. As the role of the father is undermined, so too is the strong super-ego which was born out of the conflict between father and son. In Engel's words, 'Lasch's tirade against narcissism must be seen in part as a tirade against the emergence of a pattern of male development that begins to look increasingly like the traditional pattern of female development.'[27]

Lasch, Sennett,[28] Donzelot,[29] and others who criticize narcissism and the 'policing of families' by 'welfare state' experts, ultimately come very close to the position of the Bergers and other conservative defenders of the bourgeois patriarchal family. At one level, the conservative and radical critiques of technocratic 'welfare state' intervention into family life can easily be dismissed by the post-industrial utopians. In so far as Toffler et al. call for radical alternatives to existing welfare state services, their vision of 'prosuming', 'basic communes', and local neighbourhood structures give a reply to the Bergers, Lasch and Donzelot. But at the level of intrafamilial relations, as well as the whole effect of family forms on public institutional life and the notion of citizenship, the post-industrial theorists have either remained silent, or avoided the hard issues.

While I believe that conservatives and Lasch idealize the bourgeois family, ignore (or note only perfunctorily) the enormous pain and violence inflicted on women and children in the name of authority, duty and 'civility', the whole issue of the relation between democratic institutions and family forms cannot simply be brushed under the carpet or dismissed as a conservative phobia. If the psychoanalytic theories of narcissism are riddled with sexism, it is still necessary to find alternative explanations of what causes narcissism, 'schizoid' personalities and other disturbances in private and public life. It is also necessary to discuss what kind of child–adult relations are desirable and compatible with democratic and egalitarian lifestyles. Will the post-industrial society be an extension of existing consumerism and hedonistic self-gratification? This impression could easily be given by Toffler's *The Third Wave* with its abundance of lifestyles, new forms of high-tech, demassified consumer goods and so forth. On the other hand, Toffler's vision of demarketized 'prosuming', or Bahro's depiction of 'basic communes', which put the emphasis on restoring communal relations and grass-roots democracy, do not encourage any narcissistic preoccupation with self.

## DEMOCRATIC PLURALISM, FAMILY FORMS AND STATE INSTITUTIONS

What kind of family is compatible with bourgeois parliamentary democracy on the one hand, or with post-industrial socialism on the other? This question cannot be answered with reference solely to family relations, and in fact is not even correctly posed. For example, there is enough empirical evidence to show that the existence of the bourgeois family has coincided with widespread political apathy, racism, intolerance of religious and sexual minorities, support for imperialist exploitation in Third World countries and support for brutal fascist regimes in Europe. Again, there is no conclusive evidence whether children learn faster or are more emotionally stable when at least one parent stays at home, or whether it is better that children mix with other adults, live in communes, and go to childcare centres. It is also unclear whether each child and each adult needs a room of her or his own to maximize ego identity and privacy, as opposed to learning group responsibilities and developing a public persona. If the latter condition is necessary for the cultivation of an autonomous and democratic personality, then the populations of China, India and dozens of other countries are doomed either to heteronomy or to possible ecological disaster if the massive building effort needed for individual rooms depletes forests and creates giant urban sprawls. Later on I will discuss the nature of education, law and political activity in post-industrial society. I will now discuss those services and conditions of social reproduction which cannot necessarily be produced by families – regardless of their form.

We do not want a new tyranny which prescribes the ideal family form, or ideal sexual expression and education into 'responsible citizenship'. But, to avoid it, we must first understand how the social and personal problems which inevitably arise from a plurality of lifestyles are linked to the general conditions of social reproduction. While Gorz and Jones are exceptions, Toffler, Bahro, Sale and other post-industrialists or anarchists concede little or no role to state institutions. Yet, the future of all those women, children, the aged, blacks, gays and other groups – who are currently impoverished, repressed or restricted in their material or mental capacities to participate democratically and equitably – rests very much on a transformation of 'social wage' programmes and material conditions. For example, we know that the time, energy and financial opportunities available to a single woman raising children can be radically altered if both mother and children are provided with substantial material and social support. A plurality of lifestyles and family forms is thus dependent upon the services and support network provided by 'social wage' programmes at least as much as upon the income derived from paid work.

In chapter 2 I discussed the weaknesses associated with the various guaranteed minimum income schemes proposed by the post-industrial utopians. Similarly, we must ask whether their advocacy of new and more varied lifestyles is credible, when it is not explained how these families will obtain vitally needed communal and personal services. It is not enough to say that everyone will be looked after in the 'basic commune', or that decentralized 'prosuming' and the 'electronic cottage' will provide the adequate income and economic security which was lacking in the counter-culture communes of the 1960s.[30] If there are individuals who do not live in arrangements such as the nuclear family or the extended family, then social institutions have to provide vitally needed care for those among them who are aged, young, sick or over-burdened. This alternative to the 'welfare state' cannot be relied upon if services are provided for profit, or if they are randomly supplied by volunteers and neighbours who will not always be available. Just as a sound and comprehensive GMI scheme presupposes a state-organized revenue and redistribution structure, so too post-industrial families and individuals will depend for their needs on the quality and quantity of non-wage goods and services. These 'social wage' goods and services can be organized at local, regional or national levels. But socialists err fatally, if they dispute with conservatives over family socialization processes while leaving the relevant extra-family social structures undiscussed and unchallenged.

In other words, there is little possibility of post-industrial families being free of all the pain, recrimination and violence of past and present families, if these new families are supposed to resolve all their problems in the absence of elaborately organized communal 'social wage' programmes. Just as the guaranteed minimum income is rightly seen as a more humane and rational alternative to existing poverty and discrimination, so families are more likely to cultivate autonomous and democratic individuals if the decentralized or central state institutions subsidize, nurture and support a genuine pluralism rather than the pluralism afforded by market mechanisms – that is, choice based on money, power and privilege. The positive contributions made by state-organized 'social wage' programmes must go in tandem with the protection of families and individuals from negative experiences, practices and threats. But this presupposes a notion of the post-industrial legal, educational and political arrangements that will complement a pluralistic range of family forms. While rightly opposing the bureaucratic authoritarianism and technocratic interference of existing educational, legal and welfare workers, many radicals and conservatives go to the other extreme and advocate total dismantling of 'the state'. But it is absolutely necessary to see past the glaring deficiencies of existing state institutions, and seriously develop alternative 'social wage' programmes and political–legal structures.

## WHAT KIND OF POST-INDUSTRIAL LEGAL INSTITUTIONS?

If the post-industrial society is to encourage a diverse range of family forms and individual lifestyles, it is essential to establish from the outset how it will provide protection for family members as well as problem-solving mechanisms. Toffler is once again quite contradictory when it comes to regulations and social diversity. One theme running through his work is a condemnation of regulatory mechanisms governing economic activity and private relations.[31] In this respect, Toffler merely echoes the prevailing chorus of New Right ideologists, who all demand that laws be dismantled which restrict the accumulation of capital. For Toffler, the post-industrial utopia is simultaneously an extension of private corporate activity (with new technology and social relations), and a radical post-capitalist, demarketized and decentralized new Wave. Little wonder, then, that Toffler can attack existing laws and regulations as historically obsolete and yet, at the same time, assume that the 144,000 law firms in the USA will continue to grow in number, mediating between the millions of businesses and public and private institutions.[32]

Undoubtedly, Toffler imagines that many of the workers in the new 'electronic cottages' will be lawyers or other professionals who make a living out of regulatory mechanisms or how to circumvent them! On the other hand, if many of the existing government regulations at national and local level are abolished, how does Toffler imagine that there will continue to be growth in the number of professional posts, educational institutions, consultancy agencies and so forth? Moreover, Toffler is a critic of the nation state, and favours the development of new local and supranational institutions which will supposedly reflect the 'planetary consciousness' of the post-industrial citizen of the world.[33] A critic of regulations, Toffler at the same time dons his cap as champion of minorities and advocates giving ethnic groups, local neighbourhoods and specific subcultural groups the power to regulate their own affairs, establish youth courts to discipline their young and so forth. 'Such institutions would build community and identity, and contribute to law and order, while relieving the overburdened government institutions of unnecessary work.'[34]

In advocating new self-regulatory legal institutions for local groups and subcultures, Toffler endorses a common demand made by many critics of existing state apparatuses – both from the Left and the Right. But an old dilemma immediately arises: how to meet the conflicting demands and needs of diversity, equity and democracy. Toffler appears to want his cake and eat it too. On the one hand, he advocates a radical decentralization of regulatory mechanisms and the transcendence of the nation state; yet, on the other hand, his new self-regulatory legal institutions actually still exist within the framework of national government institutions – thus enjoying the benefits of a national bill of rights, laws and regulatory mechanisms. At least Gorz recognizes the essential role of national state institutions in a post-industrial socialist society.[35] In contrast to Toffler and Bahro, Gorz wants to combine a radical anti-capitalist and anti-bureaucratic stand, with a realism which acknowledges that socialist pluralism and small-scale institutions can only thrive if there are protective institutions as well as certain large-scale economic organizations. The problem with Gorz is that he does not outline in detail how the sphere of autonomy will interact with the sphere of heteronomy (paid work, state regulation and planning, etc.). Toffler's championing of neo-conservative deregulatory principles, however, has a certain affinity with Bahro's radical 'industrial disarmament'. Both theorists emphasize the local group or 'basic commune' without indicating whether there will be a national government, or how local citizens will define their rights and needs in relation to regional and supranational bodies. After a generation of criticisms of the abuses of 'socialist legality' in Eastern Europe, China and elsewhere, it is deeply unsatisfactory to be left with little or no indication as to the nature of critically important legal institutions.

I discussed earlier the need to recognize that families could not in themselves be responsible for all the ills of society. If we have no legal institutions that transcend those self-regulatory mechanisms which Toffler advocates for local groups and subcultures, it is difficult to imagine how a great deal of personal suffering and intrafamilial disputes will be resolved. I am referring here to the need for family law, child protection, individual civil rights and so forth. One does not have to assume a society based on property rights in order to establish the need for family law. It is utopian in the worst sense to imagine that divorce, problems of custody, settlement of personal possessions, prevention of child abuse, and a host of everyday problems will all suddenly become irrelevant in a post-industrial society. Given that it is desirable to legitimate a variety of family forms and lifestyles, the issues of diversity and equity cannot be left solely in the hands of parochial groups. Cross-cultural family relations, geographical mobility, intergenerational and gender conflict all necessitate clearly specified rights at a national level. This is not an argument against radical reform of existing legal institutions. Nor is it a defence of well-paid legal parasites whose proliferation is due to the inaccessibility of legal language to ordinary people, the conversion of so many social and political problems into 'legal problems' and other self-promoting forms of legal 'empire building'. Rather, the desirable twin objectives of greatly increasing communal decision-making, and making law relevant at the grass-roots level, cannot be conceptualized as a one-way process – that is, a dismantling of national laws and regulations without their replacement by a more democratic set of structures.

A society in which private enterprise is replaced by various forms of public ownership (centrally planned enterprises, co-operatives, self-managed institutions, etc.) will at the very least require explicit *written* laws to help protect against dictatorship, regional or national hegemony, and disregard for local needs, as well as explicit laws for other areas of potential dispute. While the post-industrial economy may be entirely different from existing systems, whether capitalist or Communist, and while there may be a radical environmentalist philosophy governing the use of resources, it is most unlikely that social relations will recede to a level of non-complexity. Given that we have not yet seen a plausible scheme for the abolition of money, or a clear alternative to elaborate 'social wage' programmes (whether run locally, regionally or nationally), it is pure and simple fantasy to imagine that all these complex institutions can coexist without written laws, regulations, courts of adjudication, prisons, police forces (whether voluntary or professional) and other agencies.

What is undefined at the moment is the manner in which laws will be codified, whether there will be professionally trained lawers or not, what kind of penal sanctions and centres of rehabilitation and punishment will exist, whether there will be checks and balances between social, military, legal and political institutions at local, national and supranational levels, and other thorny problems. One thing is clear: whether the post-industrial society is made up of horizontally organized 'basic communes', or hierarchically structured forms of decentralized or centralized democratic structures, each new generation of individuals will have to learn the prevailing moral norms, boundaries of responsibility and social rights. The idea that these norms, rights, powers and boundaries can be learnt solely by word-of-mouth is both dubious and dangerous. But as soon as these norms and rights are written down, there will need to be institutions which interpret, enforce and formally change these laws. This activity entails political struggle, and a conception of private and public spheres – a crucial issue to which I later return.

## DESCHOOLING OR RESCHOOLING IN THE KNOWLEDGE-BASED SOCIETY?

When the post-industrial utopians discuss the nature and role of education, their analyses focus mainly on the major new role which educational institutions will have to play in work and leisure. One can distinguish here post-industrial notions of education as, on the one hand, the basis of new power and technological relations, and as, on the other, the vital dimension which makes possible new family forms and the new post-industrial individual. It is also possible to detect, running through these perspectives, the influence of Ivan Illich's theory of deschooling, with its sustained critique of contemporary forms of mass education and credentialism.[36] On the other hand, it is not unusual to find post-industrial theorists discussing education as the largest industry of the future, the notion being that everyone will have to be reschooled. I would therefore like to discuss briefly the consequences that changes to education would imply for work, family relations and social harmony.

Given the emphasis which various post-industrial theorists place on information, knowledge and data as the key aspects of future economies, it is surprising that their general analyses of education and work as so unsatisfactory. After all, the very notion 'post-industrial society' signifies, not the transcendence of all industry, but rather the transcendence of blue collar work as new knowledge-based industries become dominant. Consequently, Toffler, Stonier, Jones and other writers popularize an image of the future characterized by a massive expansion of educational institutions and practices. Echoing and developing Daniel Bell's seminal work on the vital role of education in the future,[37] Jones, Stonier and Toffler stress how important it is for working-class children to get a computer education, for adults to continue their education right through their lives (rather than just spend their earlier years in formal education),[38] and for varied, demassified forms of education to be available. Toffler believes educational retraining will become one of the biggest industries of all.[39] Stonier and Jones also write against the background of mass unemployment, and argue that new jobs and greater social equality will come only from a massive expansion of employment opportunities – both within the education industry, and as a by-product of increased educational resources and opportunities. Even Bahro calls for greater expenditure on education:

> We need a new overall plan for social development oriented to new values, a plan which the economy has naturally to fit into. A plan geared to the optimization of conditions of development for fully socialised human beings. This means, for example, priority for expenditure on education, it means educational planning that is no longer governed by the present state of demand for material values, or by what jobs industry has to offer. And we need the planning to be done in forms of grass-roots democracy that facilitate a process of social learning and discovery with the broadest mass participation.[40]

It is clear that everyone is in favour of education, just as they are in favour of peace, freedom and democracy. The problem is that there is no agreement as to who shall run educational institutions, who shall plan, who shall pay for education and, most importantly, what students will learn. Jones and Stonier put forward a more conventional educational scenario in that they would like to see a massive expansion of publicly financed educational institutions – even though each offers radical ideas on how education relates to lifestyle, self-fulfilment and diversity. Stonier and Jones, however, say little about how this massive expansion of education will be paid for. Like Toffler, they offer advice which the private enterprise interests in capitalist societies reject: an expanded public sector, using North Sea oil revenue for education,[41] higher budgetary deficits, and so forth. Moreover, it is difficult to reconcile Stonier and Toffler's belief that greater educational expenditure will resolve mass unemployment, with their proposals to demassify existing educational institutions. Both theorists would like to see parents play a far larger role in their children's education – supplying education at home, and drastically reducing the traditional orientation of schools to vocational education. Stonier actually proposes that all children spend the first decade of their lives being educated at home or at a neighbour's.[42] He also recommends the massive involvement of the aged – ensuring that children have cultural contact with grandparents.[43]

Each of these changes to education has intrinsic merit; there is a perfectly legitimate school of thought which values education in the home as opposed to school, as well as inter-generational contact and decentralization of education. As proposals to be implemented in capitalist societies over the next 10 to 20 years, however, they are full of contradictions and unresolved problems. First, if all children spend their first years at home instead of school, mass unemployment will be created in the teaching profession. Second, a large proportion of the population – for example, most working-class mothers (and fathers) – are ill-equipped educationally, financially and emotionally to engage in full-time education of their children in addition to all their existing (domestic) labour. Third, even if we could imagine these major obstacles being overcome, where are the new jobs for all these retrained workers and home-educated pupils? There is no doubt that a society not oriented to profit could find endless new jobs and non-vocational activities of an individual and communal nature. But educational investment in capitalist societies has always been primarily a service to the accumulation of capital and the reproduction of dominant ideology; when educational resources and practices exceeded narrow functional requirements, cultivating use-values as opposed to exchange values, and cultural challenges, public sector debt and political instability ensued. Toffler, Stonier and Jones are conscious of the socio-economic crises confronting existing capitalist societies, but almost unconscious of the social conflict which would be unleashed, if their education proposals happened to be accepted (an unlikely development) by governments in capitalist countries.

Quite apart from the vagueness of the connections they make between education and work, and their avoidance or glossing over of fundamental problems associated with gender roles, domestic labour, and education at home, the post-industrial utopians are also unconvincing in the way they relate (or fail to relate) compulsory schooling and educational content to the formation of a democratic and egalitarian citizenry. If post-industrial societies are going to be characterized by pluralistic forms of families, the connection between democratic pluralism and education will have to be better understood. For example, Toffler argues that compulsory education will be reduced in the future as children learn at home and the Third Wave moves away from 'child-centred families'.[44] What he means here is the development of new forms of childhood and youth as work and education are blended in the 'electronic cottage', as parents cease to pour all their emotional energy into their children's lives, and as the very notion of romantic love (and nuclear families) is replaced by more 'mature' and varied interpersonal relations and family forms.[45] But not all such changes in compulsory education and interpersonal relations will be necessarily compatible with democracy and universalistic values. The old disputes – whether all children should learn a core curriculum, whether varied, non-compulsory and anti-authoritarian education produces autonomous and democratic individuals – are unlikely to dissapear in post-industrial societies.

In contrast to Toffler, André Gorz favours a core curriculum which would be compulsory in his 'utopia for a possible dual society'. It is essential that all young people 'learn to cultivate the soil, to work with metal, wood, fabrics and stone, and that they learn history, science, mathematics and literature in conjunction with these activities'.[46] Gorz further argues that, after completing compulsory education, 'each individual would be required to put in 20 hours of work each week (for which he or she would earn a full salary), in addition to continuing with whatever studies or training he or she desired. The required labour would be done in one or more of the four main sectors: agriculture, mining and steelworks; construction and public works; public hygiene; and care of the sick, the aged and children'.[47] Like Stonier, Gorz favours

mixing studies with community work. But, in contrast to
Stonier, Gorz's utopia resembles Bahro's in that the four main
industrial sectors are notable for their 'industrial' rather than
'post-industrial' character – with no mention of high-technology
industries, telecommunications or elaborate information-
processing industries. Also, the compulsory core subjects
which Gorz recommends do not include televisual subjects,
computer skills, and other high-technology disciplines.
Gorz's concept of 20 hours' compulsory labour for students
would also, most probably, produce a new student rebellion.
If the work week were reduced to 20 hours for all paid
workers, and yet student labourers were expected to study
their normal courses on top of the average work week, it is
most unlikely that autonomous individuals would tolerate
this inequitable reintroduction of the puritan work ethic.
Moreover, compulsory education-labour for the duration of
a person's studies conforms more with the traditional rigid
division of life into education, work and retirement, than
with Gorz's own idea of the self-management of time and
rotation of work in the heteronomous and autonomous spheres
of society.

Both Gorz and Bahro favour decentralized consultation
and the planning of education and student labour with local
communities. While Gorz's acceptance of an important planning role for state institutions is compatible with his ideas on
education and job rotation, it is not clear how either Bahro or
Toffler can reconcile their radical 'basic communes' and
abolition of the nation state with a democratic post-industrial
society. For while one can agree or disagree with Gorz's core
curriculum, he and Jones at least envisage these changes taking
place at a national level and with the strong involvement of
state institutions. However, with Bahro it is not clear whether
he favours the retention of state institutions, national revenue
raising and resource allocation for education (even though
these would be planned at a grass-roots level), or whether
education, like most other essential needs, would be produced
from the resources of the 'basic commune'.

For all their waste of human talent and their irrational and
repressive qualities, contemporary educational institutions at

least offer an identifiable logic, a connection between education, work, ideology, retraining and so forth. In order to eliminate the negative qualities of contemporary education, the post-industrial utopians have to give more thought to the manner in which the liberation from alienated labour complements or corresponds to the new process of socialization and redistribution of political and social power. If there are no new state institutions to co-ordinate resources (in a democratic manner), then Toffler, Bahro, Sale and other advocates of stateless societies, or radical decentralization, will have to show how demarketized 'prosuming', 'basic communes' and self-sufficient towns can attain the following goals:

(1) to provide comparable education in urban and rural areas;
(2) to arrange for credentials and schooling to be recognized, to permit geographical and occupational mobility;
(3) if credentials and money are abolished, to arrange elaborate forms of barter and provision of basic needs for teachers, students and parents educating children at school or at home;
(4) to resolve fundamental differences between groups and individuals over parochial and universal values, curriculum content and the objectives of education.

If the post-industrial society becomes radically decentralized while private enterprise flourishes, then diversity in education will coexist with extensive forms of social inequality based on great disparities in income levels and in access to resources, and with incompatible religious and secular values being propagated. A free market which permits families in 'electronic cottages', or thousands of businesses, professionals and churches, to market education in a decentralized, demassified form, is a recipe for increased social atomization, isolation and conflict. On the other hand, a society structured on 'basic communes' could possible see them providing a very elementary form of education without money or external assistance; but it is most unlikely to be able to cope with the complexity of social relations which even an economy based on zero growth would require. The inability of each commune to provide its own complex technology, economies of scale, etc., would necessitate technical interaction with other communities. If there are to be no state institutions, no guaranteed income schemes, no student scholarships or teachers' wages, no local resources to make films, buy books, and so forth, then we are entitled to demand that the advocates of stateless socialism show how social conditions will not degenerate into primitive parochialism.

In other words, without the existence of new democratic state institutions, there is no way to achieve an egalitarian, but pluralistic, decentralized education. Toffler and Bahro want to have it both ways. One desires a radical form of post-industrial free enterprise which is still guaranteed protection by state institutions; the other wants a fundamentalist eco-socialist commune while still invoking the notions of planning and increased expenditure for education. But democratic planning itself presupposes the existence of public institutions of representation, of citizenship, of implicit or explicit territorial legitimacy, of communes, city states, nation states or world orders. Either we leave education to each family and individual, or we acknowledge the indispensable publicness of knowledge, the sharing of values and social objectives, the suppression or toleration of varied ideas and practices. In Gorz's case, a population simply wakes up to hear the prime minister announce the new core curriculum and compulsory education and labour for all. At the other extreme, Toffler has a fantasy world of demarketized relations with no visible signs of planning! While Bahro calls for social planning, he gives no real indication of who will be represented, apart from saying that it will be carried out at the grass roots. But will the local communards consult with regional or national governments, or just with other communes?

The issue of democratic planning, and the involvement or non-involvement of state institutions, is closely related to the content of education and the manner of education. At the technical level, there is no agreement between contemporary analysts about the social and pedagogical implications of new

computerized technology. For all his attraction to high technology, Barry Jones expresses a profound disquiet about the
new forms of communication. 'The strength of the book-
based culture was its relationship to personal autonomy,
making it possible to absorb material at one's own rate – to
stop, to go back, to ponder, note, brood and reconsider. In
an era of mass, one-way communication, where language is
persistently devalued, this view is made to seem increasingly
anachronistic.'[48] David Hawkridge is even more alarmed by
the new information technology. In a chapter entitled 'Learners
Hell',[49] Hawkridge argues that the centralizing of information (made possible by new technology), will lead to cuts
in education expenditure as course duplication is eliminated.
Also, voice recognition computers will result in technology
dominating education because children will only have to ask
the computer, rather than learn material through effort and
complex discourse. At an international level, writers such
as Herbert Schiller have long warned about the cultural
imperialism promoted by transnational corporate control of key telecommunication organizations and installations.[50]

In opposition to the worried and the pessimistic, Toffler
displays an unbridled optimism. The Third Wave will introduce new forms of 'indi-video', demassified media,
transformed scientific research, and electro-chemical forms
of communication.[51] The giant centralized computer will 'be
supplemented by myriad chips of intelligence, embedded in
one form or another in every home, hospital, and hotel, every
vehicle and appliance, virtually every building-brick. The
electronic environment will literally converse with us.'[52]
Toffler's vision is a combination of electronic poetry and
technocratic gimmickry. The future personality is both transformed and enriched by a galaxy of multi-dimensional electronic messages and stimuli. At a less futuristic level, Andrew
Feenberg (former Lukacsian and now computer freak) makes
a number of telling points against those who see computers as
simply carriers of quantitative information. Criticizing
Lyotard and other philosophers who see computers only as
one-way analytic tools and storage depots, Feenberg points to

the enhanced communication which is possible with educational teleconferencing (having himself moderated teleconferences in recent years).[53] According to Feenberg, teleconferencing liberates participants from the usual constraints of face-to-face communication – physical and mental intimidation, emotional outbursts, gender discrimination and wasted energy. Participants in social teleconferencing, whether for educational or political purposes, could exchange complex ideas through their computers, respond to issues and problems more discursively, less heatedly, while still using all the skills of reading and writing. In short, Feenberg sees teleconferencing as potentially more democratic than traditional forms of communication, not only because it minimizes intimidation and constraints, but also because the participants engage in a conscious meta-communication – that is, discussion about the means of communication – something which is less common in face-to-face interaction.[54]

Given the divergent views on the dangers of new technology, as well as its potential for liberation, it is crucial that the post-industrial theorists do not leave education as a sphere of activity inadequately conceptualized, and poorly related to radical changes in family forms, work, technology and political participation. I have tried to show that any attempt to decentralize education, extend the availability of education to all age groups, classes and regions, introduce new electronic technology or compulsory curriculum, break the division between school and home, work and leisure and so forth, demands far deeper thought and discussion than our post-industrial utopians have offered. I have said little on the key issue of educational content and philosophy. Any discussion of values and curriculum content necessarily involves a discussion of the notions of public and private spheres, of the notion of citizenship, of the new 'post-modern' personality, of the clash between unrestrained individualism and the various Right, Left and Green notions of the 'healthy' society and individual. I will therefore turn to some of these crucial issues and explore some of the contradictions of post-industrial culture.

## THE CULTURAL CONTRADICTIONS OF 'POST-MODERNITY'

For decades introductory sociology courses have emphasized the contradictions associated with the transition from pre-industrial to industrial society. Students have had to study opposed themes such as *Gemeinschaft* and *Gesellschaft*, religion and secularization, mechanical and organic solidarity, individual and community, security as opposed to freedom, the realm of freedom and the realm of necessity, ego and id. They learn how whole new lifestyles were constructed around the factory system, the automobile and the office, bringing new problems with them. The dilemmas here are self-evident. The functional order of the patriarchal family provides security for its members only so long as women and children subordinate their freedom and needs to the father. Once educational institutions fail to maintain their legitimacy in the face of persistently high unemployment, confusion and conflict over curriculum priorities, etc., the old contradictions between authority and freedom, relevance and tradition, undermine the foundations of social order. We have all become familiar with the erosion of the work ethic amongst a growing minority, of the deep hostility to legal, political and religious institutions, as new ideas and social polarization slowly undermine the seemingly stable social fabric. Nearly all the above major cultural and social tensions confronting capitalist and Communist societies (in varying degrees) have been described by our post-industrial theorists. Yet they conspicuously fail to provide any analysis of the potential cultural contradictions in post-industrial societies.

Two contrasting themes seem to be evident in both post-industrial theory and Left theory. One theme is best represented by Bahro and many anarchists, environmentalists, Maoists and various utopian socialists. It can be succinctly described as the 'revolt against modernity'.[55] Socialist society is conceived as a tranquil, simple, harmonious answer to the complex, conflict-ridden, bureaucratized, monolithic and alienated present. The 'basic commune' is basic in its very essence – back to nature, back to basic needs, back to face-to-face relations, back to small communal experiences and peace. It is not that any of these objectives is undesirable –far from it. But what is missing from these utopian longings, is an awareness that life may not be able to become so uncomplicated, so free from cultural contradictions.

The other dominant theme in post-industrial theory is the belief that all the present cultural contradictions, with their epidemics of addiction, suicide and violence, can be resolved by even more diversity, technical innovation, demassification and destandardization. In this regard, Toffler is the paradigmatic case of unreflective optimism. Every major institution – from the national government through to churches, schools, political parties, law agencies, media, hospitals – is conceived as being on its last legs or subject to radical transformation. Yet all this dissolution of the old, and reconstruction of new post-industrial institutions, is conceived in an almost problem-free manner. Certainly Toffler and others point to the millions of casualties as new family relations, work processes, cultural institutions and way of thinking upset and shake the security and power of the old. But these problems are conceived as ones of *transition*, rather than cultural and social contradictions of the fully established new order (whatever that may mean). So, while Bahro longs for the reduction of complexity, Toffler and company romanticize complexity and minimize the dysfunctional and disagreeable effects of new technology and new lifestyles.

But how can electronic environments which 'converse with you', a mass proliferation of demassified political–economic structures, individualized media outlets, the simultaneous decentralization of life and development of a 'planetary consciousness', how can all of these radical changes occur without serious cultural contradictions? This is not the place to engage in an exercise in cultural futurology. But it is possible to analyze and query some of the socio-cultural changes predicted by post-industrial theorists. Toffler's mindless pluralism is no guarantor of cultural solidarity and democracy, any more than the prevailing form of bourgeois pluralism (in OECD countries) is the answer to social inequality and social alienation. In *Future Shock* (1970), Toffler presented a smorgasbord of every conceivable lifestyle and technical innovation. Yet he also catalogued the physical and mental costs of endless novelty and diversity – anxiety, stress, mental illness, information overload, social disintegration and loss of direction.[56] Ten years later, Toffler still shows symptoms of his bout of pop sociology; but *The Third Wave* is less gimmicky, more subdued – despite the lapses into superficial bouts of futurology. Toffler proclaims that, for all the social diversity of post-industrial societies, 'any decent society must generate a feeling of community. Community offsets loneliness. It gives people a vitally necessary sense of belonging. Yet today the institutions on which community depends are crumbling in all the techno-societies.'[57] This immediately raises a fundamental question which Toffler fails to answer: If existing institutions do not provide a sense of community, and yet the future is expected to contain even more of the pluralistic forms which are thriving at the moment, how can community and meaning rise from the ashes of Second Wave social catastrophe?

The problem of community, diversity and 'decency' invariably raises the related issues of whether contemporary social movements seek to deepen and radicalize the values, institutions and promises of 'modernity' or whether they are the most visible manifestation of the 'post-modern' departure from the modern epoch. In recent years there have been at least three separate discourses involving the various notions of 'modernity' and 'post-modernity'. One of these is mainly confined within aesthetics, and continues the century-old disputes in literature, art and architecture. Another controversy has been raging, between the various conservative or neo-conservative social and political theorists and their liberal and radical opponents, over the kinds of institutions and relations which should exist in contemporary societies. The third discourse may more appropriately be described as a set of disputes arising from the Marxist tradition with proponents of post-structuralism, neo-Weberianism and post-Marxism. All three discourses in aesthetics, the future of society and the confrontation with the Marxist tradition, have overlapped with one another and with the whole discussion of post-industrialism.[58] As expressed by Jean-Francois Lyotard, one of the key disputants: 'Our working hypothesis is that the status of knowledge is altered as societies enter what is known as the post-industrial age and cultures enter what is known as the postmodern age.'[59]

While I do not propose to devote much space to discussing the multi-faceted aspects of 'post-modernity', I would like to note some of the more important points made in these debates, and how they affect any concept of a post-industrial culture and public sphere. First, it is clear that Bahro, Gorz, Toffler and Jones still adhere firmly to the tradition of the European Enlightment. Although Toffler, and to a lesser extent Gorz and Jones, flirt with various 'post-modern' aesthetic and scientific practices, it would not be unfair to say that their representative images of post-industrialism are animated and informed by the traditional historical project of bringing reason to bear on public and private life. Bahro may reject the technical rationality of industrial society, Toffler and Jones may superficially agree with Lyotard that knowledge and its legitimation is altered in post-industrial societies, and Gorz may attack the religious fundamentalism of orthodox Marxist moral absolutism; but all four theorists believe that their model of post-industrialism will maximize democracy, freedom, tolerance, equality and other rationalist values which made their appearance in Europe a few hundred years ago. In this respect they stand in stark contrast to the nihilism, relativism and loss of direction which characterizes much of post-structuralist and 'post-modern' thought.

When writers such as Habermas discuss the constituent elements of 'modernity' and the varied responses to 'modernity' – the revolt against complexity by many new social movements, the technocratic forms of crisis management by neo-conservatives, the cynical devaluation of all values and standards by the Young Conservatives and many post-structuralists – they force us to align ourselves in a partisan manner for or against 'modernity'.[60] The unfulfilled elements of 'modernity' which Habermas discusses are highly pertinent to post-industrial theory. For example, in the areas of science, art and morality, the rationalization of life and knowledge has been governed by different interests and objectives. Does the fulfilment of 'modernity' mean that science ultimately controls all forms of nature, unlocks all the mysteries of the universe? Does the fulfilment of 'modernity' mean the replacement of gods by reason, the end of moral uncertainty, the attainment of clarity and transparency in communication? Will art continue to be the repository of phantasy and the sphere of sublimation? Will art become instrumentalized and politicized, or will life become aestheticized as art, leisure and contemplation replace work, necessity and unpleasure? Finally, will 'modernity' become fulfilled when universal principles of equality, democracy and freedom replace parochial superstition, class power and privilege? Or will these universalistic goals mean the subordination of minority social movements to the dictates of objective or universal reason?

Although the discourse about 'post-modern' and post-industrial culture has raised very important issues, it is important to note that what is lacking in post-industrial theory, is precisely what is lacking in much of the discussion about 'modernity' and 'post-modernity'. There appears to be little agreement about the periodization of 'modernity', for example, whether one society, or even one part of society is 'pre-modern', 'modern' or 'post-modern'. Many of the theorists tend to periodize 'modernity' and 'post-modernity' (that is, a whole social epoch) according to changes in just one area, for example, changes in art or technology. Here, I agree with Perry Anderson when he expresses an agnostic stance towards the concept of 'modernity'. Discussing the need for a clear periodization of 'modernity', Anderson notes that:

> On the one hand, from Weber through to Ortega, Eliot to Tate, Leavis to Marcuse, 20th-century modernity has been relentlessly condemned as an iron cage of conformity and mediocrity, a spiritual wilderness of populations bleached of any organic community or vital autonomy. On the other hand, against these visions of cultural despair, in another tradition stretching from Marinetti to Le Corbusier, Buckminster Fuller to Marshall McLuhan, not to speak of outright

apologists of capitalist 'modernization theory' itself, modernity has been fulsomely touted as the last word in sensory excitement and universal satisfaction, in which a machine built civilization itself guarantees aesthetic thrills and social felicities. What each side has in common here is a simple identification of modernity with technology itself – radically excluding the people who produce and are produced by it.[61]

It is not difficult to see that Bahro has more in common with Anderson's first ('anti-modern') group while Toffler is closer to the second ('pro-modern') group. I have also tried to show how overgeneralized are the concepts of post-industrial theorists. The ease with which they file diverse political economies and cultures under a single label ('industrial', 'Second Wave', etc.) is also seen in the proponents of vague categories such as 'modern' and 'postmodern'. But to grasp the historically specific nature of uneven development, whether in the sphere of science, morality, art, particular branches of capitalist and non-capitalist industry, state administration or welfare services, is crucial to any overall understanding of the manner in which these diverse practices interconnect. For example, one only has to contrast Frederick Jameson's vague use of essentialist concepts such as 'Late Capitalism', and the 'world market' (in order to bolster his positive view of 'post modernity'),[62] with Mike Davis's more penetrating analysis of the connection between speculative finance and negative 'post-modern' developments in urban American architecture.[63] Similarly, one would like to know from Toffler and other post-industrial theorists why Japan, one of the most advanced sites of high technology, has socio-cultural relations which are either 'pre-modern', or far less 'Third Wave' than those in North America. Moreover, could the dramatic cultural changes coming with the Third Wave be compatible with Japan's dominance in commodity exports, or would these socio-cultural changes lead to less high-technology innovation, social disintegration and possible revolution or authoritarian repression?

Without clear criteria, it is difficult to know whether countries as diverse as Japan, France or the USSR are 'modern', 'post-modern', 'pre-modern' or 'post-industrial'. Of course, the extensive disagreement over the periodization of 'modernity' (did it begin five hundred, two hundred or less than one hundred years ago?), and the positive and negative responses to 'modernity' by radicals, liberals and conservatives, should not, despite the elasticity of the labels, blind us to crucial issues. While I go part of the way with various methodological attempts to 'deconstruct' overgeneralized and essentialist concepts, in their effort to gain greater historical specificity and awareness of non-identical social developments, I think that one can distrust model-building without lapsing into post-structuralist and post-modernist cynicism and relativism. For all the problems inherent in Habermas's communication theory of society, I am much closer to his project of analysing the unfulfilled elements of 'modernity', than to any post-modernist rejection of meta-narratives, and subjectivity, and overall socio-political objectives.

In 1968, Habermas noted how, in Herman Kahn's list of probable technical innovations in the next 30 years, the first 50 items included many techniques for behavioural and person-ality change, for example, genetic engineering, sex changes, drugs for various moods, electronic controls for surveillance, propaganda and so forth.[64] Many of these science fiction items have already arrived! Habermas warned that genetic engineer-ing and psycho-technic manipulation of behaviour would result in the drying-up of reflective traditions (expressed in language and culture) and the detachment of human behaviour from all value systems.[65] Without a notion of what is rational, without any priorities or hierarchies of value, how can 'post-modern' or post-industrial individuals construct non-alienated and democratic communities? One may not agree on the usefulness of the concept 'modernity', but how can one discon-nect the moral, artistic, scientific and political traditions of earlier historical periods from the struggles and dilemmas con-fronting contemporary generations? For example, will par-ticular values and practices result in social integration or in disorientation and conflict? Andreas Huyssen partially addresses this issue when he undertakes a post-structuralist critique of Habermas.

> The critical deconstruction of Enlightenment rationalism . . .
> the fight of women and gays for a legitimate social and sexual
> identity outside the parameters of male, heterosexual vision,
> the search for alternatives in our relationship with nature,
> including the nature of our bodies – all these phenomena, which
> are key to the culture of the 1970s, make Habermas's proposi-
> tion to complete the project of modernity questionable, if not
> undesirable.[66]

It appears that Huyssen has avoided the hard problems
which flow from the rejection of the Enlightenment tradition.
It is one thing to reject technical rationality, male heterosexual definitions of what is 'good' and 'desirable', undiffer-
entiated notions of social and moral progress, and other
negative legacies of the Enlightenment. It is quite another
thing to believe that, once women, gays and environmentalists have defined their values and priorities, all questions of
rationality, equality, democracy in the public, as well as interpersonal private spheres, disappear. There seems to be a
tendency to believe that, just because social movements
articulate legitimate values and concerns which are not iden-
tical with those of traditional labour movements, then
somehow all these women, gays, Greens, etc., are not living
in the same society, not encountering similar problems to do
with war, economic power, public administration, religion,
education, poverty, legal rights and other overlapping and
interconnecting public issues. The answers may be different,
but any 'post-modern' or post-industrial society will also
have to resolve issues of the public application of reason, as
well as solve the issues of how plural identities are to be
reconciled with public identities and rights. That is, it is
hoped that a future society will be much freer and diverse,
and yet each citizen in his or her sub-cultural identity must
also *share* a sense of belonging, of citizenship, of common
rights and responsibilities – unless we accept an alternative
nightmare of fragmentation, particularism and separatism.

Not all post-structuralist theorists are cynical and resigned
to a directionless future. For example, Michael Ryan attacks
the rationalist tradition using the works of Derrida and other
French deconstructionists.[67] Like Huyssen, Ryan is suppor-

tive of feminist and other alternative social movements. According to Ryan:

> Habermas' goal of restoring ego and group identity would no doubt be challenged by socialist feminists who would point out that existing models of social group identity deny validity to those who see their political interests as lying in the breaking of the coercive identity the group imposes on them, by assigning them a place defined by the rationality of the group. The breaking of group identity can be more crucial to emancipation than the restoration of group identity. And it is the metaphysical idealists, those who find such contradictions intolerable because it denies the rational categories of identity, . . . who will brand it as 'irrational' and call for its resolution in the name of rational efficiency and clear knowledge, and at the expense of those such as socialist feminists who have little to gain from the restoration of either categorical or political group identity. What is at stake, then, is a politics of multiple centers and plural strategies, less geared toward the restoration of a supposedly ideal situation held to be intact and good than to the micrological fine-tuning of questions of institutional power, work and reward distribution, sexual political dynamics, resource allocation, domination, and a broad range of problems whose solutions would be situationally and participationally defined.[68]

Ryan's critique of Habermas and 'metaphysical idealists' is of great importance to advocates of a post-industrial socialist society. Like Toffler, Ryan stresses the problems of transition. Whereas Toffler notes the many casualties as conventional Second Wave values, family structures and work practices change, Ryan positively welcomes the breaking of contemporary coercive group identities. But the emancipatory benefits when conservative group identities dissolve should not be confused with the attainment of socialist institutions and the need to maintain social reproduction. Ryan's attack on socialist rationalists such as Habermas caricatures their theory and intentions. Habermas does not want to restore some ideal ego and group identity or achieve a technical rational efficiency based on clear knowledge. Rather, Habermas, in contrast to the old Frankfurt School, recognizes that 'man and nature' can never be fully reconciled, that residual antagonisms can at best be minimized, but not completely overcome, by rational discourse. The aim of constructing a new socialist public sphere based on shared or *generalizable interests* is one which Ryan is not prepared to accept. Instead, Ryan seeks refuge in a pluralist strategy where problems will be 'situationally and participationally defined'. But this is both a relativist fiction and the politics of the moment. For while the pluralistically organized participants in specific situations must pose and resolve problems without constant reference to some a priori set of absolutes, it would be stretching the possibilities of social co-operation and mutual tolerance to believe that each situation will produce a new set of values and new solutions. Either the various pluralistically organized groups will create and redefine generalizable interests based on rational criteria such as equity and the elimination of discrimination based on gender, race, etc., while retaining their own cultural identities, or they will risk chaos and disintegration as each group denies the need to construct a larger identity of citizenship.

## RELIGION, SELF-IDENTITY AND THE POST-INDUSTRIAL PUBLIC SPHERE

If one denies the importance of rationalism and the subject, it is difficult, for example, to comprehend the role of religions in past and present societies, or to understand how a society can cohere after traditions collapse. Discussing the difference between religious and secular cultures, Bell argues that a religious culture

> has a greater unity than most because all the elements of the culture are directed toward some common end: to emphasize mystery, to create awe, to exalt, to transcend. This unity, emphasized in mood, runs like a thread through its architecture, its music, its painting, and its literature – in its spires, liturgies, litanies, spatial representation of figures, and sacred text. Secular cultures rarely have this conscious design.[69]

While Bell, like other neo-conservatives, is troubled by the 'contradictions of capitalism', the problem of cultural unity

transcends capitalist societies. Toffler argues that the proliferation of thousands of religious cults, self-help therapies
and superstitious occult practices is a clear sign of social
malaise as Second Wave societies disintegrate.[70] The problem
is that Toffler seems to have no idea about how post-
industrial changes will affect the survival of religious
thought, or what would be implied by its demise. If new concepts of time, causality, space, and new forms of decentralization topple centralized economic, political and religious
institutions, either religious thought will be reduced to a minor
role, or there will be even more cults and other therapies as life
becomes more home centred and decentralized. On the other
hand, if the 'planetary consciousness' links local people with
international communities, this presupposes either new global
religions, or an extension of secularization beyond the bounds
of existing residues of religious tradition.

While Toffler does not call for 'a new sense of the sacred' as
Bell does, he appears to be unable – like the post-modernists
– to do more than celebrate the passing of the old. I also
celebrate the passing of many undesirable practices of religious
traditions. But as an atheist, I am concerned about the
secular values which could unite people in their diversity.
José Casanova poses the problem well when he discusses
Bell's yearning to save 'modernity' from meaninglessness.

> Bell identifies the sacred with Benjamin's concept of 'aura'.
> But if art in the age of mechanical reproduction becomes 'post-
> auratic', should we not expect the same of religion? Can
> modern or post-modern religion, in the age of administrative
> and technological manipulation of symbols, rituals and
> meanings, be anything but post-auratic, i.e., post-sacral? The
> experience of the sacred presupposes a collective sacred
> cosmos. But can such a cosmos be reconstructed once it has
> been broken?[71]

If secularized post-industrial societies are to survive rampant
individualism, we cannot afford the cynical, fashion-
conscious vandalism of the post-modernists who attack not
only religious traditions, but the basis of post-sacral secularization – European rationalism. Today, even the two wings of

the Catholic church – the theological conservatives as in Poland, and the liberation theologists in the Third World – are the bearers of secularization in their fight for democracy and equality. Unless one values rationality in public life, there are no grounds for arguing that democratic participation is better than dictatorship, arbitrariness, technocratic efficiency or occult ritual.

The need to have clearly articulated principles governing public life can hardly be over-emphasized. But public life rests on more than a commitment to certain ideals – whether religious, secular, democratic or authoritarian. Historically, we have witnessed the formation of nation states out of the polar extremes of parochial fiefdoms and transnational empires. The uneven development of nationalism (with both its emancipatory and reactionary qualities) has coincided with the diverse struggles of labour movements and civil liberty groups, and with inter-imperialist rivalries. Despite the proliferation of local, regional and subcultural public spheres, most members of these local or subcultural spheres have also recognized their connection to the larger national public sphere. In talking about public spheres, I do not wish to convey the ideological impression that these spheres were the bastions of democracy, tolerance and equality. But it is necessary to ask why it is that participation in public institutions – whether establishment or oppositional – is so low in advanced capitalist countries with free electoral processes? The possibility of new forms of knowledge, the alteration of commodified time–space relations,[72] the proliferation of endless therapies and 'truths' – all signify the enormity of obstacles blocking the attainment of a new post-industrial socialist public sphere. If the cultural and interpersonal dynamics of apathy and withdrawal into private spheres are not accidental, then the continuation of certain cultural and political practices into post-industrial societies will be disastrous.

The Frankfurt School argued that the dialectic of the Enlightenment consisted of the unleashing of contradictory forces. On the one hand, the Enlightenment stimulated the belief in reason, tolerance and emancipation from enslavement. On the other hand, the Enlightenment unleashed the positivistic forces of technical rationality which sought the domination of external nature and internal human nature.[73] In recent years, writers such as Richard Sennett and Christopher Lasch have warned about the 'fall of public man' and the 'culture of narcissism'. Both Lasch and Sennett criticize people's preoccupation with self-discovery, liberation of the inner self, the transformation of social problems into problems of personality, the inability to 'feel' and so forth. The paradoxical consequence of 'getting in touch with oneself' is the 'flight from feeling', the tyranny of intimacy and the deadening of public life. People, they claim, are now unable to work with others in common struggle because of their personalities; there is a devaluation of interest in impersonal public issues, and a dangerous tendency to destroy all spheres of privacy in the quest for ultimate knowledge about the self.[74] Two issues flow from Sennett and Lasch's simplistic 'dialectic of self-enlightenment'. First, is it better that people do not attempt to discover their inner selves? Second, how can the concern with public issues and public life be revived if there is an increasing tendency toward fragmentation and decentralization?

In attacking the preoccupation with emotions and feelings, Sennett asks, 'what kind of personality develops through experiences of intimacy? Such a personality will be moulded in the expectation, if not the experience, of trust, of warmth, of comfort. How can it be strong enough to move in a world founded on injustice? . . . Is it humane to form soft selves in a hard world?'[75] These questions will undoubtedly have great appeal to all those socialists brought up in the tradition of self-discipline and hard 'outer-shells' – all necessary 'means' to a more 'humane' future. Sennett's onslaught on the transmutation or conversion of many political categories into psychological categories is only too easy to accept. One can applaud his attack on the commercial industry of self-awareness therapies and their packaged 'panaceas'. But the difficult moral questions, and hence questions of praxis, begin to appear when we have to consider the question of what should socialists struggle for in relation to social welfare services, educational policies, child-parent relations, and other vital interpersonal relations. All these areas involve precisely overcoming those bureaucratic, uncaring, non-intimate 'Therapeutic State' practices which Sennett and Lasch also attack. Above all, what kind of non-oppressive male–female relations and general social relations can be achieved if intimacy and feelings are denied as a moral good? Can socialists democratize state services if state workers and ordinary people retain alienated and impersonal relations? Can socialists ignore the central issues of 'the personal as the political' just because the need for intimacy and caring has been manipulated by commercial charlatans as well as used to promote a-political forms of escapism from the pain of living under capitalism? After all, socialists do not reject the values of equality and democracy simply because bourgeois politicians cynically use these concepts to promote their own narrow interests.

While Sennett may be correct in point out how people identify with capitalism via 'personalities', or find it difficult to oppose capitalist classes because they can not put their personal relations second to the objectives of the political struggles, there is still a very positive and radical dimension (one of the major contributions of the women's movement) to the focus on feelings, emotions and 'the self'. The focus on public personalities may produce 'stars', but the depiction of their everyday routines also reduces them to ordinary human mortals rather than abstract gods and leaders. Party or movement bureaucrats, sexists, pompous workaholics, moral blackmailers, servile toadies, and other negative personalities – which dominate traditional Left and non-Left parties, state apparatuses and public institutions – have been attacked in recent years partly because of the need to 'discover the self'. And justly so. Preoccupation with the self is always a threat (to both individuals and social movements), but a more humane and egalitarian society cannot emerge, unless those very cognitive, psycho-sexual characteristics which Sennett and Lasch indiscriminately attack, are encouraged to emerge from their historical neglect and suppression. Sennett and Lasch are forced to identify with those very pre-capitalist moral and psycho-cognitive processes which pre-date the 'culture of narcissism'. They fail to see that capitalist hegemony is parasitically dependent on those traditional non-intimate, authoritarian, puritanical work ethic and patriarchal social relations. Certainly there have been incorporations of various aspects of 'counter-culture' values into new styles of administration, management and 'public relations'. But these new modes of management have not been as widely implemented as Toffler, or 'Therapeutic State' analysts would have us believe – certainly not in most factories and offices, where old authoritarian practices used to raise productivity and maintain discipline are as entrenched as ever.

I believe that the excesses of the self-awareness movement are not a justification for a return to Victorian morality or to neglect of the self. This issue, of the balance between personal reflection and impersonal 'discipline', is very much related to the relativization of truth, the marketization of therapies and philosophies, and the failure to reflect adequately on the relation between public life and the institutionalization of participation and socialization processes. The prospect of a post-industrial socialist public sphere must, if it is to have any chance of being realized, encompass more than a ritual endorsement of pluralism. How can there be any social commitment to social movement struggles if all theories and cures are relativized? Socialist pluralism would have to be an explicit arrangement which, through the decision of diverse groups and movements, constructed the framework within which a new form of tolerance and democratic diversity prevailed. This would entail condemning those ideologies, for example, racism, which violated the interests of the new public sphere. It would also involve sorting through innumerable quack therapies and religious cults, which threaten the rights of women, patients, children and others. People are immediately frightened by prospects of censorship and 'community standards'. But these decisions will only be democratic and tolerant to the extent that the participant social movement organizations and parties construct a new pluralism which is not like traditional religious and Communist absolute moralities.

If epidemics of addiction, suicide, rape, and personal alienation are to be combatted and minimized, post-industrial theorists will have to be much clearer about the institutionalization of new democratic forms of represent-ation, education, media and cultural outlets, legal structures and welfare services. Decentralization is quite likely to add to the democratization of public life only so long as there is a clear notion of the relationship of decentralized public spheres to one another and to the whole. Just as the possibility of new plural family forms and individual lifestyles depends very much on the provision of communal 'social wage' pro-grammes, legal structures and alterations in paid working conditions, so decentralization would be disastrous if com-munities were left to their own devices and resources. The 'cultural contradictions of capitalism' are not a figment of the conservative imagination. What is wrong are their solu-tions. Similarly, a pseudo toleration of all ideas, therapies, pedagogical principles, child-raising practices, cultural messages, work practices, legal statues, etc., is both dangerous and naïve.

While the boundaries of existing nation states, regions and localities will change, it is not desirable to eliminate national institutions. To leave individuals in their 'electronic cottages' or 'basic communes', with no mediating institutional net-works between them and the global order, is equivalent to leaving isolated individuals to fend for themselves without families or kinship structures. What has to be overthrown, or drastically changed, are existing institutions which monopolize power and privileges, are insensitive to local needs and social movements, and impose discriminatory laws and regulations while destroying natural environments. But a society which has no national institutions, also has no real chance of a democratic public sphere. If one believes the age of city states is over, that the specialized division of labour will never be completely overthrown, that some form of monetary system is indispensable, that administration and social planning will be necessary to maximize equality, preserve environments and support all those unable to do paid work, that some form of defensive defence system will be necessary, and that disputes between individuals and groups will require a system of rules and rights, then either one places all humanity's hopes in a world government, or else one acknowledges the necessity for national institutions.

A problem for the Frankfurt School was that, having depicted the commodification and reification of everyday life, they were unable to explain how the agents of liberation could possibly break through this totally administered system. So, too, with Toffler, Jones and other post-industrial theorists. The old industries, lifestyles and institutions may be doomed. But how is a new social order to emerge from the cultural contradictions of the present? What is clearly missing from post-industrial theorists is a developed sense of political strategies, a sense of the political as it determines and is determined by social struggles. Commenting on Toffler's vision of the coming break-up of large, centralized political institutions, Gorz warns of the dangers ahead:

> If this decentralization and diversification of society – where a plurality of partial orders co-exists, adjusting to each other by means of successive trade-offs without ever becoming unified – is not thought out, desired and consciously prepared for, the consequence will be inescapable: either society will fragment into anarchy through violent confrontations, or a totalitarian dictatorship, in attempting to re-establish a unified order through the use of terror and constraint, will reproduce the system of 'waste, irresponsibility, inertia, corruption; in short, totalitarian inefficiency', exemplified in the Stalinist and National Socialist state models.[76]

While Gorz's warning is timely, he himself is quite vague about the crucial issues of political strategy, the future role of unions, parties and political representation in post-industrial society. In the following chapter I will endeavour to discuss these crucial political problems. But before doing this, I would like to conclude this analysis of the potential problems of new post-industrial public and private spheres with a brief look at the media.

There is little doubt that dramatic new developments in communication technology are altering the conventional forms of print and electronic media. But when individualized and global outlets and connections proliferate, this is not in itself a guarantee that ownership and control of the new media will be any less monopolized or undemocratic than at present. If we assume, however, that future societies will be much more democratic and egalitarian, there is still a fundamental issue: whether there should be only local, community-organized media outlets, or whether there should also exist national or supranational communication organizations. All the issues of 'modernity' and 'post-modernity' – decentralized educational structures or a core curriculum, multi-identities or generalizable interests, a national public sphere or endless parochial spheres – reverberate once again when we consider the media in post-industrial society.

Given the crucial role of books, newspapers, electronic media, film, theatre and other communication outlets in disseminating, constructing or inhibiting particular notions of citizenship, rights, moral values and so forth, it is difficult to imagine how a democratic socialist pluralism could survive if there were no media institutions which linked local communities into larger entities. Certainly, local groups could have their own networks for communication with other local communities. But this would not resolve the problems of political representation in larger legislatures, or the cultivation of non-parochial values, unless the model to be adopted was one of unrestrained pluralism, rigorous self-sufficiency and haphazard contact with the outside world. It is not difficult to imagine a situation where far greater access to media outlets, cultural institutions and resources was given to groups, artists and all kinds of people. This is one of the great benefits to be had from decentralizing and eliminating the political and economic monopolization of communication outlets. But the retention of national and regional media and cultural institutions does not presuppose the retention of old forms of control and ownership. At the moment, there are radio and television stations and cultural institutions which operate at more than local level, and yet are based on democratic federations of participating groups. Hence, it is possible to imagine a whole range of new organizational structures which democratize the media, but it is difficult to imagine a democratic national public sphere with no national media outlets.

If the post-industrial theorists are correct in diagnosing the demise of traditional religious views, family relations, educational practices and the relationship between home, work and leisure, it is imperative that new values and social identities not be even more fragmented, alienated and conflict ridden than at present. The unplanned nature of endless new marketable technologies and products, coupled with the almost religious faith that small-scale, decentralized institutions are inherently good, threatens to produce a post-industrial 'refeudalization' of everyday life. The resources and structures needed to mediate, facilitate and strengthen those values and practices which maximize democracy and socialist pluralism, cannot spring solely from within the boundaries of local communities. Here is perhaps the dialectic or paradoxical nature of new post-industrial public and private spheres. In order to maximize democratic decentralization, it is necessary to have the requisite institutions of democratic centralization. For while central institutions can survive without local democracy, it is most unlikely that decentralized institutions will last very long without the support of national institutions. This is the unpleasant truth which believers in stateless societies must confront. But if the new state institutions are to be much more democratic, and vastly different from existing state apparatuses in capitalist and Communist societies, the very crucial issue of political transformation will have to be accorded a much higher priority and profile than that given by our post-industrial theorists.

Finally, it is worth noting that the conflicting visions of post-industrial society are largely determined by pessimistic or optimistic views of new technology, rather than by adequate consideration of private–public relations. The pessimists point to all the developments in micro-electronics and genetic engineering which lead to Big Brother controls, loss of critical and reflective educational and cultural institutions, increased isolation and fragmentation of social life as leisure and work becomes more home centred, while public life, undermined by the new technocratic privatism, is increasingly manipulated and subjected to authoritarian rule. In contrast, the optimists depict a scenario based on varying images of a revived and committed citizenry – whether in the 'electronic cottage' or the 'basic commune' – running their own lives, overcoming private alienation, addiction and social malaise in self-help, small-scale, decentralized public and private spheres. I have tried to show that it does not matter whether one believes in Toffler's high-technology scenario or Bahro's industrial disarmament, the issue of how to construct alternative public spheres – which presuppose new definitions of the private sphere, self-identity and socialization – can be addressed only if one is prepared to confront the decisive roles played by state institutions. One may have particular interpretations of how governments maintain legitimacy, of the decisive role of religion, ideology, coercion, narcissism, exterminism and so forth. But these explanations of existing public–private relations tell us more about what is wrong with the present, than they do about the relations and institutions necessary for constructing new public spheres. If new technological and social developments lead to the abolition of nine-to-five work patterns, redefine the use of time and social space, alter the conventional life-cycle pattern of childhood to old age, will these new developments bring about the end of even limited democratic forms (as we know them today); or will they provide the ground for an enhanced and vibrant social struggle to construct the first generation of truly democratic public spheres – one of the goals of the Enlightenment as yet unfulfilled?

Most people – to the extent that they bother to think about the future at all – assume the world they know will last indefinitely. They find it difficult to imagine a truly different way of life for themselves, let alone a totally new civilization. Of course they recognize that things are changing. But they assume today's changes will somehow pass them by and that nothing will shake the familiar economic framework and political structure . . . Recent events have severely shaken this confident image of the future. As crisis after crisis has crackled across the headlines . . . large numbers of people – fed on a steady diet of bad news, disaster movies, apocalyptic Bible stories, and nightmare scenarios issued by prestigious think tanks – have apparently concluded that today's society cannot be projected into the future because there is no future.

On the surface these two visions of the future seem very different. Yet both produce similar psychological and political effects. For both lead to the paralysis of the imagination and will. If tomorrow's society is simply an enlarged, Cinerama version of the present, there is little we *need* do to prepare for it. If, on the other hand, society is inevitably destined to self-destruct within our lifetime, there is nothing we *can* do about it. In short, both these ways of looking at the future generate privatism and passivity. Both freeze us into inaction.

Alvin Toffler, The Third Wave

The first thing that struck me was how close the Social Democrats and Eurocommunists are in matters of practical politics, for all their differences in ideology and tradition. The future of both currents, as of all socialist forces, will depend on how they face up to the crisis of the capitalist *industrial* system. The old pattern of contradictions and struggle always seems to lead back into the system, serving to reproduce it in its essential aspects. What we need is an answer that goes beyond the traditional differences of approach between Social Democrats, Socialists and Communists. The old model has had its day.

Rudolf Bahro, From Red to Green

# 5

# Getting From Here to There
## *The Politics of Post-Industrialism*

Up to this point I have tried to examine the alternative proposals and visions of post-industrial society, as put forward by the post-industrial utopians in isolation from the problems associated with political strategy. That is, I have tried to evaluate the intrinsic merit and feasibility of alternative economies, welfare provisions, defence systems, environmental and cultural relations, examined purely as concepts, without considering the immediate chances of political success. While it is true that I have argued against the feasibility of various proposals within existing capitalist and Communist societies, I have not yet discussed the vital issues of political agency and the politics of transition. Instead, I tried to show that many of the proposed alternatives were intrinsically flawed or poorly thought through, even if it were assumed that no major political obstacles existed to prevent their implementation. Really, of course, the likely role of any proposed social institution or alternative practice cannot be properly foreseen unless one also takes into account the social agents who must bring them about – usually under circumstances not of their own choosing. Therefore, it is also necessary to examine whether the post-industrial theorists have a political strategy which is any better than their exciting, but problem-ridden ideas. Before discussing this major issue, I would like to set the scene by briefly highlighting some of the key social and political changes now in train, which must be reckoned with in any strategy aiming for a post-industrial socialist society.

First, there is little doubt that the reorganization of labour processes, introduction of new technology, increase in part-time work and persistently high levels of unemployment, will all have significant effects on trade unions and Left of centre political parties in capitalist countries. The conflicting objectives and priorities that appear – when some seek some more leisure time as opposed to higher wages, or better conditions for women and blacks as opposed to traditional male demands, or environmentally safe production as opposed to consumerist or job-creation schemes – make labour movement solidarity an increasingly difficult goal to achieve.[1]

Second, the range of policy choices available to leaders of Communist countries seems to present them with the unpalatable mixes of stagnation, further marketization and erosion of planning, growing authoritarianism and deepening dissent. In the Third World, the social costs of the imperialist exploitation of the South by the capitalist North are just as heavy, and as resistant to reform as ever. Meanwhile, the Maoist and Soviet roads to development have largely been discredited, even though civil war still rages in a number of countries with military and social aid coming from the USSR, Cuba and China. On the other hand, the 1980s have witnessed a crisis in newly industrializing capitalist countries (for example, Brazil, Phillipines, Mexico) as authoritarian regimes have been rocked or overthrown by a combination of political revolt, enormous debt, falling commodity prices and limits to the export of new technology consumer goods to OECD countries.

Third, social movements in OECD countries – especially the peace, womens' and environmental movements – have made little change to actual practices and government policies, despite massive mobilization and the spread of a new social consciousness in the past decade or so. The burning issue of class power and social movement strategy 'outside the state' will be discussed later on. Meanwhile, a succession of conservative and social democratic governments has presided over essentially stagnant social formations, characterized by urban blight, environmental damage, social malaise and the failure even to keep pace with the increasing numbers of poor and alienated. Confronted with these intractable problems, even the New Right have lost a lot of their evangelical optimism about reforming capitalism, while social democratic and Communist parties have largely abandoned their traditional sense of direction and many of the ideals to which they were formerly committed. The malaise in both Left and Right political organizations varies in severity from country to country. However, this malaise is not only due to an aversion to many traditional political practices and policies; the fall in party membership and traditional loyalties is also partly due to a significant increase in privatized forms of consumption (for example, home video recorders, computer games and other leisure activities).[2]

Political loyalties are realigning; public participation has declined; industries, lifestyles and government policies have been transformed in a largely unplanned manner. All these developments prejudice and limit the chances that traditional Left parties can successfully alter the major direction of socio-economic change.

A very bleak picture emerges when some of the key aspects of contemporary societies are sketched but, on the other hand, it would be irresponsibly defeatist to ignore all the positive political developments of new social forces in recent years. Also, it is precisely during periods of profound social malaise, that opportunities arise to mobilize citizens around new programmes ignored by traditional parties and organizations. The positive contribution made by writers such as Bahro and Gorz lies in their attempt to transcend conventional politics and in getting us to think about new social relations and new priorities. In this sense, even their glaring theoretical and practical weaknesses are invaluable, because they force us to explore and find stronger and more plausible alternatives and strategies. I will therefore divide this chapter around two themes: (a) the usefulness of traditional theories of class, civil society and state; and (b) the role of parties, labour movements and new social movements in post-industrial theory.

## CONFRONTING 'THE STATE' AND 'CIVIL SOCIETY' IN POST-INDUSTRIAL THEORY

It is not surprising that various conceptions of how post-industrial societies will come into being are themselves inseparably connected to particular analyses: of the role of state institutions, the relevance of class conflict, the belief in a 'new class', a 'knowledge elite', or the importance of specific social structures for the nature and health of new social movements. Most post-industrial theorists share – along with many Greens, anarchists and alternative movement activists – a one-sided understanding of the complex roles and functions carried out by contemporary state institutions. Moreover, their visions of political and social life in post-industrial societies are still far too tightly organized around the traditional concepts of 'the state' and 'civil society'. What I am referring to here is the widespread tendency to reduce state institutions to mere political–administrative apparatuses or machines which are separate from 'the economy' or the 'civil' and 'cultural' relations and institutions of particular social formations.[3] This one-dimensional interpretation of 'state' and 'civil society' is, paradoxically, at odds with exactly those social–political developments seen by the post-industrial utopians as the wave of the future, for example, the 'electronic cottage'. I will try to explain the political implications in more detail.

If one examines the history of social theory during the past two hundred years of capitalist societies, it is quite common to find human relations divided into the spheres of 'the state', 'the economy' and 'civil society'. In various Marxist and non-Marxist theories, there is often an overlap between the categories 'market' (or 'the economy') and 'civil society'. But these are nearly always clearly differentiated from 'the state'. Thus, social analysis is often based on the degree of domination, control or penetration of 'civil society' by 'the state'. It is usual to find social theorists treating 'the family', for example, as a sphere or unit within 'civil society' which is outside 'the economy'. In reality, however, these conceptual divisions are a caricature of the infinitely more complicated social interactions of everyday life. In most leading capitalist societies, millions of workers are employed in state institutions which are an inseparable part of 'the economy'. Also, the so-called cultural institutions of 'civil society' such as the media, education, theatre, etc., are integral parts of many national and local state structures.

One of the major problems with the traditional division of social life into 'the state' and 'civil society' is that, while most theorists and activists are quick to recognize the political–administrative roles and functions of state institutions (even though most ignore the economic and socio-cultural roles of states), there is no agreement about all those relations and institutions which are supposed to come under the heading 'civil society'. Consequently, generations of Left and Right political theorists have talked about the 'withering away of the state', the 'minimal state', 'civil society versus the state' and so forth. Bahro, Toffler et al. echo the desires of all those who wish for a society free of bureaucratic state apparatuses, where citizens control their local, small-scale institutions and 'civil society' is once again left to live in peace outside the shadow of 'the state'. But the very social forces and new technological developments which Toffler and Jones describe, render the neat divisions between 'the family', 'the economy' and 'the state' more and more obsolete historically. For as 'the economy' moves into the home, and as the transformation of service industries, leisure activities, social welfare, media and education (brought about by the micro-electronic revolution) breaks down the old spheres of 'civil society' and 'the state', the political objective of liberating 'civil society' from 'the state' becomes more and more dubious. Either one aims for a stateless society – possibly organized around 'basic communes' – and argues for the feasibility of this post-industrial utopia; or else, one is forced to recognize that state institutions are not mere political–administrative apparatuses (that is, there is much more to states than the parties, bureaucrats, etc., who make the laws), and will continue to be heavily involved in many social relations normally defined as belonging to 'civil society'. If this reality is acknowledged, the issue becomes one of working out what kind of state institutions are desirable, who should control them, how can their size and scale enhance equality and freedom, and how can these new post-industrial state institutions be brought into being?

Of course, there are many others who believe that it is vital to retain the notion of 'civil society' so that it can be democratized and made socialist. For example, David Held and John Keane argue that the Left must campaign for a revitalized 'civil society' in order to meet the New Right critique of old-fashioned 'big-state' Labourism, ('socialism equals nationalized industry').[4] I fully endorse their vision of democratized local community institutions as well as the need for democratized national state institutions. However, nearly all the examples which Held and Keane cite as models for a revitalized 'socialist civil society' – for example, the social investment funds in Sweden, Green Party proposals to change the relationship between paid work and unpaid housework, and the 'lease back' of social institutions from states – are proposed without any adequate consideration of what the main principles of a 'socialist civil society' economy will be. That is, the 'Swedish model' of social investment funds presupposes market socialist mechanisms, while Green Party proposals are based on a mixture of market mechanisms, marketless allocations and simple barter. If one believes in a clear sphere of 'civil society', then it is also vital to know whether a 'socialist civil society' will be principally based on market mechanisms, central planning, a mixture of central and decentralized planning and market mechanisms, or some other mechanism. Whether a post-industrial society is radically decentralized, or has a GMI scheme, or is centrally planned in key areas, or has market socialist institutions, will crucially affect the very nature of state institutions.

The battle-cry 'civil society against the state' will not resolve the fundamental problems of income redistribution, self-management and other key issues if there is no clear analysis of the manner in which production, consumption and control are to be organized. For example, the Solidarity movement was based on workers employed within *state* institutions (in factories, universities, hospitals, television stations, offices), even though they proclaimed their opposition to 'the state' in the name of 'civil society'! If Solidarity had not been outlawed, the movement would still have had to resolve the problem of planning, market mechanisms and so forth. This will also remain true of any struggle which tries to bring about a post-industrial socialism or a 'socialist civil society' – regardless of what it is called! Hence, there is a need to clarify the difference between the exercise of power within state institutions (by one party or multi-party rule, military and bureaucratic personnel), and the state-organized socio-economic and cultural practices which constitute an indispensable part of the contemporary social reproduction of everyday life.

I will try to show that the problems inherent in the post-industrial theorists' notions of alternative economies, defence systems, cultural institutions and social welfare, are closely related to their inadequate conception of the vital role of state institutions. This usually signals their undeveloped sense of the 'political dimension', which in turn stems from failure to think through the vital issues of planning or market mechanisms, and the relationship between political power and social reproduction. In this sense some post-industrial theorists see alternative societies in simple terms (the reduction of complexity), while others see future societies based on increasing social differentiation and complexity. These contrasting views also reveal the likelihood that a particular theorist will tend to be more, or less aware of political–economic complications, dangers, obstacles and potential crises. Finally, these same notions of reduced or enhanced complexity are themselves closely tied to theories of social power and action. To appreciate adequately the role of state institutions, whether in the present or future, requires a corresponding appreciation of the existing organization of power and the likely agents of social transformation.

In the previous chapter I tried to show why a stateless or purely decentralized society, or even a combination of local and global institutions, would face formidable difficulties if national state institutions were lacking. It is paradoxical that Toffler sees a diminished role for state institutions precisely at that stage of history when social life becomes infinitely more complex. It is also paradoxical when Gorz argues that state institutions are indispensable, and yet sees the post-industrial state as competely amoral. In rejecting the traditional view which equates the state with the supreme good, Gorz goes to the other extreme and proclaims that 'there is no 'good' government, 'good' state or 'good' form of power, and that society can never be 'good' in its own organization but only by virtue of the space of self-organization, autonomy, co-operation and voluntary exchange which that organization offers to individuals.'[5] This means that social forces have nothing to fight for, as the denial of good state institutions, or a good society, disarms the Left and relativizes all states – whether fascist or democratic – as not better than one another. Gorz's position also makes a virtue out of self-organization and *laissez-faire*. But the self-organization of racists or profiteers is the antithesis of those socialist moral principles which Gorz himself promotes. In actual fact, Gorz advocates a socialist morality as the basis for a good society, even though he denies any connection between morality and politics.

It is important to emphasize that the historical polemics between Left and Right over the relationship between 'the state' and 'civil society' have often depended upon ideal-type beliefs: in the 'individual', in the virtues of private property, or in the inherently 'progressive' quality of the proletariat. In so far as much of the post-industrial literature continues classical sociology and political theory, extending it to a new stage of history and new technological and cultural developments, it preserves the old stereotypes of social-contract theory and Marxist concepts of 'civil society'. Yet, if we look at what state institutions actually do, we find that the artificial boundaries which demarcated 'the state' from 'civil society' have long since crumbled, if indeed they were ever truly operative. Once the sphere of 'civil society' is seen to lack clear and coherent definition, the hopes and expectations of social relations within post-industrial society must alter accordingly, for example, the belief in a stateless, self-managed, small-is-beautiful society. The interesting thing about post-industrial theory is that, while the old ideal types of 'civil society' and 'the state' are invoked either implicitly or explicitly, there is an almost unanimous rejection of classical Marxist class theory. It is to this issue that I now turn.

## IS CLASS THEORY RELEVANT TO 'INDUSTRIAL SOCIETY' ONLY?

There are weighty socio-political consequences, both immediate and long-term, when we accept, modify or reject class theory. In the immediate or short run, to reject class theory means we must explain contemporary social relations otherwise and, more importantly, must provide an alternative theory of political agency and strategy. Of course, the belief that class struggle is central does not, in itself, give rise to one clear and unanimous political strategy – witness the prolifer-ation of Left parties and sects, each offering the 'correct path' to socialism. But if class theory is replaced by some other theory – of social movements or whatever – questions immediately arise as to the nature of the alternative future society. Most class theorists, despite their major differences over political strategy, have acknowledged the importance of parties and unions based on the labour movement. Non-class theorists are faced with the tasks of explaining, not only how workers will be represented in policy-making struggles and institutional processes, but also, in broader terms, whether the new post-industrial societies will continue to have political parties, trade unions, national elections and other means of representative or direct democracy. I will discuss later the vital issue of political institutions in post-industrial societies, but wish first to examine the rejection of class theory by the post-industrial utopians.

There is little needing explanation in the attitudes of Jones and Toffler towards Marxist class theory. Both recognize the contributions made by Marxists, the historical importance of labour movements and the great gaps in wealth and privilege which exist between rich and poor. Both seem content, however, with an eclectic grab-bag of concepts, and avoid or reject the notion that capitalist ruling classes dominate the power structures in Western countries. Conflict and decision-making is depicted in non-class terms as the outcome of the sum total of pluralistically organized pressure groups, inter-acting with technology and the natural environment. Toffler explicitly attacks the Marxist 'obsession' with ownership of private property and stresses the importance of the 'techno-structure' (Galbraith) and managerial control (following his teacher Burnham).[6] Toffler not only rejects the idea that private corporations seek to maximize profit, but believes that, in contrast to Second Wave society where the machines or 'means of production' were owned, in Third Wave societies the essential property becomes information. This new form of property, claims Toffler, is revolutionary because information is non-material, non-tangible, and potentially infinite.[7] In contrast to the finite and scarce property typical of capitalism, Toffler proclaims the science fiction of an unbounded new property form (meta-symbolic information) in the post-industrial society. Somehow, the dominance of the eight hundred plus transnational capitalist corporations (accounting at present for over 80 per cent of world trade),[8] the private control of hardware and software production and sales, the monopolization and control by private firms of scarce resources (the symbolic at least as much as the material) – somehow, all this will disappear in the new utopia just because production supposedly moves from goods to information! Toffler's attempt to deny the nature of capitalist production – that is, the development of new commodities and techniques of production for exchange-value rather than just use-value – is matched only by his attempt to deny the existence of ruling capitalist classes by using the old and exploded argument of the 'managerial revolution' having made capitalism obsolete. When, and if, the Third Wave eliminates stock exchanges and the investment by businesses, pension funds, and individuals in profit-making enterprises – with all the associated aspects of exploitative labour processes, domination of Third World resources, wasteful consumption and advertising, etc. – then, and only then, can we begin to consider whether Toffler's image of 'infinite' non-privately owned and controlled property can provide a revolutionary basis for the new society.

Barry Jones and Alvin Toffler are representative of many social democrats, liberals and Left of centre analysts in their attitude to Marxism. They accept the importance of class conflict when referring to the development of industrial society in the nineteenth century, they acknowledge Marx's important insights into the capitalist economy and social relations such as alienated labour,[9] and they even acknowledge that many workers in various countries are still the victims of class exploitation. But the prevailing impression conveyed by

Jones and Toffler is that Marxist class conflict is either historically obsolete, or just one among many forms of conflict in modern societies.[10] Toffler rightly rejects the economic determinist Marxism which treats all non-economic phenomena as derivative 'superstructures' emanating from the economic 'base'. Like Toffler, Jones tries to salvage the positive contributions made by Marx, but draws class analysis from the veritable rag-bag of quite disparate theories, uneasily jostling each other as he takes us on the road from industrial to post-industrial society.

Whereas Jones and Toffler have never been renowned for their Leftism, it gave rise to widespread debate when Bahro and Gorz broke with orthodox class theory.[11] *Farewell to the Working Class* tended to polarize Left opinion, as it was published at a time when there was extensive discussion about the 'crisis in Marxism' and the disillusionment with Eurocommunist and Leninist strategies. Depending on one's perspective, Gorz's recent work can be read as one more attack on Marxist class theory, or as a critique of the dubious aspects of orthodox Marxism rather than a total rejection. I do not believe that Gorz has totally rejected Marxist class theory, despite his highly critical comments on both aspects of Marx's theory and on conventional class struggle political practice. In 1964, Gorz published *Strategy For Labor*, while his friend Marcuse published *One Dimensional Man*.[12] The contrast between the two books was remarkable. Marcuse argued that the proletariat were tending to become co-opted into the totally administered society and no longer constituted the clear opposite or negation of capitalism. Although Marcuse believed that this tendency to proletarian integration was currently dominant, he placed more hope in the outsiders and outcasts – the unemployed, unemployable, poor and victims of discrimination – to oppose the system. In contrast, Gorz developed a strategy for the European labour movement – a set of radical reforms – because he saw this movement as the best hope for bringing about an end to capitalist class domination.

By 1980, Gorz had come around to Marcuse's 1964 position, while Marcuse, before he died in 1979, was more sympathetic to Marxist class struggle than he had been prior to the political upheavals in the mid-1960s. But whereas Marcuse argued that the 'outcasts' were only a minority, Gorz argues that the new 'non-class of post-industrial neo-proletarians' are the majority of the population.[13] The traditional proletariat, according to Gorz, were not only a privileged minority, but had ceased to constitute the negation of capitalism. In language reminiscent of Marcuse's *One Dimensional Man*, Gorz proclaims:

> We are left in a one-dimensional universe. In its struggle with capital, the proletariat takes on the indentity capital itself has given it. Rather than internalizing their complete dispossession and setting out to construct the universal proletarian society on the ruins of the bourgeois order, proletarians have internalized their dispossession in order to affirm their complete dependence and their need to be taken charge of completely.[14]

Given the new relations between proletarians and capitalists, Gorz argues that, for workers,

> it is no longer a question of freeing themselves *within* work, putting themselves in control of work, or seizing power within the framework of their work. The point now is to free oneself *from* work by rejecting its nature, content, necessity and modalities. But to reject work is also to reject the traditional strategy and organizational forms of the working-class movement. It is no longer a question of winning power as a worker, but of winning the power no longer to function as a worker. The power at issue is not at all the same as before. The class itself has entered into crisis.[15]

According to Gorz, modern capitalist industry has become bureaucratized and converted into a technostructure where nobody holds power.[16] Traditional workers have become deskilled and reduced to reified cogs in the machine. The new 'post-industrial non-class of neo-proletarians' have no class identity, and are over-qualified for the temporary, contract and part-time jobs which are constantly being eliminated or changed by new technology.[17] Because work has ceased to be permanent and central to a person's life career, two social consequences – a negative and a positive development – are envisaged by Gorz. The negative future is one of increasing automation which in turn increases the 'neo-proletariat'. Forced to live in a state of unemployment or marginalized contract work, the 'neo-proletariat' do not see themselves as members of the working class or as having a useful role in society, because the future is devoid of promise and is becoming less and less meaningful. 'Whole areas of economic life now have the sole function of 'providing work', or of producing for the sake of keeping people working. But when a society produces in order to provide work rather than works in order to produce, then work as a whole has no meaning.'[18] It is because the 'neo-proletariat' see no future in capitalist post-industrial society, that positive consequences may result from their opposition to the 'productivist' machine. In not identifying with the production of waste, destruction and meaningless work to fill in time, the 'non-class of neo-proletarians' are the only ones, Gorz believes, who will break through the 'accumulation ethic' of 'productivism' and bring into being the post-industrial socialist society.[19]

While I would agree with Gorz that there are many people in Western countries bearing the characteristics of the new 'neo-proletarian' outcasts, and that Gorz's depiction of the irrationality of key areas of capitalist economies and meaningless jobs has much validity, I also agree with many of the criticisms made by Gorz's critics. These criticisms can be divided into two basic charges:

(1) Gorz misinterprets Marx and creates a false or idealized picture of the proletariat;
(2) Gorz's new 'non-class' of 'neo-proletarians' are not a majority and do not constitute the only agent of revolutionary change.

Without going into a discussion of Marx's writings or actual historical studies of working classes, let me summarize the main weaknesses in Gorz's analysis. First, the working class have always been alienated from their labour and have not all been skilled artisans.[20] High unemployment rates, temporary work·and marginalized existences have characterized earlier generations and not just the new 'neo-proletariat'. Second, Gorz exaggerates the degree of deskilling which has taken place. Labour-process studies reveal a much more complex picture – depending on the industry studied – where workers have actually acquired new complex skills and not simply suffered an inevitable deskilling.[21] Third, many of the 'neo-proletariat' – in contrast to Gorz – do feel guilty about being unemployed, do still identify with waste consumption and the work ethic, and are not mainly oriented to an alternative vision of autonomous free time – a life without work.

The issue of how large the traditional proletariat or the new 'neo-proletariat' is has major implications for political strategy and the transition to a post-industrial socialist society. It is not a matter of endorsing conventional Left labour movement strategies and denying that there have been significant changes in technology, labour processes, or major forms of rejection of lifestyles associated with consumerism, the work ethic and so forth. Rather, Gorz's beliefs in the 'neo-proletariat', as the new revolutionary agent of change, seems to be both misplaced and poorly grounded. It is paradoxical, and far from clear why a 'non-class of neo-proletarians' (who do not identify with the working class) should struggle to bring about a classless society – given that they have no class consciousness! If we subscribe to a notion of capitalism as a bureaucratic technostructure with 'nobody holding power', how can we expect Gorz's 'neo-proletarians' to identify the capitalist class as the dominant class to be overthrown, when the 'system' is almost self-propelling? Equally important: in claiming that the proletariat is now a privileged minority, Gorz distorts the reality of capitalist societies where wage-labour proletarians (even if working in new occupations and industries – whether private or public) still constitute with their dependants the overwhelming majority of the population.

When Gorz advocates that workers free themselves *from* work rather than *within* work, he is not advancing the possibility of life without work. It is clear that what Gorz wants is an end to the work ethic, the self-management of

ime and an increase in the amount of autonomous work
nstituted, not the total abolition of work. But strategically,
Gorz's apparent abandonment of the working class is self-
defeating.[22] This can be seen from *Farewell to the Working
Class*, where Gorz gives the strong impression that all struggles
by workers to control their workplaces, to change the commodities produced (for example, the Lucas experiment)
*within* workplaces are futile because the majority of 'neo-
proletarians' are unable to identify with a minority of
privileged workers.

Yet at the same time, Gorz warns about the construction of
a Rightwing semi-automated capitalist nightmare (a 'South
Africanization' of society) consisting of a minority elite of
paid workers and a majority of the unemployed and
marginalized.[23] Gorz would like workers to fight for non-
economistic alternatives and radically alter their priorities
- that is, reject consumerism and promote ecologically harmonious solidarity and greater autonomous free time for
communal and individual pursuits. But how can Gorz see this
Rightwing nightmare being prevented (let alone a post-
industrial socialism constructed), when he dismisses even the
limited struggles of the working class today? Either Gorz still
supports class struggle (and had a momentary bout of
pessimistic anti-proletarianism in *Farewell to the Working
Class*), or he has thrown in his lot with the 'neo-proletariat'
regardless of the fact that they are not a majority as he
claims. Whatever the actual truth, Gorz's positive attempt to
emphasize the need for new anti-capitalist struggles will only
be useful to the degree that he can specify in much more
detail who should carry these struggles out, and how the rest
of the population will be affected.

It appears to me that Gorz has exaggerated the number of
people suffering from 'neo-proletarian' symptoms and hence
created a new social category the 'neo-proletariat' which,
strictly speaking, is not a clear rejection of class theory. In
actual fact, Gorz still largely works within the Marxist framework, even though his analyses are highly critical of
'workerist' strategies and his writings are partly infused with
ideas emanating from non-Marxist sources, for example,

Illich and Toffler. Gorz is not the only person who has developed new categories in response to the changing social developments in capitalist societies. Post-industrial theory has also given us concepts such as the 'new class' and 'knowledge-based elites' – concepts which attempt to explain the increased numbers of white-collared, professional and technical strata working in private and public institutions. Like the concept of 'neo-proletariat', the theory of the 'new class' tends to exaggerate both the numbers and the distinction from other classes, of people classified as 'new class'. While I do not dispute the growth in numbers of new middle-class individuals pursuing a lifestyle and career different from those of workers in low-paid factory and office jobs, it is another matter to assume that the 'new class' has replaced the capitalist class as the dominant class or rendered obsolete the theory of class conflict. But from the strategic and policy-making point of view, the disproportionate influence of professional, middle-class individuals in parties and social movements, and the widespread disaffection with political and trade-union activity by people whom Gorz calls the 'neo-proletariat', are both, in contrasting respects, highly important contemporary phenomena which class theorists cannot afford to ignore. I will discuss the political implications of new social strata shortly.

If Gorz has modified class theory and almost abandoned the class struggle by bidding farewell to the proletariat in favour of the 'neo-proletariat', Bahro has gone all the way. As Bahro puts it: 'I have moved from a class-dimensional to a populist orientation.'[24] In Bahro's opinion, Marx is still a man of the bourgeois period.[25] Like Gorz, Bahro does not deny the existence of class struggle, but he does not see the proletariat as the revolutionary agent which will bring about a new society.[26] On the contrary, the working class have been politically pacified. Moreover, the working class collaborate with capital to maintain the 'alienated Megamachine'.[27] According to Bahro,

> without the support of the metropolitan working class colonialism would not have been possible, and it is the position

and strength of the trade unions which have given stability to the whole system here. It is the industrial system itself which is about to undo us – not the bourgeois class but the system as a whole in which the working class plays the role of housewife. It would therefore be a most inappropriate strategy for survival to appeal to the interests of the working class. Expansion during the time of the Caesars was driven forward by the need to pacify the lower classes: . . . The working class here is the richest lower class in the world. And if I look at the problem from the point of view of the whole of humanity, not just from that of Europe, then I must say that the metropolitan working class is the worst exploiting class in history.[28]

Given Bahro' sweeping attack on the 'expoitative' role of the working class, it is not surprising that he finds alternative workers' plans, such as the Lucas plan, very limited at best, and no real attack upon the industrial system despite the idea of creating useful technology.[29] Bahro is not hostile to workers as people, but rather to workers who demand jobs in the industrial system at the expense of the environment and global survival. Bahro constantly uses examples from ancient Rome or the middle ages to make points about social relations in contemporary societies. This has also resulted in Bahro abandoning the Marxist concept of the proletariat for Arnold Toynbee's all-embracing concept of the 'internal proletariat'.[30] The 'internal proletariat' are the vast majority (whether poor or in possession of material goods) who reject the ruling minority because it violates the rights of the majority and has also ceased being a creative force. Toynbee's concern for the rise and fall of whole civilizations has undoubted appeal for Bahro, especially as the latter tends to think in sweeping religious and grand cultural and psycho-social terms.[31]

Both Gorz and Bahro still see capitalism as the primary enemy. But both have significantly changed their attitude to the working class and the traditional organizations of the Left. Most post-industrial theorists operate with non-class or anti-class theoretical concepts. Gorz and Bahro have moved in this direction, but are peculiar in that they are just as critical of the Left as they are of capitalist classes and other social conservatives. However, their revision or rejection of Marx's concept of the proletariat, in favour of the 'neo-proletariat' and the 'internal proletariat', is ultimately unsatisfactory. It is unsatisfactory for both conceptual and strategic reasons.

Conceptually, it is historically possible to have industrial societies without dominant capitalist classes, for example, Eastern European societies. It is also possible to have working classes exploited by non-capitalist bureaucracies, elites or classes. But we have never had a dominant capitalist class without a majority class of dominated proletarians. Gorz admits to a capitalist class, but denies the existence of a majority working class. Bahro tries to fit all industrial societies – whether the USSR or the USA – into the 'capitalist system', and hence is also forced to expand the concept of proletariat to the metaphorical, but much more sociologically loose term of 'internal proletariat'. Despite the pertinence of Gorz and Bahro's criticisms of trade unions, of the conservative social attitudes of many workers and so forth, their conceptual abandonment or modification of class theory poses serious problems for all those interested in radical change and the vexing problem of agency and political strategy. It is to the strategic problems that I now turn.

## TRADE UNIONS, PARTIES AND THE TRANSITION TO POST-INDUSTRIAL SOCIETY

The post-industrial utopians represent, in their various personal activities and careers, typical forms of political activism in Western capitalist societies. Barry Jones represents all those who believe that a more humane post-industrial society can be brought about by being active in a reform-oriented, mainstream parliamentary party. Alvin Toffler tries to influence policy makers – in the private corporate and government sectors – through his individualistic activity via journalism, books and lectures. His faith, typical of many non-class theorists, lies in the so-called creative energy and talents of a free enterprise system – a system which will supposedly transform existing structures and social relations into a radical alternative. Andre Gorz is also a journalist and publicist; but his work is not oriented to the corporate sector or to existing governments (although Gorz did support Mitterand's policies) as is Toffler's energy. Rather, Gorz has played a Left-maverick role in alternating between acting as theorist for the labour movement, and being a harsh critic of the Left for what he sees as its conservatism, myopia and lack of imagination. The main difference between Gorz and Rudolf Bahro is that the latter is active in an alternative, 'post-Marxist' movement, whereas Gorz pursues unattached intellectual activity. Each theorist, not surprisingly, places an emphasis on conventional parties or on alternative movements correlated with his individual involvement or free-floating intellectual activity. Yet all four theorists are distant from revolutionary movements in Third World countries and from agents of social change – whether dissidents or party members – in Communist countries. The post-industrial theorists, like their strategies, are Western or Eurocentric, despite their analyses of the transition to a post-industrial society as a global phenomenon.

While I do not believe that the post-industrial theorists have presented a convincing case for the obsolescence of class theory (despite their focus on several very important limitations and glaring weaknesses in class theory and practice), the continued use of concepts such as 'capitalist society' begs the question as to what the post-industrial theorists regard the agents of change to be, and how these agents can transform or overthrow 'capitalism' without the traditional proletariat? Of course, a political strategy cannot be itself reduced to a belief in class struggle. As one class does not actually confront another class as two subjects in conflict, there is no 'correct path' or inherent class strategy just because one acknowledges the importance of class theory. Not only are there numerous parties each claiming to speak on behalf of the working class, but there is just as much conflict between organizations of the working class as between Left and Right parties, if not more. Similarly, a rejection of class theory in favour of new social movements or new social issues, for example, environmentalism or feminism, has not resulted in an unambiguous environmental or feminist consciousness, let alone a commonly accepted strategy. The old divisions within the Left between revolutionaries and reformists are just as evident in the new social movements, as 'fundamentalists' and 'realists' split over theory and practice. As I will discuss later on, some of the divisions in new social movements are even deeper than the old divisions between Leninists and social democrats.

Toffler argues that the old Left–Right divisions are as obsolete as the present capitalist and Communist Second Wave industrial systems.[32] He is also highly critical of those members of the West German Green movement who are nostalgic for the pre-industrial past and who attack technology indiscriminately.[33] In typical Toffler fashion, one can read in his works support for quite incompatible practices and theories. For example, Toffler supports the workers' plan at Lucas;[34] he advocates marketization of social welfare and education,[35] and deregulation of industry, and yet he wants new supranational agencies to control currencies, the side effects of new technology and pollution of the oceans and outer space.[36]

More importantly, Toffler sees two political wars going on simultaneously. The first war or struggle is 'politics-as-usual' – that is, battles between classes and groups for immediate gain. The second and larger form of struggle is the 'super struggle' between supporters of the old Second Wave social relations and promoters of the new Third Wave.[37] While the battle lines are not yet clearly drawn, the most basic cleavage 'is no longer between rich and poor, or between the middle class and the extremes, or between racial or ethnic minorities, or between Right and Left in the conventional sense'.[38] Rather, Toffler sees new and unusual alliances between all sorts of groups and individuals. Generally, supporters of the Second Wave will tend to be existing power wielders, supporters of conventional politics – of entrenched unions, businesses and parties. These people and groups will oppose diversity, demassified politics, direct democracy, alternatives to the nuclear family, greater care for the environment, the break-up of the large bureaucracies and a fairer world economic order.[39] On the other hand, Toffler argues that the supporters of the Third Wave are harder to characterize.

Some are drawn from the Second Wave 'right', others from the Second Wave 'left' – free marketeers and libertarians, neo-socialists, feminists, and civil rights activists, former flower children and the straightest of straight-arrows. Some are long-time activists in the peace movement; others have never marched or demonstrated for anything in their lives. Some are devoutly religious, others diehard atheists.[40]

The interesting thing about Toffler's analysis is that, in contrast to most non-class and anti-conflict theorists, his pluralist and 'non-aligned' perspective (in Left – Right terms) promises much conflict and instability.

The super-struggle between these Second and Third Wave forces, therefore, cuts like a jagged line across class and party, across age and ethnic groups, sexual preferences and subcultures. It reorganizes and realigns our political life. And, instead of a harmonious, classless, conflict-free, non-ideological future society, it points towards escalating crises and deep social unrest in the near-term future. Pitched political battles will be waged in many nations, not merely over who will benefit from what is left of industrial society but over who participates in shaping, and ultimately controlling, its successor.[41]

Despite the violence, economic depression and social conflict which Toffler predicts in the short-term future, the struggle between the forces of the Second and Third Waves will not be like earlier struggles of vanguard parties overthrowing ruling elites, nor will the Third Wave society come about through a single climactic upheaval.[42] Instead, Toffler envisages the new society as a product of thousands of tiny 'innovations and collisions at many levels and at many places over a period of decades'.[43] Ultimately, Toffler falls back on the educated 'new class' of the information society to lead the way through greater public education and the creation of new political and social structures ignored or opposed by defenders of the Second Wave.[44]

Toffler's analysis is simultaneously superficial and perceptive. It is superficial in that it is easy to point to a multiplicity of conflicts without specifying how important or relevant particular conflicts are to one another. It is perceptive in that it is true that millions of people are disillusioned with conventional politics, that there are new alliances developing, and that former champions of social change in unions or Left parties are often just as strong opponents of new social movements as old conservatives and reactionaries. Gorz and Bahro also share Toffler's disillusionment with conventional political parties, although they are far more critical of them than is Toffler. Like Toffler, they also advocate greater decentralization and direct and semi-direct democratic participation by the people in their everyday institutions. Gorz attacks the manner in which political parties have been converted into 'transmission belts' for state policies rather than arenas of debate and policy determination by party members.[45] Bahro is even more scathing. Not only has he attacked the policies and structures of Left parties,[46] but he has also broken with the so-called anti-party – the West German Green Party. In his June 1985 resignation letter, Bahro states:

> This experience is the end of traditional political existence for me altogether. At last I have understood that a party is a counterproductive tool, that the given political space is a trap into which life energy disappears, indeed, where it is rededicated to the spiral of death. This is not a general but a quite concrete type of despair. It is directed not at the original project which is today called 'fundamental', but at the party. I've finished with it now. I wouldn't consider it right just to withdraw silently. I am not becoming unpolitical. I am not saying goodbye to the intellectual process. I want to contribute to creating a new place and a new practice. Clearly we have to take a longer run-up. We must risk some cold water if we want to assemble the necessary substance for our withdrawal from the industrial system, first of all within ourselves.[47]

There must be thousands of party members and ex-members who know what Bahro means when he describes parties as 'a trap into which life energy disappears'. But the post-industrial utopians' critique of the conventional political process raises more questions than it answers. If the goal is to create an egalitarian society based on grass-roots participation in decentralized, small-scale institutions, how will this be achieved outside parties? Moreover, if political parties are in fact 'transmission belts' for state policies, how can social movements not only challenge this state of affairs, but create an alternative form of public policy process if they reject any involvement in state institutions? Several theories and strategies have been pursued in recent years. First, reject all parties and unions and build new movements based on a new consciousness and new lifestyle. Second, build new parties out of new social movements which will be opposed to the old political practices – a new organization which is simultaneously party and social movement. Third, struggle to transform existing parties and unions so that they either reflect the interests of the old 'Red' labour movement and the new 'Green' social movements, or are the basis for a new alliance with these new movements. Fourth, reject all movements – whether old or new – and build the new society via micro-activity at the interpersonal level in small communes and new child-rearing practices. Fifth, concentrate on single issues or subcultural values as the only meaningful form of political expression at the expense of a broader range of issues which only dilute ones' energy. Let me examine some of these strategies in relation to both parties and social movements, and also in relation to the goals of building new post-industrial public or private practices and forms of participation.

### Trade unions

The post-industrial utopians are much more critical than supportive of trade unions. Toffler sees great battles between 'prosumers' and unions, as parents struggle with teacher unions, do-it-yourself tradespeople clash with building unions, and so forth.[48] There is no doubt that incompatible interests exist between many people working in the informal sector for low wages or barter, and unionists defending hard won wage rates and working conditions. Not only does

Toffler fail to tell us how living standards can be preserved for millions of workers if unions are weakened or abolished, but also his notion of the Third Wave worker is highly romantic. According to Toffler, the new worker in the Third Wave will be like an artisan compared with the unskilled factory worker. These new individualistic 'mind workers' are not easy for unions to recruit. They will, claims Toffler, 'invent their own new forms of organization – more associational, less homogenizing. And if they do join unions, they will force important changes in union structure, practice and ideology.'[49] What these new organizations will look like, Toffler does not tell us. But in opposition to Marx, who argued that the factory system created the conditions of working class unity, Toffler argues that

> the end of the factory system, in its traditional form, and the shift to de-massified production and distribution, creates counter-conditions – they lay the base for de-massified political movements . . . The idea that the mind-workers will unite to oppress the rest of society is, I believe, wrong. They may have a harder time forming a unified majority than any other group.[50]

Toffler is undoubtedly correct in pointing to the difficulty which many unions are having in recruiting new 'mind-workers'. But is the difficulty due to the nature of the new work processes, or to the anti-union climate in countries such as the USA and the UK in recent years? There seems to be no clear evidence that information sector workers in strong union countries such as Sweden are resisting union recruitment in overwhelming numbers. Moreover, Toffler is highly premature in his prognosis that the mass production factory system is nearing its end. On the contrary, capitalist production will continue to remain mass production in character, but the trend is towards highly automated factories based on the convergence of three key technologies – computer-aided design (CAD), the grouping of machine tools into flexible manufacturing systems (FMS) and computer-integrated manufacturing (CIM). Even if this unlikely event (the end of the mass production factory system) were to happen in the next 40 years, it is certainly not true that most 'service sector' or 'mind workers' jobs will be highly creative and non-routine.

There is a parallel between Toffler's Third Wave society and the communist society depicted by many Marxists. As trade unions were seen by Marx and Lenin to be defensive organizations in a class-exploitative society, there was a need either to justify the trade-union movement's existence in a 'class-less society' such as the Soviet Union, or redefine the role of trade unions according to party needs. Similarly, Toffler and the other post-industrial theorists do not seem to be able to deal with the problem of workers' rights and conditions. Even in the best of societies where the working week has been drastically reduced, where gender relations and race relations do not result in grossly unequal work conditions, etc., there will still be many labour disputes. If one does not envisage a radically decentralized society based on tiny communes, a democratic public sphere will, at the very least, be based upon workers organized and represented through their own unions. This does not mean that the many existing bureaucratized and conservative union movements – with their authoritarianism, sexism, racism and abuse of nature –will be tolerated or remain in control. But any social order which requires a certain minimum division of labour, a certain minimum level of social and geographical diversity, will be far less democratic if there is not strong, direct representation of workers in their own democratically controlled unions.

If Toffler's Third Wave has minimal room for trade unions, Bahro's strategy is openly anti-union. His attitude to unions is well expressed in a reply he gave to a question about the importance of class struggle.

If I discuss with a factory worker who wants to get involved in politics, I would advise him to invest one little finger on one hand in the trade union and to invest the rest in the new social movement. Trade union activity is a retrograde step. It's not good when Capital takes more than it should, but this whole defensive struggle takes place on a carousel which guarantees the reproduction of the system.[51]

However, the Green movement has had to battle with unions in the chemical, nuclear power and other environmentally polluting industries, and there is much truth in Bahro's criticism that trade unions defend the old system. In response to a critique by the Fourth International that the ecology movement was a single-issue movement, Bahro states: 'If there is anything today that really does deserve the label of a single-issue movement, it is the institutionalized wage struggle which is ultimately subordinated completely to the overall process of capitalist reproduction.'[52] On the other hand, it is also quite clear that many unionists are justifiably opposed to Bahro's position – given the failure of alternative movements to spell out in detail how these workers would survive the loss of their jobs in the short run (which could last a worker's lifetime). While Bahro and other members of the Green movement are more than happy to co-operate with unions on commonly shared issues and objectives, the overall goal of 'industrial disarmament' will never mobilize millions of workers dependent on the system for their wages – short of an enormous catastrophe.

All those activists in new social movements who believe that it is not worth bothering with trade unionists, and that it is better if unions decay and wither away, appear to have a poor understanding of the power relations in contemporary capitalist societies. If strong trade-union movements are severely weakened or become insignificant, it is most unlikely that new social movements will be the beneficiaries of this development. If millions of unionists deserted their unions and Left parties in favour of alternative movement issues and values, this would indeed be a major boost to the prospects of a post-industrial socialist society. But a combined attack on unions by the New Right and new social movements would almost certainly weaken radical social movements once the union movements were defeated. This is because many social conditions necessary for an egalitarian post-industrial society, for example, a reduced working week, greater control over production by the workers, adequate social welfare, education, health and safety, etc., would all be almost impossible to achieve without a strong and organized workforce. Not only that, but a victorious and aggressive private corporate sector would revoke even those minimal, hard-won existing environmental, consumer and health controls and regulations in the quest for higher profits and uncontrolled growth. Despite their conservative nature, many unions and conventional Left parties provide an invaluable buffer for new social movements against Rightwing governments and businesses. It is also true that union involvement in corporatist management with governments and businesses excludes and attacks new social movements, for example, in pitting unionist against environmentalists. Labour, Communist and Socialist parties and unions are themselves divided between sympathizers and opponents of new social movements – a division which constantly recurs on feminist, environmentalist and peace issues among others.

To sum up, if unions are to be rejected or to play no significant role in the transition to a post-industrial socialist society, the main actors will have to be existing conservative parties, businesses, churches and other social groupings, and the new alternative social movement organizations. Given the domination of state apparatuses and the material means of production by the capitalist classes and their political allies, this would, most likely, be no contest. The outcome would be a spread of Rightwing post-industrial societies marked by authoritarian technocratic rule and marginalized masses – the latter with a shortened life expectancy, given the further growth of high-technology military–industrial complexes and the increased risks of nuclear catastrophe. The destruction or significant weakening of trade unions in Western Europe, Australia, New Zealand and Japan would destroy the Left of centre political parties whose fortunes are closely integrated with national labour movements. Those theorists who welcome this development and point to the American model – weak trade unions, no social democratic parties and thriving deregulation, a plurality of social movements, and innovative private enterprises – tend to remain silent about the poor welfare services, large urban ghettos and glaring forms of inequality, corruption, violence and commercialism, not to mention the massive American exploitation of other countries and support for the most brutal regimes from El Salvador to South Korea. While it is perfectly true that various Rightwing Labour and Social Democratic parties also support these brutal regimes, or close their eyes to atrocities and repression for the sake of trade relations or the American alliance, it is safe to say that the defeat of Left unions and Left parties would do little to advance democracy abroad or equality at home.

Stressing the need for trade unions is not equivalent to an apology for existing union policies and structures. Just as Bahro rejects the dismantling of the welfare state before an alternative form of social welfare is created, so the dismantling or rejection of unions would be extremely short-sighted and counter-productive for the forces of greater equity and democracy. There is a tendency within post-industrial theory to treat unions and workers as the equivalent of those peasants who resisted the development of industrial societies. I agree with Bahro when he argues against the Marxists' belief that the interests of the European working class coincide with the interests of the rest of humanity.[53] But then no class or social movement has an a priori or inherent claim to stand for everyone else in the world. Just as there is no pure class perspective, so there is no single trade-union viewpoint, organizational structure and form of action. Unions are themselves subject to numerous divisions, and are the sites of struggles over how to respond to new technologies, unemployment, gender and 'social wage' issues. The belief that unions are merely the historical expression of a particular stage of history – the industrial or Second Wave – and that just as peasants disappeared, so too will unions, is both simplistic and dangerous to the future interests of 'post-industrial workers'.

### Political parties

Bahro, Gorz and Toffler agree – unlike Barry Jones – that existing political parties are either obsolete, or are failing to express and represent an increasingly large number of people angered or disillusioned by the parties' neglect of issues raised by new social movements. Bahro is particularly scathing in his critique of Social Democratic, Labour and Communist parties who keep the industrial system going and borrow the rhetoric of social movements (for example, the environmental and peace movements) without delivering fundamental changes in policy.[54] The tensions within the West German Green movement over whether the party should be an 'anti-party', a social movement or a radical parliamentary party, is well expressed in Bahro's writings in the past few years.[55] I will discuss Bahro's position in relation to the role of social movements later on.

In the previous chapter, I discussed the problems arising in new societies based upon a plethora of decentralized groups and lacking a national public sphere. The role of political parties is particularly important in any conception of a post-industrial society – and especially, of the transition towards this new society. All the post-industrial theorists are in favour of a peaceful transition even though they recognize that many conflicts, including violent ones, may take place.[56] Yet, apart from Jones who sees the post-industrial transition being assisted by conventional parties, unions, businesses and social movements in a slowly evolving 'mixed economy', the post-industrial theorists appear to have no real sense of the political dimension. That is, one can read much in their writings about the need for new social relations, organizations and practices, one can also read much about how existing societies fail to work properly; but one reads very little about how to get there from here. Toffler calls for a new type of sensitive political leadership and paints a picture of demassified local political organizations coexisting with new supranational parties.[57] This scenario accords with Toffler's belief in the obsolescene of the nation state and the rise of a new decentralization combined with internationalism. But the mediating institutions are absent – as is any account of the manner in which national party structures are integrated into a national set of state institutions with all their corresponding juridical, political–economic and cultural relations.

It is quite likely that new political forces, new styles of organization and new issues will continue to emerge while socio-economic relations alter as a result of intentional and unintentional current developments. But this vague prognostication obscures or evades the decisive issues of the existing roles of major political parties and how their power structures can be demassified, disassembled or abolished in favour of decentralized new social forces, or new global co-ordinating parties. Somehow, Toffler, Gorz and Bahro believe that we will get to the post-industrial utopia via a leap in consciousness, a total disengagement from the existing system, or a spontaneous or conscious self-destruct mechanism triggered by all the politically entrenched interests dominating existing private and public institutions! Even if we assumed with Toffler that the transition would take place via countless battles at all levels between the supporters of Second Wave and Third Wave relations, this evolutionary process tends to relegate political conflicts to a secondary or epiphenomenal by-product of micro- and macro-processes in the economic and social spheres. For example, it is acknowledged by many writers that national state institutions and large private corporations have considerably more power and influence than thousands of local councils, groups and small businesses. The post-industrial theorists do not tell us how decentralized or demassified politics take over from mass, bureaucratized political parties if citizens increasingly opt out of national political struggles. Similarly, at the supra-national level (for example, in the European Parliament and bureaucracies), there is no indication that the major ideological blocs of Euro-MPs pursue policies which are at odds with their national conservative, socialist or other party loyalties. In other words, how are all the dissatisfied and alienated citizens to empower themselves if existing policy-making powers remain in the hands of conventional party machines? Three responses are possible:

(1) mass disengagement from the party political system;
(2) pressuring existing parties from inside and outside by mass mobilization and the long march through the institutions;
(3) building a new radical party based on the principles of

implementing decentralization and devolution of power from the centre to the grass roots.

Prior to his resignation from the Green Party in 1985, Bahro advocated a combination of the third and second strategies, in so far as he still believed that a political party was a valuable though not unique means of bringing about change. Bahro in fact oscillated between building a radical party or movement and abhorring the co-opting power of parliamentary politics. It should not be forgotten that the perspectives and strategies advocated by the post-industrial theorists have been very much influenced by the electoral processes in their own countries. For example, Bahro's ultimate rejection of the Green Party had much to do with the internal disputes within the Green movement, over whether it should remain a fundamental opposition or enter into coalition with the Social Democrats in return for policy concessions.[58] Bahro attacked the SPD and the unions as 'institutional prisons' whose walls should not be freshly cemented by the Green movement. Instead, Bahro advocated that the Green movement 'should welcome, encourage, permit this inner decay of these old, state-bearing organizations, which presupposes putting our confidence into something completely different from a junior partnership'.[59]

The rejection of coalition with the SPD or similar parties in other Western countries need not mean the rejection of party politics *per se*. In rejecting party politics forever, Bahro has now to conceptualize a strategy which brings about the end of the system from outside the 'walls of the state'. Before he left the Green Party, Bahro advocated a new version of the old Leninist theory of 'dual power'. Instead of workers' councils constituting the alternative power base to the bourgeois state, Bahro supported the idea of a parallel institution – a 'citizen's parliament' – which would articulate the values of alternative social movements as opposed to the vested interests represented by traditional parties.[60] Even though this 'citizen's parliament' was not conceived as an actual alternative parliament, Bahro nevertheless still operated within the historical framework of parliamentary political representation. If parties, whether traditional or Green, are totally rejected, fundamental answers must be given to questions about policy-making in an alternative society. It is true that other earlier political traditions, like anarchism, also advocated the organization of society without parties and bureaucracies. Bahro's theory has affinity with these notions of small-scale, face-to-face politics, of delegates and federated structures, which avoided routinized party platforms, national elections and all the traditional trappings associated with conventional party machines. But while I also believe that many new forms of local, regional and national decision-making are possible, that existing forms of representative democracy are highly bureaucratized, restrictive and in many respects undemocratic, I do not believe that political parties as such can be dispensed with in a genuinely democratic and pluralistically constituted socialist society.

Just as Bahro has failed to indicate how his 'basic communes' would relate with one another at the economic and socio-cultural levels, so too the notion of a plethora of decentralized communes without regional or national parliaments (or legislatures or councils – the names are not so important) is a recipe for dictatorship or chaos. In so far as new 'citizen's parliaments' are created, the chances of new groupings, factions, blocs or parties are almost guaranteed – and this is a positive, healthy sign of democracy. In other words, Bahro wants a transition to a new society without activity through parties; but he appears to want a society where politics as an activity ceases – that is, a society of permanent harmony, reconciliation with nature and so forth. This is an anti-democracy, a social order of spontaneous or 'natural' agreement – something which is foreign to human theory and practice.

As I mentioned in chapter 4, a new democratic public sphere of empowered, decentralized and diverse local communities needs a set of national and regional state structures to facilitate legal, economic, educational and cultural values and practices, to support those local citizens lacking in material and cultural resources, and to settle the many disputes and conflicts which will continue to be a part of any foreseeable social formation. A combination of local, direct democracy and new semi-direct democratic structures at the national level will make life for traditional political parties very difficult if not impossible. This development is to be applauded because too many citizens in contemporary societies have an impoverished notion of the possibilities of democratic participation and often equate democracy with voting rituals. But new, democratic parties have an important role to play as organizations which articulate a range of interests and as facilitators of major policy changes in the long transition from bureaucratic to grass-roots democracy. It is quite possible that new democratic legislatures and local councils will see parties reduced to a status where they are barely distinguishable from other lobby groups, minority organizations or collectivities. But what is important, for the survival of new post-industrial democratic public spheres, is the institutional possibility of citizens self-constituting themselves into parties or any other organizations in the pursuit of policies democratically arrived at.

Like Bahro, who wishes to transcend the corrupting effect of institutionalized party politics, so Toffler and Gorz, each in his own way, are unable to propose an adequate institutional mechanism or process as a viable alternative to the political party. Toffler's vision of a proliferation of endless demassified pressure groups – a new minority politics in contrast to majority party politics – is a utopian extension of the old American dream.[61] This dream of American pluralism has always foundered on the rocks of 'big government' and 'big business'. It is the small-town folks against the politicians in Washington. The trouble is that Toffler does not explain how the billion dollar packaging of politicians, the whole professional lobbying industry and the electoral system which is loaded against third parties, will be broken by the new surge of Third Wave struggles. Toffler's transitional politics are just as implausible as his notion of transnational private corporations building a peaceful post-industrial society lacking the whole destructive activity of profitable high technology military–industrial complexes. Even if the traditional political system were broken by Toffler's endless struggles, his vague notion of supranational structures and local democracy leaves the whole vital area of taxation and representation unresolved once the national political institutions cease to exist. Like Bahro, Toffler's emphasis on decentralization and 'prosuming' almost implies a locally self-contained or self-sufficient politics. Co-ordinating and mediating institutions, so necessary for the peaceful co-operation of one community with another, are provided no institutional space within which to flourish – other than distant, supranational structures.

Gorz is even more ambiguous when it comes to transitional politics. On the one hand, Gorz is one of the few post-industrial theorists to argue for the necessity of state institutions. On the other hand, his dual society of heteronomous and autonomous spheres makes no clear provision for political mediation. According to Gorz, everyone will have three levels of activity:

> (1) Heteronomous, macro-social work, organized across society as a whole, enabling it to function and providing for basic needs: (2) Micro-social activity, self-organized on a local level and based on voluntary participation, except where it replaces macro-social work in providing for basic needs: (3) Autonomous activity which corresponds to the particular desires and projects of individuals, families and small groups. As an intermediary level connecting socially necessary, heteronomous work and autonomous activity entirely determined by individual choice, the second level thus constitutes the social fabric of civil society. It is the level of debates and trade-offs; the level where decisions are reached as to what is necessary and what is desirable; the level of conflicts and plans for the future . . .[62]

This scheme sounds reasonable until we realize that Gorz's micro-social level is only constituted at the local level, while heteronomous macro-work is constituted at the national or global level. If all the conflicts, trade-offs, and debates take place at the intermediate level, how is Gorz's macro-level co-ordinated, and how are macro-political decisions determined? How can Gorz leave the vital national state institutions and heteronomous work spheres to the infinite micro-spheres of local communities, when he himself argues for the necessity of larger state institutions? If we are not to have a utopia run by presidential decrees, then Gorz's alternative society had better provide the political institutional processes whereby macro-social policies are self-organized and democratically implemented.

Perhaps it is no accident that Gorz is much better at articulating what is wrong with traditional party politics and trade unions, than in formulating a democratic public institutional process which accommodates state planning on the one hand, and local and individual autonomous activity on the other. His attraction to the concept of the 'neo-proletariat' signifies the degree to which Gorz has moved from institutionalized class politics to the amorphous and unorganized 'anti-systemic' existentialism of the 'neo-proletariat'. It is interesting to note that Gorz was attracted to Antonio Negri's writings. Negri and other Italian theorists of Autonomia Operaia also argued that a new proletariat based on the unemployed, students and other strata had emerged in the advanced capitalist 'social factory'.[63] The division of society into new proletariat (or 'neo-proletariat') and privileged traditional workers, led various Italian radicals (during the 1970s and 1980s) into a range of confrontationist acts with the traditional Left – ranging from verbal abuse to terrorism. In opting out of the traditional political system, the terrorists in Italy and other capitalist countries practised the 'end of politics', replacing democratic discussion and mass movement activities by violent 'decisionism' (all in the name of the proletariat). Gorz's analysis lies midway between the violent response of the marginalized, and the privatized withdrawal of all those who believe that social change can be brought about by alternative lifestyles at the interpersonal level. Gorz recognizes that both terrorism and private withdrawal are recipes for the triumph of the status quo. But his post-industrial 'neo-proletariat' are simply described as existing, armed with no theory of organization or political expression. How can the 'neo-proletariat' bring into being a post-industrial socialism when they have opted out of the system?

Gorz bids farewell to class politics but greets an a-political and unorganized mass. He talks about reconstructing the Left around new issues (for example, self-managed work time), yet posits no new organizations or processes; Gorz's choice appears to be either a renewed Left political activism based upon parties, unions and social movements, or an unorganized spontaneous rebellion. We know what Gorz wants, but not how be believes we will get it.

## SOCIAL MOVEMENTS, STATE POWER AND ALTERNATIVE POLITICS

In recent years it has become highly fashionable to replace class theory with the theory of new social movements. Writers such as Touraine, Cohen, Eder and many others have focused on Solidarity, the peace movement, the Greens, and the women's movement as examples of a new politics which reflects the obsolescence of class struggle.[64] But, despite the many valuable insights which these theorists offer us in relation to the nature and practice of these movements, their work provides endless typologies and descriptive contrasts between the old and new political movements yet little on the ability of social movements to replace the existing structural differentiation and institutionalization of political decision-making in state and private organizations and apparatuses. It is one thing to propose new social movements as the agents of the transition from industrial to post-industrial society; it is quite another matter to concentrate on the political struggle at the expense of evaluating whether the end goals of these struggles are feasible. That is, new social movements are generally conceived to be reactions against bureaucratization, statism, corporatism and 'the colonization of the life-world' or technocratic interference into all aspects of civic life and physical existence. Moreover, the struggle between social movements and traditional political processes is erroneously depicted as the struggle of 'civil society against the state'. This is because new social movement theorists do not adequately differentiate between 'the state' in the narrow sense of political administration (that is, government by

freely elected ministers, one party dictators or military–
bureaucratic regimes), and state institutions in the larger
sense as part of what is called 'civil society', for example, the
vital educational, social welfare, transport, media and other
national and local services, not to mention nationalized
industries in telecommunications, electricity, manufacturing
and so forth. Hence, social movements exist both *inside* the
larger state (for example, Solidarity or student movements in
state-run universities), and outside state institutions, just as
workers and their unions exist both within private businesses
and also in state institutions.

At one level it is clear, for example, that many environmentalist or feminist organizations are directly opposing
government policies, practices and potential legislation. But
at another level, social movements have no more 'natural'
coherence or existence than pure classes. That is, women,
environmentalists, peace activists, gays, etc., do not have a
ready-formed identity as a social movement any more than
workers have an innate class consciousness. Rather,
individuals become active within particular organizations or
support in a looser manner (via protest marches or lifestyle
practices) some, or all of the demands, made by particular
organizations or coalitions. There are just as many political
divisions within new social movements – divisions between
revolutionaries, reformists, fundamentalists and pragmatists
– as there are within labour movements. Claus Offe points
out that social movements are often unable to make compromises in the way that political parties or unions can
because they articulate non-negotiable values, for example,
less nuclear power is just as unacceptable as full reliance upon
nuclear power generation.[65] While Offe and other new social
movement theorists note all the tensions and divisions within
social movements, they do not emphasize that a social movement cannot function as an organization or as an actor who
enters into negotiations with other organizations or forms
alliances. For example, particular groups of women (not the
'feminist movement') enter into negotiations or struggles.
This theoretical distinction is important as a great deal of the
literature on social movements is so unsatisfactory. In

treating social movements as historical actors, there is a real danger of succumbing to a new form of substitutionalism. That is, new social movements are substituted for the proletarian class as the subject of historical change. This misconception repeats all the old problems associated with treating classes as coherent social actors.

The major divisions within the West German Green movement are a good illustration of the limits of new social movement theory and practice. At the practical level, Bahro represents all those fundamentalists in the Green movement who reject compromise with the system, who oppose 'limits' on armaments or animal experiments and want to do away with them completely.[66] Bahro's fundamentalism is qualitatively distinct from the old division between revolutionaries and reformists. Whereas revolutionaries attacked reformists for working in the system, they did not necessarily believe that parliamentary tactics were bad, and argued that strategic alliances were at times necessary with non-working class organizations. But the Green fundamentalists oppose the 'realists', not because of their methods, but because of the impending 'eco-catastrophe' which 'limited reforms' will delay but not avert. If Bahro and his supporters believe that the whole industrial system is doomed, and that compromise with this system is a replay or renewal of conventional politics, all contact with state institutions is self-defeating unless this contact is one of fundamental opposition. But how is a transitional politics to be exercised by social movements who play an all-or-nothing game? Leninists believe in the need for a vanguard party which grows in size until dual power results in the bourgeois state being overthrown. But believers in new social movements must either hope for the system to weaken and wither away, or come into major confrontation with state power.

If one does not believe in either violence or compromise, as Bahro does, there can be no transitional politics, but only collapse of the old and replacement by the new. Life in a social movement must then become increasingly oriented to consciousness-raising, messianic prophecy about the impending *catastrophe* (nuclear war or ecological devastation) and withdrawal into a micro-politics of small face-to-face relations, or quasi-religious, sect-like activities. Bahro actually sees spiritualist and religious orders of the past as examples for the present generation.[67] But the history of humanity reveals no examples of societies reverting to much simpler and less complex organizational forms of life save after a natural or social catastrophe (usually war). Religious groups have long preached the renunciation of worldly possessions without much success. Mass mobilization of earlier generations of peasants or workers was possible through the promise of a richer material life and greater freedom, rather than a dismantling of the whole production system.

I must agree with Bahro: the orthodox Marxist belief that socialists can utilize the means of production developed by capitalists is not only profoundly conservative, but totally incompatible with the construction of a post-industrial socialist society. But while I support the dismantling of military–industrial complexes and other anti-human means of production, this is not equivalent to support for total 'industrial disarmament'. If Bahro is correct about the industrial system (and there is great merit in many of his warnings), then the political conclusions must be profoundly pessimistic – given his opting out of conventional politics. For if millions of workers cannot be assured of alternative jobs, social welfare, etc., in the peaceful transition from eco-doomed industrialism to eco-pacifist post-industrialism – and there is no indication whatsoever that Bahro wants or is able to address and resolve this massive problem – then the end result, if we subscribe to Bahro's analysis, must be the end of the world.

I do not believe that things are as bad as Bahro makes them out to be, although I can fully agree with many specific examples of environmental damage which alarm Bahro and all other sensitive people. More importantly, even though I agree with many of the critiques from feminists, environmentalists, gays and other new social activists, there is a vast difference between those who wish to extend and democratize existing undemocratic and bureaucratic public institutions, and the other members of new movements who reject any form of state institution and seek a radically decentralized and diffused stateless society. New social movement organizations have tried to implement, with mixed success, a 'new politics'. But they are also plagued by 'old politics' problems: bureaucratic tendencies, tension between the rank-and-file and the leaders or media 'stars', intolerance of dissenters or ideological divisions, funding crises, and co-option into neo-corporatist policy-making processes. These problems often arise from having to oppose the system, while at the same time trying to gain concessions or new policies by using whatever resources or institutions are available.

Most organizations in new social movements actually accept to a lesser or greater extent the prevailing public and private political processes, rather than advocate a total dismantling of the whole state institutional system. Others have a naïve disregard or ignorance of the massive repressive state apparatuses and private corporate resources which can be (and often are) deployed against critics of prevailing socio-political orders. But those members of new social movements who advocate a radical anti-statism and the end of the 'welfare state', appear to ignore important members of their own diverse constituency. Sociologically, many members of new social movements are drawn from what Offe calls 'decommodified' groups: students, retired persons, middle-class housewives and unemployed or marginalized people who are not engaged in the labour market, as well as many public sector workers (for example, teachers, social workers) whom conservatives call 'the new class'.[68] Consider, then, a transition to post-industrial society in which new social movement organizations dismantle the very 'social wage' services that keep 'new class' members employed, or the revenue structures which provide pensions, student allowances and dole payments for the 'decommodified' groups. Such a process is bound to promote a Rightwing post-industrialism – or, somewhat less plausibly, a stateless society without mass support in either the labour movement or the 'decommodified' groups.

If we assume that contemporary Western societies are based upon complex relations between a dominant private

sector and a broad range of local and national state institutions (which perform the contradictory roles of assisting and
preserving capitalist enterprise as well as maintaining
legitimacy and crisis managing), then social movement
theorists have to be able to show that class relations, and
hence the relationship between class power and state power is
much less decisive than the relationship between social
movements and state power. If we still live in a capitalist
society, what has happened to class domination and exploitation? Social movements are made up of members who come
from more than one class; yet there is little to suggest (as is
implied in social movement theory) that new social movements have replaced classes as the sociological basis of contemporary societies. If a post-industrial society is to be a
classless society, it would have to be shown how the political
organizations (which express new social movement values
and interests) can overthrow or negate the power of ruling
capitalist classes.

It has become evident, in recent years, that members of
what is called 'the new class', now play a highly influential
role both in traditional Left parties and in new social
movements. It is also clear, since the influx of 'new class'
members, that many Left parties in OECD countries have
tended to become less radical and more technocratic or corporatist – as 'professionals' have replaced socialist policies
with crisis management 'fine-tuning'. On the other hand,
there are many 'new class' members who are opposed to technocratic practices; these people have joined new social
movements (often the same people belong both to Left
parties and to new social movements). There are noticeably
few cases, however, where new social movement organizations have pursued objectives in clear conflict with the income  and jobs of 'new class' members. The majority of
peace activists, feminists, gays, environmentalists and animal
liberationists have tended to focus their activities on capitalist
enterprises and those state apparatuses (for example, defence
departments) which do not necessarily threaten jobs in the
'social wage' services of local and national state sectors. This
is not to argue that all 'new class' activists in social

movements are self-interested protestors who campaign only on issues that allow them to maintain their comfortable lifestyles. But when post-industrial theorists hail the new 'knowledge-based elites' and 'new class' members as the agents of social change, it is important not to have illusions about how far these professionals are prepared to struggle. We need to recognize realistically those issues on which they may enter into coalition with Offe's 'decommodified' groups and traditional sectors of the labour movement, and those issues on which they almost certainly will not.

The important point about new social movements is that too many theorists give these movements a life of their own – beyond the actual organized groups who champion particular causes. But social movements cannot enter into alliances any more than classes can. Rather, particular organizations or individuals expressing feminist or other values can make alliances with other groups. When Offe speculates on the three possible alliances in Western countries – an alliance between the conservative–liberal Right and new movements, an alliance of Right and social democratic Left parties against new movements, or an alliance of traditional Left parties and new social movements – he is actually implying that new social movements have no coherent life or values outside their manifestation via particular organizations or individual actions.[69] That is, the varying class backgrounds and beliefs of social movement members can attract them to Right or Left coalitions. The distinction is important because of the immediate and long-term implications. In the short run, an awareness that social movements are *not coherent* actors (for example, the peace movement is made up of new organizations and old ones such as churches and parties) will focus attention on the institutional processes open to social activism. That is, social groups will either work through legal channels or fight the system by obstruction, resistance, violence or withdrawal. In the long run, it does not matter whether one believes in class struggle, new social movement action, or combinations of both forms of struggle. What counts is the manner of political and social representation which movement organizations theorize, or set up if victorious. If new social groups cannot provide a feasible set of institutional political–economic structures able to sustain a non-technocratic, eco-feminist and decentralized non-bureaucratic democracy, all moral critiques of the present will be in vain. Post-industrial societies can emerge only out of existing capitalist and Communist industrial societies. To be acceptable, any project of social change must provide for the minimum conditions and structures needed to maintain open, democratic public spheres, maximum social equality and commitment to social solidarity through cultural diversity. This cannot be plausibly achieved if one ignores the indispensable role of state institutions. If this vital point is neglected, then social activists will be unintentionally promoting an authoritarian or dictatorial nightmare.

In this chapter I have tried to show that the post-industrial theorists seriously neglect some vital questions concerning transitional politics and alternative forms of representation and participation. Their theories vary from more of the same (for example, Jones), to quasi-religious withdrawal combined with strong opposition to the system (Bahro). All these theorists reject class struggle as the primary conflict in contemporary societies, and yet all wish to get beyond capitalist societies as we know them today. Despite all the important issues raised and struggles waged by new social organizations, the post-industrial theorists have failed to address adequately the vital issue of state power, as well as the related strategic issue of how class-dominated and bureaucratized state institutions can be transformed into their post-industrial opposites. While policies and practices developed by feminists, environmentalists and other movements can never all be reduced back to class politics, the post-industrial theorists conspicuously fail to explain how working-class organizations fit into their transitional scenarios. It is also asserted, but not clearly shown, that workers will benefit from the micro-electronic revolution, 'industrial disarmament', 'prosuming', 'electronic cottages' and other such potential changes. Wage workers constitute the vast majority of all existing populations in capitalist countries, yet the post-industrial theorists are either openly hostile to workers' organizations, or regard them as irrelevant to the shaping of the future. Such short-sightedness or antagonism is both un-justified and self-defeating.

Despite all the negative characteristics of unions and other workers' organizations, it is most unlikely that the vital campaigns and values of the new social movements will succeed without mass support from paid workers. But this implies that social movement activists must come to terms with the political–economic structures of existing state institutions – if the old structures are to be replaced with the new. Many activists in new social movements recognize the need to co-operate wherever possible with worker's organiz-ations. It is a pity that most of the post-industrial theorists have remained utopian in not emphasizing the importance of these strategic relations, and have instead almost foresaken the political process for the comfort of moral critique and futurology.

If capitalist industrial society won't let us abandon its chosen growth path, then we need to use all means and all motivations – the workers' movement, the women's movement *and* the ecologists' Green movement – to change direction. In the last resort what the Marxists, the feminists and the Green movement are saying is that we have to find ways of bringing decision-making down to the base, to the people themselves where they are with their own hopes and fears, desires and dislikes, expectations and frustrations. The problem of making social change is a whole one, complex and inter-related, not a question of tackling first the bomb, then the biosphere, then exploitation, then self-management. We have to find ways of relating all these together in our own consciousness and in our own models of an alternative political economy.

Michael Barratt Brown, *Models in Political Economy*

A society that offers few other sources of psychic security and little other means of material support is likely to throw people together into little defensive groups and to leave those who do not form such groups isolated and deprived. A male-dominated society is likely to produce a form of private life in which men are privileged and powerful. What is needed is not to build up an alternative to the family – new forms of household that would fulfil all the needs that families are supposed to fulfil today – but to make the family less necessary, by building up all sorts of other ways of meeting people's needs, ways less volatile and inadequate than those based on the assumption that 'blood is thicker than water'.

Michele Barrett and Mary McIntosh, *The Anti-social Family*

# Conclusion

Throughout this book I have tried to distinguish between two issues arising from the various models or notions of post-industrial society: how intrinsically desirable they may be, on the one hand, and how feasible they are, on the other. I have frequently criticized the analyses and alternative institutional arrangements proposed by the post-industrial utopians, but it would be a serious mistake, and myopic, to treat their writings as worthy of anything less than the fullest consideration. Personally, I share and endorse many of their criticisms of contemporary societies. I too desire many of the alternative eco-socialist social relations advocated by writers such as Bahro, Galtung and Gorz, but I differ strongly on key aspects of their theoretical and practical proposals. Having already expressed many of these criticisms in the preceding chapters, I would like to conclude this book on a positive note by outlining some characteristics of what I would call a feasible 'concrete utopia'. This 'concrete utopia' is based upon important aspects of existing societies and implicitly the potential they hold for alternative social relations.

First, while I have accepted the term 'post-industrial' as a short-hand expression for a variety of models which describe new, post-capitalist societies, I do not believe that we have in fact ceased to live in capitalist societies with identifiable ruling classes. Second, I do not believe that capitalist and Communist countries are converging into a new post-industrial social formation. The political–economic relations and structures in Communist countries are marked by political conflicts and processes quite different from the contradictions experienced in capitalist societies. However, *all* societies are affected by military conflict and the devastation of environmental resources, whose global scale transcends geo-political boundaries. Third, while I do not believe that capitalist societies have given way to classless societies dominated by 'knowledge-based elites', it would be stupid and short-sighted to deny the major changes in social relations, both actual and potential, due to micro-electronics, genetic engineering, robotics, high-technology engineering and other technological innovations.[1]

A technological revolution is not equivalent to a social revolution. But the transformation of labour processes and information processes, along with the continued destruction of natural resources, are all giving rise to new forms of social organization, political protest and defensive response. Even if the society in which all these developments are taking place remains capitalist and class dominated, this certainly does not mean that the old forms of class politics, practised by Left parties and unions, adequately confront the actual and potential socio-technological innovations. The post-industrial theorists are not convincing in their over-hasty celebration of the new (Toffler and Jones), or their quick dismissal of the old political movements (Bahro and Gorz). But then neither are the orthodox varieties of Marxist–Leninist who dismiss all talk of post-industrial trends as 'bourgeois ideology'. Just as socialists have waited in vain for the inevitable immiseration of the proletariat which would result in the proletarian revolution, it would also be a serious mistake to believe that capitalist classes cannot harness new technology to their own continued prosperous development. I would agree with Gorz (although not in all details) that a post-industrial society could also be a Rightwing nightmare of technocratic authoritarianism, characterized by a minority privileged élite and a mass of marginalized unemployed. I do not believe, however, that this Rightwing version of post-industrialism would endure very long – although the alternative could very well be barbarism rather than socialism. The important point is that we are living in a crucial period of social transition, where the restructuring of production, consumption and administration by dominant political–economic forces is far too fluid to predict possible outcomes.

But while we do not know the outcome, it is not too difficult to estimate the likely result of a particular form of development or model of a desirable alternative. I would like to put forward a sketch of a 'concrete utopia' – a utopia which recognizes that we have to make clear choices between the opposing tendencies of our day. Each tendency is supported (or opposed) by social groups and individuals distributed over both Left and Right, in conventional labelling. I can agree with Toffler that we are witnessing a struggle between the advocates of the new and the supporters of the old order. But the struggle is not primarily between the supporters of the Second and Third Waves. Rather, it is a much more complicated struggle between the various opponents within an existing capitalist or Communist society, on the one hand, and the defenders of this status quo on the other. Among the opponents of existing social formations are to be found groups and individuals who differ between themselves on some fundamental principles, images and organizational conceptions of alternative societies. These issues of conflict include:

(1) more global integration – or more self-sufficiency;
(2) centralization – or decentralization;
(3) state planning – or market mechanisms, simple barter, other co-ordinating mechanisms;
(4) eco-pacificism – or defensive defence systems;
(5) regional and national legal and political structures – or stateless, direct forms of small-scale democracy;
(6) one global standard of living – or continued differences between North and South;
(7) fulfilment of the humanist–rationalist tradition – or greater affinity with spiritualist, irrational and naturalist cultural values.

It is difficult to find any one group which subscribes consistently to one or the other of these sets of values (which I have deliberately formulated into polar opposites). This is because very few groups and individuals have articulated coherent philosophies or political programmes spanning all the major issues – attitudes to technology, implementation of 'social wage' services, the connection between planning and democratic structures, and so on. Similarly, there is no automatic correspondence between socio-political practice and beliefs – for example, traditional Left party politics, catastrophe politics, new social movement values – and support for state planning, eco-pacifism, new technology or spiritualist values. All these varied perspectives and partial programmatic goals can be found in oppositional groups and parties currently active. That various perspectives and end goals are incompatible must be recognized, if a viable 'concrete utopia' is to be made more coherent and plausible and to gain the support of populations unhappy with the present but frightened of the new. Let me outline which new developments I believe should be supported and which opposed, and which long-cherished ideals we may be forced to recognize as not compatible with a democratic socialist society.

## IN DEFENCE OF SEMI-AUTARKY

For generations, socialists and humanists have advanced the notion of global solutions to the irrationality and conflict induced by imperialist and nationalist institutions and practices. It was never quite clear how this world government, federation of councils, or other institutional arrangement could guarantee local grass-roots democracy while at the same time bringing order to the world through global planning. I would argue that the objective of continental central government (for example, one government for the whole of Europe), let alone world government, is an anti-democratic nightmare. Given the vital role which local, regional and national state institutions play in all facets of everyday life, it would be disastrous if these national institutions were replaced by even more remote supranational bureaucracies. Certainly, there is a pressing need for eco-socialists to organize co-ordinated institutional responses to political–economic, environmental and military problems. But supranational co-ordination and co-operation is *not* equivalent to the replacement of national and local governments by a world government.

Since state institutions are necessary for any genuinely democratic socialist alternative (as argued above), it is essential to prevent the growth of those political–economic developments which minimize or destroy indigenous local and national control over vital assets, resources, skills, technology – whether natural or humanly constructed. This process of destruction is occurring as the major private corporations and government institutions promote a variety of supranational political–economic forms of integration. Integration is also promoted by many Left parties and individuals. The notion of a fully integrated 'socialist Europe', to replace the capitalist European Common Market, is a powerful illusion. Many socialists have advanced the idea of a 'socialist Europe' in the spirit of internationalism, and as a direct critique of the worst forms of parochialism and national chauvinism. For example, Gorz favoured European planning in his *Strategy For Labour* (1964), and European Left parties continue to propound a market socialist or neo-Keynesian European solution to persistently high unemployment, poverty and social malaise.

In chapter 1 I argued that all visions of a post-industrial society based upon global integration (Toffler and Jones), would give us a world shaped by transnational corporations and with the existing military–industrial complexes strengthened. On the other hand, those socialists who believe in supranational solutions would have to reverse the trends to industry rationalization and to enslavement by market forces, which supranational agreements in the EEC, GATT and other structures have imposed. Market socialism – which is promoted as the alternative to capitalist market forces – would also be driven by the need to cut and rationalize industries and resources, local or national, given the problems of market competition induced by over-production. This would not necessarily be a negative phenomenon if the particular industries cut were destructive of the environment or wasteful; however, market-socialist principles operating at a supranational level would inevitably promote profitable 'socialist industries' at the expense of local needs. If we are to transcend the permanent 'fiscal crises' of national states and supranational institutions (cf. the EEC budget), it is imperative that state finances do not depend on the market efficiency of post-industrial enterprises – whether socialist or capitalist. All those vitally needed 'social wage' programmes and GMI schemes would be faced with cut-backs, if revenue depended on the success of enterprises in an increasingly cut-throat competitive global economic environment.

If one wishes to have a society where social relations are not dependent on the success of institutions in a socialist or capitalist market, then social relations have to be planned. If, on the other hand, one is also committed to maximizing democratic control, then state planning should be confined to geo-political and bio-regional areas of manageable proportions. Hence the virtues of semi-autarky or semi-self-sufficiency. I do not share Bahro's belief in the need for 'basic communes' of no more than a few thousand people. While I have no objection to the development of these 'basic communes', a 'concrete utopia' will need much more elaborate urban and other administrative units of organization straddling the local, regional and national levels.

Small-scale social institutions have their best chance of thriving, inside the boundaries of nation states themselves democratically organized, along lines which aim at self-sufficiency. Yet most nations are, I believe, incapable of full self-sufficiency. Nor do I espouse semi-autarky or full self-sufficiency as a desirable goal in itself. Currently there are semi-autarkies which fail to satisfy a wide range of eco-socialist and democratic criteria. For example, the USA has achieved high levels of self-sufficiency in that only a small part of its overall GDP consists of imports and exports. But the USA is hardly a model of equality, environmental protection or peaceful coexistence! Similarly, the USSR has achieved high levels of self-sufficiency and self-reliance. But its political economy is characterized by one-party dictatorship, intolerance, bureaucratic waste and disregard for environmental and alternative, life-enhancing practices. Finally, there are semi-autarkies in the Third World, most notably Burma, which lack economic resources and democratic political structures – thus making these non-industrialized and undemocratic societies inappropriate and irrelevant models for eco-socialists.

For a combination of environmental, technological and other material reasons, many nation states lack the resources to become fully self-sufficient. That is why a feasible 'concrete utopia' must, in most cases, be a *semi*-autarky. Hence, a certain proportion of vitally needed food, raw materials or other material goods and services will have to be imported from other nations or localities. The social objective of *full* self-sufficiency can also result in narrow parochialism and the selfish neglect of other (less well-endowed) peoples' needs. International trade and assistance are indispensable links between the nations of the world. The limitation to a semi-autarky is therefore both a necessity (due to lack of natural and technical resources), and a positive condition in that greater co-operation between diverse communities can be fostered in all those domains which are non-exploitative.

Because most Left and Right theorists of state institutions have tended to emphasize their political–administrative aspects while neglecting their vital economic and social roles, an unreal anti-statist perspective (the withering away of the state, the minimal state) has dominated contemporary political strategies. A semi-autarkic strategy would recognize that an alternative, eco-socialist society must have new democratic state institutions at the local, regional and national levels. These new state institutions may be organized along federal and non-federal lines, depending on the particular society concerned, for example, Australia or France. New state institutions will employ most (but not all) of the paid workforce and also provide 'social wage' programmes and guaranteed minimum incomes. If one believes that greater democracy also requires the corresponding material structures for local and national sovereignty, then semi-autarky is the only means whereby the political economy of direct and semi-direct democracy can flourish. A socialist internationalism is unlikely to develop from conditions where local co-operation is absent, let alone international co-operation. Greater global integration of productive and administrative forces will inevitably further weaken the structures of local, regional and national control before citizens have even acquired an opportunity to practice local democracy. Advocates of internationalism and socialist global integration usually stress the liberating and broadening effects of supranational planning. But a semi-autarky would encourage vitally needed cultural, political and other relations without individual national and local economies losing control or identity. The onus is on all opponents of semi-autarky to show how hyper-centralization and global integration of the vital material means of production can preserve local democracy.

What we have at the moment is a world dominated by partially democratic or totally undemocratic local, national and supranational government and private bodies. The political task is to democratize these state institutions radically by abolishing all those overt and covert mechanisms whereby power has tended to remain within the hands of small minorities. But a 'political' solution would be self-defeating if the material resources were organized at supranational levels, thus nullifying local and regional democratic forces. This raises the related issues of planning or non-planning, and centralization or decentralization.

## THE NEED FOR CENTRALIZED AND DECENTRALIZED PLANNING

If one desires a society where energy is conserved, where unnecessarily large volumes of raw materials, food and manufactured goods are no longer transported across long distances in millions of environmentally destructive land, sea and air vehicles, where a majority of citizens (rather than private companies and government bureaucracies) determine what, where, and how goods and services are produced, then social planning and open public discourse becomes essential. I have argued that a post-industrial socialist society cannot be based solely upon the inadequate mechanisms of simple barter, moneyless exchanges and other informal sector principles. All those who believe that 'prosuming', simple barter or other forms of socio-economic interaction can replace capitalist markets and state planning – and yet guarantee equity and democracy – are profoundly wrong. Money will continue to be necessary for the foreseeable future – although an increasing number of 'social wage' goods and services could be communally provided, thereby reducing the proportion of necessary material goods or services demanding money.

An alternative society must provide not only wage security but also social security. This is particularly crucial for all those people – especially women and children – not engaged in paid labour. A society committed to social equity and democracy *must* provide the appropriate material floors necessary to eliminate regional and social inequality, and the administrative ceilings or controls to prevent new forms of social inequality and abuse from arising. Each locality and region must have sufficient capital resources for infrastructure and production, and income for recurring expenditure such as wages and 'social wage' programmes. Without *national* state institutions, wage security, social security, and adequate income for recurring expenditure would be most unlikely; the individual's social and labour mobility would be restricted, or undertaken only at risk of poverty, homelessness and unemployment.

I do not propose to discuss in detail all the inadequacies and social inequalities which would develop if market socialism (as proposed by writers such as Alec Nove)[2] were adopted. Instead, I would argue that the best chance of realizing desirable values and social practices, as espoused by eco-socialists, eco-feminists and other supporters of greater equality and democracy, is to be found in the strategy of combined centralized – decentralized planning with minimal market mechanisms. Furthermore, these planning mechanisms would be far more likely to succeed in nation states with populations of less than one hundred million than in countries with very large territorial boundaries and hundreds of millions such as the USSR, USA, China or India. Of course, there are countries with large territories and small populations (for example, Australia or Canada) and countries with small territories and large populations (for example, Japan). There is no ideal size or solution to these problems. The long-term political objective should be the rational break-up of very large societies into genuinely autonomous republics based on ethnic, linguistic, socio-cultural or bio-regional criteria. Of course, such sub-division into more manageable, smaller nation states is politically improbable in the short term. But in the dozens of small to medium sized nation states which currently exist, the following political–economic objectives are highly desirable and, given mass political struggle, realizable within the next few decades.

### Central planning at national level

Several vital roles and functions would have to be institutionalized at the central level because it would either be impracticable, or create unnecessary extra problems, if they were decentralized. Among these centrally planned activities would be: certain forms of tax revenue collection (tax collection would be shared with local and regional bodies to prevent too much fiscal power being concentrated); domestic and foreign currency controls; international trade controls and exchange mechanisms; national post and telecommunications; central budgeting co-ordination; military defence; the administration of a national guaranteed minimum income scheme; and other areas of activity which require national co-ordination and development. The production and circulation activities which would be centrally planned include: raw materials; energy and fuel (except where local, small-scale renewable sources like wind or solar power were more efficient and manageable); key productive elements such as steel; and means of transportation such as national rail, air and sea networks. It is also very important that a large proportion of the manufactured means of production – for example, machine tools, heavy equipment and national research and development – be centrally planned. Small-scale means of production could be left in the hands of decentralized enterprises.

The principal aim of central planning would be to provide the capital goods, raw materials and social income which decentralized social and productive bodies lacked. Central planning would also give vital coherence to national investment strategy – not in the sense of promoting competitive growth in foreign markets, but rather for the necessary task of dividing national resources into areas of need and urgency, emphasizing redistribution, repair, new developments, public works and recurring expenditure. Since no country will be fully self-sufficient, national planning will be needed if foreign trade, aid to less well-endowed countries, and international co-operation in supranational organizations is not to be carried out in a divisive, wasteful and unco-ordinated manner by thousands of local organizations.

### Decentralized planning at local and regional levels

Within regions, cities or localities covered by decentralized planning, there will be three main forms of employment in production, co-ordination, exchange and provision of services:

(1) Employment in democratically controlled state sector institutions and enterprises, for example, 'social wage' programmes in health, education, childcare, factories producing consumer goods, farms, public administration, local transport, cultural institutions and so forth. These facilities will be subjected to *non-market mechanisms* and will be steered by public political deliberation (direct or semi-direct) of all involved citizens, consumers and producers.

(2) Self-organized workers' co-operatives, which will produce goods or deliver services for the local and regional state sector institutions. These co-operatives will operate according to a *mixture* of market mechanisms and state planning. In contracting to provide goods and services for decentralized state sector institutions, co-operatives in the locality and region will be free to compete with one another. But the market mechanisms governing co-operatives will be *limited* and *constrained* by the *non-market* mechanisms of

decentralized and central planning. Planning mechanisms will provide clear guidelines for co-operatives (for example, quantity and quality of goods and services, for which co-operatives can submit tenders), so that market mechanisms will not exhibit the ruthless features of capitalist markets, based as they are on unregulated mechanisms or monopoly corporate price fixing.

(3) Finally, individual and family producers, operating outside planning guidelines and subjected to the following mechanisms: (a) market mechanisms of supply and demand, which determine size of income and the provision of goods and services, for example, food, crafts, personal services and repairs; (b) 'prosuming' or simple barter, whereby individuals, families and small groups provide goods and services in moneyless, self-sufficient transactions.

Several additional explanations are necessary. If one wishes to minimize or avoid the negative social consequences which are inherently part of the competitive struggles associated with market mechanisms – whether capitalist or socialist – market mechanisms have to be reduced to the bare minimum. As I do not believe that stateless societies are either feasible or desirable (if one values democracy and equality), planning must be shared between central and decentralized points of administration. People should not confuse the principle of central planning with command central planning in Eastern Europe. There is no inherent quality in central planning which makes it undemocratic, just as there is no inherent mechanism in market exchange which makes the latter democratic. Rather, planning must be evaluated within the context of a broad range of political-economic institutions and practices. The virtue of a semi-autarky strategy is that political–economic institutions are geared to the short- and long-term objective of *maximizing self-sufficiency* – an objective which is the opposite to central control and dependency favoured by party bureaucrats in the USSR. As to the objective of zero growth, I do not believe that this is an appropriate goal in the short- and medium-term future. Rather, there should be limitation or actual cessation of production in particular industries which are destructive to health and the environment, and significant growth in other areas of the economy such as 'social wage' programmes. There is far too much inequality within nations and between nations to endorse zero growth. The establishment of a semi-autarkic society will not be accomplished in a few years. Hence the vital role of central planning, in directing and increasing socially useful production and the redistribution of resources and income to less privileged regions, groups and individuals – domestically and externally.

Under the system I propose, the main difficulties will arise in those areas of production and distribution where responsibility is shared by central and decentralized authorites. This conflict and clash over priorities is both necessary and healthy. Local and regional authorities will be responsible for planning the bulk of 'social wage' programmes, consumer durables and food production; the more these decentralized communities maximize self-sufficiency, the more the decision-making will occur locally rather than centrally. Central planning will continue to be necessary in the areas of national resource allocation and income maintenance; but the greater the build-up of *local* technological infrastructure in the form of producer goods – that is, the means of production needed to produce consumer goods – the greater the freedom of consumer goods industries from the restrictions imposed by the central planning of scarce resources. In contrast to existing economies which are constantly pressurized to compete – to grow bigger or go bust – or integrate their production with other national economies, the whole *reproductive* thrust of a semi-autarky is towards democratic control over those resources which are considered most important to the people concerned. Existing proposals for market socialist strategies also emphasize the important role of central planning. But these latter models rely far too heavily on market mechanisms for most consumer goods and producer goods, thereby assuring that all the negative aspects of income inequality, rapid industrial growth, pollution and unemployment carry over from capitalist to 'socialist' markets. More importantly, these market socialist models say very little about the vitally needed 'social wage' programmes, which cannot afford to depend on the continued profitability of 'socialist market forces'.

Under the political–economic model that I propose, there is room for individuals and groups to work in co-operatives, engage in simple barter or operate very small market services and alternative forms of small-scale enterprises. Market mechanisms and informal exchanges will always persist in some form or another. The social objective should be one which encourages the provision of personal services, food, repairs and other essentials or leisure requisites in an informal manner. Just as the central planners must aim to maximize local and regional self-sufficiency, so too decentralized planning will aim to produce both wage goods and services *and* 'social wage' essentials in a manner which best combines local knowledge and resources with national concepts of equity, co-operation and environmental sensitivity. Vertical forms of administration and decision-making will continue to be necessary, but limited horizontal exchanges (between enterprises or co-operatives) at local and regional levels will be desirable.

Given the pivotal role of both central and decentralized planning, a form of dual political control will be in-built into the decision-making processes. Those state sector institutions and enterprises governed by *decentralized* planning mechanisms will have to reckon with the activities of two polar opposites: the individuals and groups in the *micro* informal and market sectors, and the *macro*-planners at the central level. This will require local and regional governing bodies to impose administrative ceilings and public control mechanisms upon all those market and bureaucratic activities which threaten to abuse social standards in favour of greed, corruption and privilege; it will also require centrally planned national institutions and enterprises to provide those essential material floors under local and regional communities, to allow equality and democratic socialist pluralism to thrive. In contrast to all those who believe in small-is-beautiful and informal alternative practices without state institutions, a 'concrete utopia' which permits the flourishing of small-scale institutions and limited forms of barter becomes feasible precisely because there are complex local, regional and national institutions governed by decentralized and central planning mechanisms. Each component element at the micro level, the intermediate local and the regional level, as well as at the central level, is oriented towards empowering individuals and groups with structures, facilities and resources necessary for realizing those values promoted by eco-socialists and other contemporary peace-seeking and democratizing movements.

It could be argued that a combination of planning and market mechanisms at decentralized levels would actually result in the dominance of market mechanisms, as co-operatives, small-scale market activities and barter flourished. This is unlikely to eventuate because, in a society oriented to maximizing self-sufficiency, decentralized planning decisions will strictly limit the growth potential of market forces. The more the relevant central and decentralized authorities implement redistributive policies, maximize equity through non-marketable 'social wage' programmes and so on, the less opportunity there will be for market mechanisms to generate continually a culture of consumers avid for over-produced goods. Democratic control of local and national institutions – especially decentralized state institutions – will entail regular public debate over the level of goods and services which should be left to market mechanisms at the micro level, or which could be produced by competing co-operatives. If market mechanisms became dominant, there would soon be increased unemployment, undesirable gaps in income and wealth and a growth in 'socialist businesses' seeking customers at national and international levels. In contrast, the emphasis on semi-autarky undermines the dynamics of perpetual growth, and limits income inequalities through GMI schemes and egalitarian tax systems (thus severely reducing the incentives for profit-making). On the other hand, scarcity of natural and social resources acts as a disciplining incentive for local communities to decide democratically to minimize waste, inefficiency and corruption. Moral incentives are inadequate by themselves; market discipline entails unemployment and social inequality. But, the self-learning processes of decentralized or centralized planning will hold market mechanisms in check, simply because it will be in the citizens' own interests to maintain maximum social equality and democracy through realizing the objectives of semi-self-sufficiency.

## DISARMAMENT AND DEFENSIVE DEFENCE

A post-industrial socialist society is simply not possible if existing military–industrial complexes continue as they are, or are just slightly cut back. I thus share with Bahro and other members of the Green movement a strong opposition to all forms of nuclear deterrence systems and offensive weapons strategies. Nuclear and chemical weapons, and the high-technology innovations with lasers, satellites and so on, are in no way peripheral to contemporary social orders. They cannot be excised without profoundly altering the nature of political–economic power relations. As explained in chapter 3, military R & D is an integral part of the major new forms of high technology development. Local and national democracy depends more and more on reversing all those integrating tendencies which lock economic institutions into technological dependency and military blackmail. A strategy of semi-autarky is impossible if the key technological, fiscal, political and military resources of a nation are pre-empted by membership of military pacts such as NATO or ANZUS. The struggle against nuclear war must inherently be a struggle for unilateral nuclear disarmament, for neutrality, disengagement from the arms race, and disengagement from the competitive pressures of economic and technological rivalry-cum-dependency.

But, while stressing the essential need to disarm existing offensive military establishments, I do not believe that eco-pacifism is a realizable objective in the coming decades. For the foreseeable future there will have to be new national *defensive* defence systems which are integral parts of a planned semi-autarky. Co-operation with other nations will be necessary if supranational treaties, demilitarized zones and conflict-preventing mechanisms are to be introduced. The whole world will not convert to pacifism uniformly or chronologically; hence the need for limited military defence structures organized through central-planning mechanisms. Decentralized regional and local authorities will have a major role in mobilizing citizens, resources and communication channels. Central planning will be essential, since technology or raw materials unavailable domestically will have to be imported from friendly nations until defence preparedness and maximum self-sufficiency are achieved. This will be an extremely difficult transition as economic and military self-sufficiency will be bitterly opposed by the superpowers. Ultimately, the proportion of national resources allocated to defensive defence systems can significantly decline only if the international environment is substantially pacified, and reoriented to co-operation instead of conflict.

## A GLOBAL STANDARD OF LIVING OR CONTINUED INEQUALITY BETWEEN NORTH AND SOUTH?

Figures published in 1984 show that the 1.2 billion people in the North (both West and East) had an economic output of over 11 thousand billion US dollars, compared with less than 3 thousand billion dollars for the 3.6 billion people in the South.[3] Even allowing for a social revolution in the North, the huge gap in living standards between the peoples of the South and the North is unlikely to be fully bridged in our time. This would remain true even if the Northern economies entirely ceased to expand in the future, given their elaborate industrial and technological infrastructure and the material possessions of their citizens. Certainly, an eco-socialist network of Northern semi-autarkies would do a great deal to eliminate exploitative relations between North and South; such countries would minimize the use of imported raw materials and give large amounts of aid to the peoples of the South. But it is far from clear whether the limited industrialization of most Third World countries is ecologically feasible and durable. On the other hand, it is also clear that without massive investment in new fuel and energy sources (whether conventional or alternative) many Third World countries will suffer ecological devastation as impoverished peoples deplete the remaining forests and shrubs for cooking and heating – thus causing deserts, soil erosion and more famine. In the foreseeable future there is no real prospect of radical social change in the South without violence and mass conflict. Third World debt would have to be abolished, transnational corporate domination ended, and militarization of Third World countries reversed. All these changes are inconceivable, or highly improbable, unless major social change occurs in the North. At the moment, the strategy of greater global or supranational economic integration, promoted by Labour, Socialist and Communist parties in OECD countries, runs directly counter to any prospect of fundamental changes in the South. In so far as European or other Left parties support their own private or nationalized transnational companies earning those profits in the South they see as vital, or militarizing the South by exporting arms, competing for new agribusiness markets and so forth, there is no prospect of their 'socialism' becoming anything but a sham.

Contemporary world trade figures show also that approximately 70 per cent of value is embodied in manufactured goods and services, while around 30 per cent is made up of food and primary products such as fuel. A semi-autarkic strategy could significantly alter this ratio (which works to the detriment of nations in the South), by either drastically reducing manufactured exports (from Northern countries) and thus reducing primary product imports from the South, or paying higher prices for primary commodities from the South and thereby generating more income for the internal development of Third World economies. Because of the uneven industrial development of countries in the South, some would import significantly more raw materials as they industrialized further, while others would export less manufactured goods and concentrate on maximizing national self-sufficiency. Semi-autarky presupposes diversity of the means of production which single-crop economies currently lack. An altered ecological consciousness in the North, massive military disarmament and the abolition or minimization of dominant market mechanisms in OECD countries, would greatly transform international trade figures as domestic national economies moved to new forms of co-operation based upon planned semi-autarkic, eco-socialist objectives.

Radicals in the North have veered from belief that revolution in the imperialist countries of the North would liberate the South, to hope that Third World revolutions would engulf the imperialist metropolises. By the 1980s it had become clear that relatively 'peaceful' change in the South can mean only deeper integration into the disastrous policies pursued by the dominant OECD countries. Unless mass politics in the North is significantly radicalized, real social change in the South will be thwarted and distorted by imperial intervention (for example, US intervention in Central America). There can be no effective skipping of the capitalist industrial 'stage' or implementation of alternative 'appropriate technology' as the dominant form of production, until and unless the countries of the South are freed from economic and political exploitation by the capitalist and Communist North. It may sound a cliché, but an annual allocation of just half the 800 billion US dollar world military budget to egalitarian, socially useful expenditure in Third World countries, would eradicate the worst forms of poverty and disease within 10 to 20 years. Little wonder that post-industrial socialism cannot emerge without an end of the world arms race.

## SOCIALIST PLURALISM AND THE NEED FOR NEW STATE INSTITUTIONS

Throughout this book I have tried to show that, despite the positive and desirable images of stateless, radically decentralized, face-to-face alternatives which permeate many new social movements and radical parties, democracy would not survive the abolition of state institutions. Healthy democratic, post-industrial socialist public spheres require all the corresponding legal, cultural, educational and administrative structures which guarantee adjudication, mediation, representation, and checks and balances. I also support the notion of direct democracy in small-scale institutions, and semi-direct democratic representation and recallable delegates in state institutions at city, regional and national levels. There are many imaginative alternatives based on federations of consumer and producer councils, mixes of individual, group and institutional representation, dual forms of checks and balances at regional and national levels, and other realizable proposals for the expansion of citizen democracy. In short, neither representative or direct democratic structures are adequate on their own; combinations of the two are necessary and feasible.

In a semi-autarky based upon central and decentralized planning, there is no escaping the need for bureaucratic administration. But all complex, genuine democracies will require administration. Parties, unions, social pressure groups, international cultural and social organizations must all flourish in an open manner if regulation and dictatorship are not to predominate. Too many radicals think that, to achieve a pluralist democracy, one simply creates the appropriate political institutions, and that 'the economy' will then somehow fit in with the new socialist or Green political mechanisms. But, first, there will not be one form of socialism for all societies, but many variations depending on the country and political forces involved. Second, if any socialist society fails to maximize equity and participation in decision-making, by providing the necessary material floors for all citizens in all regions, its 'socialism' will be just a hollow formality. Third, I believe that the political goal of a semi-autarkic society (rather than market socialism) offers the best hope of realizing direct and semi-direct democratic structures – in other words, the vital material means of political–economic reproduction necessary for an eco-socialist democracy. Fourth, there is no one form of central planning and no one form of market. Even in the dictatorial and unfavourable circumstances of Eastern Europe, the central plan in East Germany has worked much more efficiently than planning in the USSR. The centralization of planning and energy always brings with it the risk of the centralization of political and social power; institutions and organizations have a tendency to want autonomy.[4] There is also the danger that local bodies will avoid difficult problems by 'passing the buck' to central authorities – thus weakening local democracy. However, the desire for institutional autonomy also applies to local and regional bodies. An active citizenry with real decision-making powers would be most unlikely to surrender local power to central authorities without a major public struggle (witness the struggle between local councils and the Thatcher government). In a system where self-sufficiency is in-built into the planning directives of central and decentralized planning bodies, political pluralism is given a vital material base of support in a manner which Soviet command planning, market socialism and private enterprise fail to provide.

Ultimately, any political economic strategy which fails to recognize the central needs of women, the importance of 'social wage' programmes, the need to transform radically public and private forms of consumption and the relationship to the environment, will have failed to break away from the destructive and undemocratic traditions of existing power relations. We often forget that the mere achievement of a peaceful world, free of starvation, homelessness and poverty, is a radical utopia that is practically feasible at this very moment. To construct a new democratic public sphere will not be possible, if a majority of people find greater psychic security in privatized arrangements, irrationalist traditions and occult practices. It can well be a positive thing for socialists to learn the best traditions of alternative medicine and art, to gain psychological insights and so on. But those spiritualist and occult beliefs which de-emphasize the need for democratic public institutions, by cultivating an over-emphasis on emotional feelings, gurus, hyper-anti-rationalism, and exaggerated introspection, only weaken the development of a democratically active socialist citizenry. Weber argued that the Protestant ethic was an important catalyst in the development of capitalist production. What contemporary ideas (including religious ones) assist in the development of a post-industrial socialist society? Bahro challenges the prevailing forms of hedonism and consumerism with a new post-industrial asceticism and

spiritualism. In contrast, I do not believe that the new asceticism embodied in the goal of 'basic communes' and 'industrial
disarmament' will triumph. Nor do I believe that to over-
compensate for the anti-humanism and anti-naturalism of
technical rationality, by a turn to Eastern religions and
spiritualism, will help to bring about a democratic, eco-
socialist future. What is needed is a new rationalism – the
promotion of a cultural diversity and naturalism which
rejects the exploitative and censorial elements of puritanism,
racism, sexism, homophobia and the domination of nature
–while not succumbing to an aimless hedonistic and drug-
addicted pseudo-democracy. Not all theories are equally
truthful, and not all practices are conducive to a vibrant
democracy. Socialist pluralism needs laws to protect the civil
rights of its citizens against unjustifiable encroachments
whether religious or secular. A feasible 'concrete utopia'
must be based upon citizens who are consciously attached to
those social relations and values which assist the democratic
polity, and just as consciously wary of the negative and
destructive ideas and practices that can eat away from within.

## IS THERE A POLITICS OF FEASIBLE
## POST-INDUSTRIAL SOCIALISM?

Given the deep-seated political–economic trends which seem
to push us strongly towards the further global integration of
technological and socio-economic forces, is it not utopian to
advocate a strategy of semi-autarky? The answer is yes. But
then, it is even more utopian to believe that conventional
political–economic policies in capitalist societies will resolve
the major problems of unemployment, poverty, ecological
devastation and threat of nuclear war. There is not much confidence that any of the dominant Rightwing think-tank
reports or conventional Left parliamentary parties' electoral
policies are addressing the major problems of industrial
restructuring, fiscal crises, the arms race, Third World debt,
and other urgent issues which need resolution. *Ad hoc*, short-
term policies, ineffective budgetary incrementalism or fiscal
cuts, token posturing on issues of peace, the environment and

poverty are no substitutes for radically alternative policies. Post-industrial socialism will not come about by leaving change to existing market forces (Toffler), the Fabian evolution of the 'mixed economy' (Jones), by bidding farewell to the proletariat (Gorz), or by rejecting parties because they still have to make strategic compromises (Bahro).

If one rejects eco-catastrophe politics of the Bahro school, then there must be engagement and struggle with the organizations, policies and structures of existing public and private spheres. The major problem is: How can one be politically effective without succumbing to the logic of conventional Left parties and unions, themselves constituent elements of the system to be opposed? In capitalist societies with free electoral processes, there are still only a few political options open to those who desire a post-industrial socialist society. These options revolve around the positive or negative consequences of planning and regulation. By withdrawing from political struggle within existing state institutions, one leaves the future to be determined by conservative forces and non-radical Labour, Socialist and Communist parties. No social movement can hope to implement policies on unilateral nuclear disarmament, equal wages for women, stringent environmental controls and other eco-socialist policies, without organizations which affect state power. If we withdraw from electoral politics, then we must simply stand by while New Right forces carry out their dreams of a totally deregulated market system, or else traditional Left governments assimilate the labour and new social movements in a new neo-corporatism, by blackmailing them with the New Right threat. For most future struggles will be about the degree of planned, political regulation over socio-economic activities, and the degree of corporate evasion and of minimization of regulatory controls over profit-making enterprises.

To withdraw from party politics is of course mandatory, if one believes in a crisis collapse theory or one wishes to remain uncontaminated by conventional problems in the decadent system. From this view, social movement struggles 'outside' the existing political system can only hope to weaken existing orders until they supposedly collapse (a variety of catastrophe politics, in which one believes the system approaches its doom but still needs a strong push). A similar ineffectiveness awaits new radical political parties without a mass grass-roots base, who will most likely dwindle like existing Left parties if they pursue a strategy based solely upon electoral politics. It is true that new social organizations can advance equality and democracy by struggles outside the party system (for example, the movements of the 1960s and early 1970s). These pace-setting struggles and new political agendas influenced even Left parliamentary parties. But the general failure of Left parliamentary parties (with some minor exceptions) actively to encourage mass non-electoral campaigns and struggles, is mirrored by many new social movement organizations who disavow electoral politics and relations with state institutions. Both practices are ultimately ineffective and conservative.

It is clear that no single party or movement can bring about radical social change in capitalist societies characterized by a plurality of social organizations and of subcultural values and practices. But to urge increased control over current economic, military and general socio-environmental policies, as I do, does not imply any belief that capitalist societies can be successfully managed as they peacefully transform themselves into post-industrial socialist societies. In rejecting the belief that capitalist societies are inevitably doomed to collapse in catastrophe, whether economic, ecological or military, I do not wish to go to the other extreme and approve those pragmatic Left technocrats who naïvely or cynically tout their capacities to crisis manage. First, ecological or military catastrophe would hardly provide the conditions for socialist renewal – even if we assumed some human life survived. In the second place, economic catastrophe would not in itself bring about socialist change without a mass mobilized coalition of new social movements, unions and radical parties.

One may therefore ask what is the point of increasing regulatory controls over more and more parts of national political economies if these capitalist systems cannot be successfully managed? The answer has much to do with my belief that the immediate defensive struggles of workers and representative organizations of new social movements are absolutely essential, whether one believes in the successful management or crisis collapse of capitalism. The fluctuating fortunes of capital or labour cannot be predicted; capitalist societies may collapse, full-employment may one day return, or revolution may eventuate. In the meantime, the enormous problems posed by social welfare, the threat of nuclear annihilation, chemical pollution and so forth, demand immediate intervention if any alternative 'concrete utopia' is to have a real chance of being realized in the medium to long term. Without political and social forces intervening in all the relevant state and private institutions, the future will be shaped by our opponents. If one believes that a strategy oriented towards an eco-socialist semi-autarky offers the best hope for humanity, then there are a thousand tasks and policies which can be pursued at the moment – all necessary preconditions for maximizing local and national self-sufficiency. These policy objectives – which will vary from country to country – will undoubtedly be incompatible with the profitable activities of many (though not all) private firms. Alternative economic strategies which appear to promote semi-autarkic solutions, but are based on slight variations of existing capitalist 'mixed economies' are doomed to fail. I mention this, as there is always the danger that coalitions of workers and chauvinistic business organizations, championing narrow, national capitalist interests may prove to be popular in times of crisis. On the other hand, it would be naïve to believe that market forces will suddenly cease operating simply because eco-socialist political forces triumph in local and national electoral *and* non-electoral struggles. Short of revolution, many businesses will continue to exist – either in opposition to new radical coalitions, or in an uneasy relationship marked perhaps by some limited form of co-operation from small-scale enterprises.

There can be no illusion, however, about the general thrust of electoral and non-electoral struggles oriented towards eco-socialist semi-self-sufficiency. The more controls limit the dangerous and inequitable activities of private corporations and individuals, the more capitalist societies will be polarized and conflict-ridden. This scenario may alarm many well-intentioned reformers whose support is vitally needed if radical environmental, anti-nuclear and egalitarian policies (especially in the reorganization of work and social income) are to succeed. But it is better to be honest about the potential dangers and the conflicts which will arise, than to manipulate large numbers of people into following paternalistic leaders and parties.

The failure of traditional revolutionary parties is apparent to all but their incorrigible faithful. The few which are mass parties find their appeal dwindling; the majority remain insignificant; for all, their time has long since passed. Any new radical party must be able to incorporate the contemporary eco-feminist and eco-socialist concerns of the large numbers of concerned individuals fed up with the limits and abuses of traditional parties. The Green parties in West Germany and other countries are indeed welcome developments in this direction. But they too are still highly influenced by many of the unfeasible ideas which I have analysed in earlier chapters. We have yet to see the emergence of new parties and groups which will strongly champion many of the eco-socialist strategies associated with central–decentralized socialist state planning, and which will recognize the indispensable role of state institutions in providing adequate 'social wage' programmes and co-ordinating semi-autarkic forms of material reproduction. Until individuals and groups accept the unpalatable news that stateless, decentralized, moneyless, small-scale communes or other informal alternatives are not viable without the complex administrative and social structures necessary to guarantee democratic participation, civil rights and egalitarian co-ordination of economic resources, there is not much hope of strong coalitions between labour movements and new social movements. Similarly, there is little prospect of new coalitions until trade unions abandon their conservative opposition to values and practices promoted by new social movements.

Given the steady diet of bad news which radical individuals and groups confront on a daily basis, expectations often develop that some group or individual will theorize and develop an ultimate answer to the problems of theory and practice. Such idle wishfulness evades the painful reality of the hard grind. There will be no smooth transition to a society based on principles entirely opposed to the present destructive and irrational social orders. In Eastern Europe, political rebellion caused by stagnation or crisis may result in further democratization. But in the USSR there is no likelihood of political rebellion succeeding or internal changes in the direction of democracy and equity (implemented from above), without a significant reversal of the arms race and Cold War hostility. However, to achieve nuclear disarmament in the West (or even *détente* between West and East), to defeat the New Right thrust, to discredit those forces within Left parliamentary parties which are moving steadily to the right, and to advance those causes championed by feminists, ecologists, ethnic and racial minorities and other social movements, will require every ounce of energy and determination. If most Third World countries are unlikely to change without social revolution or drastic reforms at the very least, the protracted stalemate between opposing social forces in OECD countries is destined to simmer and erupt as new political alignments and crises unfold.

To sum up, we need a new vision and a new sense of direction. Labour, Socialist and Communist parties are generally bankrupt. It is difficult to think of a single, major innovative policy which has originated from within the ranks of these parties in recent years. But so many of these party spokespersons heap scorn upon radical critics because politics, they claim, is about the hard grind and the 'art of the possible'. Yet without the imaginative ideas of people like the post-industrial utopians, politics becomes nothing more than the myopic, self-justifying and often cynical hard grind. If earlier generations had not dared to think the impossible, we would not have achieved much that is now taken for granted. Yet, if the alternatives are not feasible, all the passion in the world will go tragically astray. It is for this reason that a 'concrete utopia' based upon eco-socialist, semi-autarkic principles – and geared to existing, but surmountable problems – combines passion and perspective with steadfastness of heart.

# Notes

## INTRODUCTION

1 K. Kumar, *Prophecy and Progress* (Harmondsworth: Penguin, 1978), pp. 193–4; for a general survey also see R. Badham, 'The Sociology of Industrial and Post-Industrial Societies' in *Current Sociology*, 32, 1984, pp. 1–141.
2 See B. S. Page, 'Anatomy of a Theory: The Post Industrial Theory' in *Critical Anthropology*, 2 (2), 1972, pp. 29–57; S. Michael Miller, 'Notes on Neo-Capitalism' in *Theory and Society*, 2 (1), 1975, pp. 1–35; and T. Schroyer, 'Review of The Coming of Post–Industrial Society' in *Telos* (19), 1974, pp. 162–76.
3 See D. Bell, *The End of Ideology* (Glencoe: Free Press, 1960).
4 D. Bell, *The Cultural Contradictions of Capitalism* (New York: Basic Books, 1976).
5 See the Trilateral Task Force on the Governability of Democracies, *The Governability of Democracies* (New York: Trilateral Commission, 1975).
6 H. Kahn *The Coming Boom* (London: Hutchinson, 1983), and also J. Simon and H. Kahn, (eds), *The Resourceful Earth A Response to Global 2000* (Oxford: Basil Blackwell, 1984).
7 D. Bell, *The Cultural Contradictions of Capitalism*, pp. xxx–xxxi; for an appreciative study of Bell's writings, see J. A. Hall, *Diagnoses of Our Time* (London: Heinemann, 1981), ch. 4.
8 See R. J. Bernstein (ed.), *Habermas and Modernity* (Oxford: Polity Press, 1985).
9 D. Bell, *The Coming of Post-Industrial Society* (Harmondsworth: Penguin, 1976), p. 488.
10 See Kahn, *The Coming Boom*, ch. 9.

11 P. Shack, 'How the Utopian Vision Can Make Things Happen' in *The Australian*, 28 September 1985, p. 10.

12 R. Nozick, *Arnarchy, State, And Utopia* (New York: Basic Books, 1974). In a review of Nozick I wrote that his philosophy of 'rightwing anarchism' is 'a strange amalgam of some of the worst features of the "counter culture" (e.g. do your own thing and other escapist and egoistical, disinterested "tolerance") as well as Wall Street ethics. While his theory is "ahistorical" in its acceptance of the state-of-nature original position, behind the "veil of ignorance" is the actual historical logic of ruthless, manipulative business practice. Nozick's abstract analysis of socialism in one factory, or "socialism in one suburb" is a public relations handout for academics seeking refuge from their tarnished "Community of scholars" which, in earlier days, was also conceived as a harmonious utopia.' See Review Symposium on Anarchy, State, And Utopia in *Theory and Society*, 3, 1976, p. 448.

13 E. F. Schumacher, *Small Is Beautiful: A Study of Economics as if People Mattered* (London: Abacus, 1974).

14 I. Illich, *Tools for Conviviality* (London: Fontana, 1975).

15 J. Galtung, *The True Worlds: A Transnational Perspective* (New York: Free Press, 1980).

16 Ralf Nader's campaign for safe products, corruption-free politicians and other reforms, has spawned numerous consumer activist and citizen initiatives against big business and big government.

17 S. Nora and A. Minc, *The Computerization of Society* (Cambridge, Mass: MIT Press, 1981).

18 E.g. see the journal *Alternatives* and R. Falk, *A Study of Future Worlds* (New York: Free Press, 1975). Also see R. Kothari, *Towards A Just World* (New York: Institute for World Order, 1980).

19 There has been a considerable proliferation of organizations, journals and books on North–South relations, the food crisis and energy consumption, e.g. The New Internationalist, Institute For Food and Development Policy/Food First, Worldwatch Institute, Greenpeace, Agenor, Future in Our Hands, etc.

20 See Bell, *The Coming of Post-Industrial Society*, p. 37 and also M. Marien, 'The Two Visions of Post-Industrial Society' in *Futures*, October 1977, pp. 415–31, for a brief discussion of Penty.

21 See Peter Fuller's and Mike Cooley's contributions in ICA (eds) *William Morris Today* (London: Journeyman Press, 1984).

22 See H. Marcuse, *An Essay on Liberation* (Harmondsworth: Penguin, 1969), and M. Bookchin, *Post-Scarcity Anarchism* (Berkeley: Ramparts Press, 1971).
23 Published by Random House, New York, 1971.
24 R. Richta (ed.), *Civilization at the Cross-Roads* (Sydney: Australian Left Review Publications, 1967).
25 R. Jungk and J. Galtung (eds), *Mankind 2000* (London: George Allen and Unwin, 1969).
26 C. Lasch, 'Toward a Theory of Post-Industrial Society' in M. D. Hancock and C. Sjoberg (eds), *Politics in the Post-Welfare State* (New York: Columbia University Press, 1971), pp. 36–50.
27 Ibid., p. 37.
28 L. Hirschhorn, *Two Essays on the Transition to Post-Industrialism* (Working Paper No. 170, May 1972); *Towards a Political Economy of the Service Sector* (Working Paper No. 229, February 1974); *The Social Service Crisis and the New Subjectivity* (Working Paper No. 224, December 1974); *The Social Crisis – The Crisis of Work and Social Services Part 1* (Working Paper No. 251, March 1975) and Part 2 (Working Paper No. 252, May 1975) Institute of Urban and Regional Development, Berkeley.
29 Hirschhorn, *The Social Crisis – The Crisis of Work and Social Services Part 1*, p. iv.
30 Hirschhorn, *Toward a Political Economy of the Service Sector*, p. 10.
31 Hirschhorn, *The Social Service Crisis and the New Subjectivity*, p. 32.
32 The Centre was intended to be an institute for the analysis of changing patterns in capitalist societies.
33 See J. Baudrillard et al. in K. Woodward (ed.), *The Myths of Information: Technology and Postindustrial Culture* (London: Routledge & Kegan Paul, 1980). For a critique of Baudrillard, see G. Gill, 'Post-Structuralism as Ideology' in *Arena* (69) 1984, pp. 60–96.
34 J. F. Lyotard, *The Postmodern Condition*, trans. by G. Bennington and B. Massumi. (Manchester: Manchester University Press, 1984), p. 3.
35 See F. Jameson 'Postmodernism or the Cultural Logic of Late Capital' in *New Left Review* (146) 1984, pp. 53–92; M. Davis, 'Urban Renaissance and the Spirit of Postmodernism' in *New Left Review* (151), 1985, pp. 106–13; M. Berman, *All That is Solid melts into Air* (London: Verso, 1983); P. Anderson,

'Modernity and Revolution' in *New Left Review* (144), 1984, pp. 96–113 and Berman's reply, 'The Signs in the Street', in ibid, pp. 114–23; and R. Rorty, 'Habermas and Lyotard on Post-Modernity' in *Praxis International*, 4 (1), 1984, pp. 32–44.

36 See A. Touraine, *The Voice and the Eye: An Analysis of Social Movements* (Cambridge: Cambridge University Press, 1981).

37 See F. Capra and C. Spretnak, *Green Politics* (New York: E. P. Dutton, 1984); and W. Hulsberg, 'The Greens at the Cross-Roads' in *New Left Review* (152), 1985, pp. 5–29.

38 J. Gershuny, *Social Innovation and the Division of Labour* (Oxford: Oxford University Press, 1983); T. Stonier, *The Wealth of Information* (London: Methuen, 1983) and K. Sale, *Human Scale* (New York: Coward, McCann & Geoghegan, 1980.

39 Published by New Left Books, London, 1978.

40 Trans. by M. Nicolaus and V. Ortiz and published by Beacon Press, Boston, 1967.

41 Published by Pan Books, London, 1985.

42 South End Press and Pan Books, London, 1984.

43 See *Farewell to the Working Class* (London: Pluto Press, 1982), pp. 145–52.

44 R. Bahro, *From Red to Green* (London: Verso, 1984), p. 220.

45 Toffler, *Previews and Premises*, p. 36.

46 Ibid., p. 46, and *The Third Wave*, (London: Pan Books, 1981), p. 50.

47 Toffler, *The Third Wave*, p. 368.

48 Touraine, *The Voice and the Eye*, p. 19.

49 Quoted by Kumar, *Prophecy and Progress*, p. 241.

50 H. Marcuse, 'The End of Utopia' in *Ramparts*, April 1970, pp. 28–34.

51 Ibid., p. 28.

52 G. Lukacs, *Tactics and Ethics* (New York: Harper & Row, 1975), pp. 15–16.

53 H. Gintis, 'Towards A Political Economy of Education: A Radical Critique of Ivan Illich's Deschooling Society' in *Harvard Education Review*, 42 (1), February 1972, pp. 70–96.

54 F. Engels, *Herr Eugen Duhring's Revolution in Science (Anti-Duhring)*, trans. by E. Burns (New York: International Publishers, 1970), p. 290.

55 Quoted by Frank and Fritzie Manuel, *Utopian Thought in the Western World*, (Cambridge, Mass.: Harvard University Press, 1979), p. 702. Also see S. Lukes, 'Marxism and Utopianism' in P. Alexander and R. Gill (eds), *Utopians* (London: Duckworth, 1984), pp. 153–67.

## 1 MORE INTEGRATION OR MORE AUTARKY

1 I. Kristol, 'Capitalism, Socialism, and Nihilism' in R. Kirk (ed.), *The Portable Conservative Reader* (Harmondsworth: Penguin, 1982), p. 630.

2 D. Bell, *The Coming of Post-Industrial Society* (Harmondsworth: Penguin, 1973); H. Kahn and A. J. Weiner, *The Year 2000* (New York: Macmillan Co., 1967); and Z. Brzezinski, *Between Two Ages: America's Role in the Technetronic Era* (New York: Viking Press, 1970).

3 See B. Jones's citation of Gross's work in *Sleepers Wake!* (Oxford University Press: Melbourne, 1982), p. 6.

4 Ibid.

5 Ibid., pp. 11–14.

6 See my critique of Long Wave theory in *Beyond the State?* (London: Macmillan, 1983), pp. 47–55.

7 Jones, *Sleepers Wake!* p. 44.

8 Toffler, *The Third Wave*, p. 274.

9 Ibid., p. 24.

10 Ibid., p. 335.

11 See ibid., chs 18 and 19.

12 Ibid., pp. 241–3.

13 Ibid., p. 227.

14 See ibid., ch. 20.

15 Ibid., pp. 295–9.

16 Ibid., p. 296.

17 Ibid., chs 16 and 22.

18 P. and P. Goodman, *Communitas: Means of Livelihood and Ways of Life* (New York: Vintage Books, 1960).

19 See M. Bookchin, *Post-Scarcity Anarchism* (Berkeley: Ramparts Press, 1971); G. Boyle and P. Harper (eds), *Radical Technology* (Ringwood: Penguin, 1976); *Programme of the German Green Party* (London: Heretic Books, 1983); D. Dickson, *Alternative Technology and the Politics of Technical Change* (London: Fontana, 1974) or journals such as *Undercurrents* and *Chain Reaction*.

20 J. Gershuny and I. Miles, *The New Service Economy* (London: Pinter, 1983).

21 See Jones, *Sleepers Wake!* pp. 50–2.

22 See ibid.; also see T. Stonier, *The Wealth of Information* (London: Methuen, 1983), chs 11 and 12.

23 R. Bahro, 'Fundamental Green Positions: For an Ecological Response to the Economic Crisis', October 1982 (Mimeo), p. 2.

24 A. Gorz, 'The Reconquest of Time' in *Telos* (55), Spring 1983, pp. 213–14.

25 Ibid.; also see *Farewell to the Working Class*, Appendix 1.

26 Bahro, 'Fundamental Green Positions', p. 2, also see R. Bahro, *Building The Green Movement*, trans. by Mary Tyler (London: Heretic Books, 1986), pp. 17–19 and 86–91.

27 Published in New York by Coward, McCann & Geoghegan, 1980.

28 See part 2 of my *Beyond The State*?

29 See R. Carlson, W. Harman, P. Schwartz and Associates, *Energy Futures, Human Values and Lifestyles* (Boulder: Westview Press, 1982).

30 Ibid., chs 3, 4 and 5.

31 Toffler, *The Third Wave*, pp. 441–4.

32 A. Gorz, 'The Limits of Self-Determination and Self-Management: An Interview' in *Telos* (55), 1983, p. 222.

33 Stonier, *The Wealth of Information*, and B. Jones, 'Australia as Post-Industrial Society' (Melbourne: Commission for the Future, 1986).

34 E.g. see W. P. Dizard Jr, *The Coming Information Age* (New York: Longman, 1982).

35 R. H. S. Crossman (ed.), *The New Fabian Essays* (London: Turnstile Press, 1952), p. 42.

36 K. Windschuttle, 'High Tech and Jobs' in *Australian Society*, November 1984, pp. 11–13. Windschuttle draws upon the work of Henry Levin and Russell Rumberger of Stanford University who have shown that most new jobs in the USA will not be in high skilled occupations. Rather, unskilled jobs such as janitors, guards, hospital orderlies and fast food salespersons will increase in the new 'high tech' society. Windschuttle cites Levin and Rumberger's analysis in order to criticize Barry Jones and other advocates of high technology solutions to current economic crises. Yet, amazingly, Windschuttle concludes that a high technology future is 'the only pathway' despite his earlier arguments against the promise of skilled jobs put forward by post-industrial theorists. Jones and Windschuttle are hoping that a minority of skilled, high technology jobs will produce many unskilled jobs (the multiplier effect). This hope is based more on faith than on any firmly based analysis of political economic trends, i.e. which new industries will emerge, or how to finance expanded public sectors and improved social welfare programes, etc.

37 A. Gorz, 'The American Model and the French Left' in *Socialist Review* (84), November–December 1985, pp. 101–8.

38 See A. Etzioni and P. Jargowsky, 'High Tech, Basic Industry and the Future of the American Economy' in *Human Resource Management*, 23 (3), 1984, pp. 229–40; M. Harrington and M. Levison, 'The Perils of a Dual Economy' in *Dissent*, Fall 1985, pp. 417–26; and R. Gordon and L. M. Kimball, 'High Technology, Employment and Challenges to Education' in *Prometheus*, 3 (2), December 1985, pp. 315–30.

39 Figures cited in Harrigton and Levinson, 'Perils of a Dual Economy'.

40 See OECD figures reported in *The Economist*, 1 September 1984, p. 83.

41 Ibid.

42 See 'Nirvana by Numbers' in *The Economist*, 24 December 1983, p. 54.

43 See OECD figures for social security expenditure in leading capitalist countries reproduced in *The German Tribune*, 4 March 1984, p. 5. For example, in 1981, social security costs as a percentage of national product were 33.5% and 31.5% in Sweden and West Germany compared with only 21% in the USA. Also, public sector or state employees made up 37% of the paid workforce in Sweden, 30% in Britain, 26% in Australia, compared with only 18% in the USA – from OECD figures quoted by G. Therborn, 'Britain Left Out' in *New Socialist* May/June 1984, pp. 24–8.

44 For a good analysis of the nature and form of basic research and R & D in the USA – where about 70% of government research money goes to military R & D – see D. Dickson, *The New Politics of Science* (New York: Pantheon, 1984), p. 21.

45 For a survey of cost cutting in OECD public sectors, see D. Tarschys, 'Curbing Public Expenditure: Current Trends' in *Journal of Public Policy*, 5 (1), 1985, pp. 23–67. While tax revenue as a percentage of GDP varied from 27% to over 50% in different OECD countries, there is no simple equation between tax rates and socio-economic policy. For example, Holland and Belgium have high tax rates and high unemployment, while Sweden and Norway have high tax rates and low unemployment rates. For tax revenue as a percentage of GDP to go up from 27% and 30.5% (in Japan and the USA respectively) to over 50% would require major political changes. Even then, broad aggregate tax figures do not in themselves constitute radical changes if the burden of extra taxes

continues to fall on workers' shoulders (rather than on
corporations and the rich) and if state expenditure is allocated
in the same old patterns. Too many commentators repeat the
mistake of citing broad budgetary figures (such as the size of the
deficit), rather than examining the qualitative aspects of
individual national budgetary revenue and expenditure items.
The key question is not the size of the state sector, but in what
way these institutions and processes assist or undermine the
power and social relations of dominant classes.

46  See *The Economist*, 15 June 1985, p. 32.
47  B. Lozano, 'Informal Sector Workers; Walking Out of the
    System's Front Door?' in *International Journal of Urban and
    Regional Research*, September 1983, pp. 340–61; also see
    N. Redclift and E. Mingione (eds), *Beyond Employment*
    (Oxford: Blackwell, 1985), especially P. Connolly's chapter,
    pp. 55–91, for a good critique of the ideology of informal sectors.
48  For a comprehensive study of the historical origins and relative
    strengths and weaknesses of co-operatives in European capitalist
    societies, see J. Thornley, *Workers and Co-operatives*: *Jobs
    and Dreams* (London: Heinemann, 1981).
49  E.g. in the USA there have recently been about 108,000 co-
    operatives and 5 of these were large enough to be on Fortune
    Magazine's top 500 companies in the early 1970s – see
    E. Etzioni-Halevy, *Social Change* (London: Routledge & Kegan
    Paul, 1981), p. 251.
50  See Frankel, *Beyond the State?*, pp. 194–6.
51  See R. Oakeshott, 'The Group of Mondragon Co-operatives in
    the Basque Provinces of Spain as an Intriguing and Working
    Model for Small and Medium-Sized Enterprises' in E. Goodman
    (ed.), *Non-Conforming Radicals of Europe* (London:
    Duckworth & Co., 1983), pp. 218–34. Also see Collective
    Design/Project (ed.), *Very Nice Work If you Can Get It*
    (Nottingham: Spokesman, 1985), for a collection which praises
    Mondragon and other co-operatives.
52  See D. Zwerdling, 'The Uncertain Revival of Food Co-
    operatives' in J. Case and R. C. R. Taylor (eds), *Co-ops,
    Communes and Collectives Experiments in Social  Change in
    the 1960s and 1970s* (New York: Pantheon Books, 1979),
    pp. 89–111, and A. Gorz, *Paths To Paradise on the Liberation
    From Work*, trans. by M. Imrie (London: Pluto Press, 1985),
    p. 20.
53  See P. Jay, 'The Workers' Co-operative Economy' and general
    discussion of Peter Jay's proposals in A. Clayre (ed.), *The*

*Political Economy of Co-operation and Participation* (Oxford: Oxford University Press, 1980).

54 R. Bahro, *The Alternative* (London: New Left Books, 1978).

55 Ibid., p. 447.

56 See *Programme of the German Green Party* (London: Heretic Books, 1983). As long-term objectives, most of the policies in the Green Programme are realistic to the extent that they presuppose the non-existence of capitalist production. It is the short-term policies (to be implemented in capitalist West Germany) which appear unrealistic, e.g., abolition of low pay, etc. Many of these worthy policies can only be implemented by defeating capitalist classes.

57 Bahro, *Building the Green Movement*, p. 18.

58 See *Beyond The State?*, ch. 12, for a discussion of decentralized planning options put forward by writers such as Albert and Hahnel.

59 Sale, *Human Scale*, parts 4 and 5.

60 Gorz, *Farewell to the Working Class*, ch. 8.

61 Ibid., p. 102.

62 Ibid., p. 98; also see *Paths to Paradise*, pp. 64–77.

63 Gorz, *Farewell to the Working Class*, p. 101.

64 See J. Berger and N. Kostede, 'Review of Farewell to the Working Class' in *Telos* (51), Spring 1982, p. 232.

65 See Gorz, *Paths to Paradise*, pp. 24–8.

66 See Gorz, *Farewell to the Working Class*, pp. 114–15.

67 A. Gorz, 'Security. Against What? For What? With What?' in *Telos* (58), Winter 1983–4, pp. 158–68.

68 M. Bookchin, 'Review of A. Gorz Ecology as Politics' in *Telos* (46), Winter 1980–1, p. 188. While I do not share many of Bookchin's views, he is a very perceptive critic and manages to highlight a number of glaring inconsistencies in 'Gorzutopia' such as his embarrassing praise for non-radical Californians like Jerry Brown.

## 2   THE FEASIBILITY OF ALTERNATIVES TO BUREAUCRATIC WELFARE STATES

1 For an analysis of New Right values and practices, see N. Bosanquet, *After the New Right* (London: Heinemann, 1983); S. Hall et al., *Policing the Crisis: Mugging, the State, and Law and Order* (London: Macmillan, 1978); P. Armstrong, A. Glyn and J. Harrison, *Capitalism Since World War II*

(London: Fontana, 1984), ch. 18; B. Jessop et al. 'Authoritarian Populism, Two Nations, and Thatcherism' in *New Left Review* (147), 1984, pp. 32–60.

2 See H. Marcuse, *One Dimensional Man* (London: Routledge & Kegan Paul, 1964); I. Illich, *Tools for Conviviality* (London: Calder & Boyars, 1973); C. Lasch, *The Culture of Narcissism* (New York: Warner Books, 1979); C. Offe, *Contradictions in the Welfare State*, ed. by J. Keane (London: Hutchinson, 1984); J. Donzelot, *The Policing of Families* (New York: Pantheon Books, 1979); S. Bolger et al., *Towards Socialist Welfare Work* (London: Macmillan, 1981); P. Carlen and M. Collison (eds), *Radical Issues in Criminology* (Oxford: Martin Robertson, 1980), and F. F. Piven and R. Cloward, *Regulating the Poor* (New York: Vintage, 1972).

3 O. Giarini, *Dialogue on Wealth and Welfare* (Oxford: Pergamon Press, 1980), p. 369. For similar views see S. Bergstrom (ed.), *Economic Growth and the Role of Science Proceeding From a Symposium in Stockholm 1983* (Stockholm: Swedish Research Councils, 1984).

4 See H. Henderson, *The Politics of the Solar Age Alternatives to Economics* (New York: Anchor Press, 1981), also see Bergstrom (ed.), *Economic Growth*.

5 E.g. see P. Corrigan and P. Leonard, *Social Work Practice Under Capitalism* (London: Macmillan, 1978); B. Deacon, *Social Policy and Socialism* (London: Pluto Press, 1983); I. Gough, *The Political Economy of the Welfare State* (London: Macmillan, 1979); Offe, *Contradictions in the Welfare State*; Piven and Cloward, *Regulating the Poor*; D. Massey, L. Segal and H. Wainwright, 'And Now for the Good News' in J. Curran (ed.), *The Future of the Left* (Cambridge: Polity Press, 1984), pp. 211–27, and A. Coote, 'A New Starting Point' in ibid. pp. 316–22.

6 See J. Stephens, *The Transition From Capitalism to Socialism* (London: Macmillan, 1979); G. Therborn, 'The Prospects of Labour and the Transformation of Advanced Capitalism' in *New Left Review* (145), 1984, pp. 5–38; V. George and P. Wilding, *The Impact of Social Policy* (London: Routledge & Kegan Paul, 1984); I. Gough, *The Political Economy of the Welfare State* (London: Macmillan, 1979), and F. Castles, *The Working Class and Welfare* (Sydney: George Allen and Unwin, 1985).

7 E.g. see A. Brown and M. Kaser (eds), *Soviet Policy for the 1980s* (London: Macmillan, 1982), chs 6, 7 and 8 by A. McAuley,

A. Nove and M. Kaser; also see Deacon *Social Policy and Socialism*, chs 3–7, and G. Littlejohn, *A Sociology of the Soviet Union* (London: Macmillan, 1984).

8 E.g. see the debate over the US social security system, P. Peterson, 'Social Security: the Coming Crash' and 'The Salvation of Social Security' both in *New York Review of Books*, 2 December 1982, pp. 34–8 and 16 December 1982, pp. 50–7; also see replies to Peterson in ibid. by A. H. Mannell and R. Rinder, 'The Future of Social Security: An Exchange', 17 March 1983, pp. 41–57.

9 For a comparative survey of social security costs and the aged, see 'A Granny Crisis is Coming' in *The Economist*, 19 May 1984, pp. 55–8. While the ageing population will certainly impose severe strains on particular national welfare budgets in the next 30 years, there is a tendency to exaggerate the burden of the aged and use this demographic change as an ideological justification for cutting welfare spending or increasing private responsibility for income security.

10 See 'Big Government – How Big is It? in *The OECD Observer*, March 1983, pp. 6–12, for a survey of employment in state institutions.

11 For detailed analyses which show why existing 'social wage' programmes have failed to eradicate poverty, see J. LeGrand, *The Strategy of Equality: Redistribution and Social Services* (London: George Allen and Unwin, 1982) and George and Wilding, *The Impact of Social Policy*. While these authors concentrate on the British experience, many of their observations are equally applicable to other OECD countries.

12 E.g. see P. Smith (ed.), *Seminar on Guaranteed Minimum Income* (Sydney: ACOSS, 1975).

13 K. Hinrichs, C. Offe and H. Wiesenthal, 'The Crisis of the Welfare State and Alternative Modes of Work Redistribution' in *Thesis Eleven* (10/11), 1984–5, pp. 37–55.

14 See P. K. Robins, R. G. Spiegelman and S. Weiner (eds), *A Guaranteed Annual Income: Evidence From a Social Experiment* (New York: Academic Press, 1980); S. Masters and I. Garfinkel, *Estimating the Labour Supply Effects of Income Maintenance Alternatives* (New York: Academic Press, 1977); and M. Rein, *Dilemmas of Welfare Policy: Why Work Strategies Haven't Worked* (New York: Praeger, 1982).

15 Gorz, *Farewell to the Working Class*, p. 149.

16 Jones, *Sleepers Wake!*, pp. 242–3.

17 *Programme of the German Green Party*, p. 41.

18 A. Toffler, *Previews and Premises* (London: Pan Books, 1984), p. 58.
19 Ibid.
20 Ibid.
21 J. Gershuny and I. Miles, *The New Service Economy* (London: Pinter, 1983), ch. 9.
22 Jones, *Sleepers Wake!*, ch. 11.
23 Gershuny and Miles, *The New Service Economy*, ch. 10.
24 Jones, *Sleepers Wake!*, ch. 11.
25 As Minister for Science, Jones was reported to have been very upset and as having threatened to resign from the Hawke Government over the very poor funding allocations for his ministry in the 1984–5 budget.
26 E.g. see H. Kahn, *The Coming Boom* (London: Hutchinson, 1983).
27 Jones, *Sleepers Wake!*, p. 243 and pp. 204–5.
28 Toffler, *The Third Wave*, ch. 17.
29 See Toffler, *Previews and Premises*, ch. 5, where he talks of the 'cognitariat' replacing the proletariat.
30 Toffler, *The Third Wave*, p. 220.
31 Gorz, *Farewell to the Working Class*, p. 4.
32 A. Gorz, *Paths to Paradise On the Liberation from Work*, trans. by M. Imrie (London: Pluto Press, 1985), p. 48.
33 Ibid., p. 58.
34 Ibid., p. 57.
35 Ibid., p. 62.
36 Ibid.
37 Ibid., pp. 44–5.
38 See Bahro, *Socialism and Survival*, p. 130, and *From Red to Green*, pp. 212–13.
39 Bahro, *From Red to Green*, p. 171.
40 Ibid., pp. 171–2.
41 Ibid., p. 173. Another German, Thomas Schmidt, has also produced a book on the need to free people from 'false labour' via the provision of a GMI. For a discussion of Schmidt and other Greens, see W. Hulsberg, 'The Greens at the Cross-Roads' in *New Left Review* (152), 1985, pp. 5–29.
42 Gorz, *Farewell to the Working Class*, pp. 150–1.
43 Ibid., p. 103.
44 Ibid., p. 83.
45 Ibid., p. 84.
46 See Toffler *The Third Wave*, chs 16 and 17, and Jones, *Sleepers Wake!*, ch. 11.

47 E.g. see B. Ehrenreich and F. Fox Piven, 'The Feminization of Poverty' in *Dissent*, Spring 1984, pp. 162–70, and B. Campbell, *Wigan Pier Revisited: Poverty and Politics in the 80s* (London: Virago Press, 1984).

48 Jones supports reproductive technology as part of his drive to boost high technology exports – see *The Age*, 12 December 1985, p. 20; also see Toffler, *The Third Wave*, p. 220.

49 I. Illich, *Gender* (New York: Pantheon Books, 1982), p. 65.

50 A. Nove, *The Economics of Feasible Socialism* (London: George Allen and Unwin, 1983), p. 200.

51 See ibid. and also G. Hodgson, *The Democratic Economy* (Harmondsworth: Penguin, 1984), and G. Kitching, *Rethinking Socialism* (London: Methuen, 1983).

52 See my critique of Nove in *Radical Philosophy* (39), 1985, in the Frankel/Nove Debate on Market Socialism, and also a further reply to Nove in *Radical Philosophy* (41), 1982.

53 Nove, *Economics of Feasible Socialism*, p. 216.

54 See *Beyond the State?*, ch. 12.

55 E.g. see J. Rothschild-Whitt, 'Conditions for Democracy: Making Participatory Organizations Work' in J. Case and R. C. R. Taylor (eds), *Co-ops, Communes and Collectives Experiments in Social Change in the 1960s and 1970s* (New York: Pantheon, 1979), pp. 215–44.

56 Nove, *Economics of Feasible Socialism*, p. 200.

## 3  ECO-PACIFISM OR POST-INDUSTRIAL MILITARISM AND EXPLOITATIVE NORTH–SOUTH RELATIONS

1 See Bahro, *Socialism and Survival*, pp. 108–9; A. Gorz, *Ecology as Politics* (Boston: South End Press, 1980), part 3; Toffler, *The Third Wave*, p. 145, and Jones, *Sleepers, Wake!*, p. 233.

2 See Gorz's analysis, 'From Nuclear Electricity to Electric Fascism', in *Ecology as Politics*.

3 Barry Jones was a critic of uranium mining but has remained silent since the Hawke government reversed Labour policy and proceeded to support the mining and export of uranium.

4 See Toffler, *Previews and Premises*, p. 78.

5 Ibid., pp. 78–9.

6 See e.g. D. Dickson, *The New Politics of Science* (New York: Pantheon, 1984).

7 See 'American Science Spending' in *The Economist*, 11 February 1984, p. 72.

8 See 'US defence spending: the price is more than dollars' in *The Age*, 2 December 1985, p. 1 and p. 9.

9 See J. Falk, *Global Fission* (Melbourne: Oxford University Press, 1982), ch. 10.

10 The Bahro–Gorz debate has been translated and reprinted in *Telos* (51), 1982.

11 For a critique of the French Left's attitude to the peace movement, see my Open Letter to the French Left (written with Alan Roberts) which was ignored by most French Left journals but reprinted in *Arena* (65), 1983, pp. 154–61, and D. Johnstone, 'How the French Left Learned to Love the Bomb' in *New Left Review* (146), 1984, pp. 5–36.

12 Gorz and other French Leftists have attacked West Germans as having a 'willingness to accept despotism', depicting West Germany as a nation lacking a cultural relation to freedom. See A. Gorz in *Telos* (51), 1982, pp. 117–22.

13 A. Gorz, 'Security: Against What? For What? With What?' in *Telos* (58), Winter 1983–4, p. 167.

14 Ibid., p. 161.

15 For a powerful critique of nuclear arms strategy and why deterrence has been used as a cover-up by American leaders for war-fighting strategies, see D. MacKenzie, 'Nuclear War Planning and Strategies of Coercion' in *New Left Review* (148), 1984, pp. 31–56.

16 See 'On the German Non-Response to the Polish Crisis: An Interview with André Gorz' in *Telos* (51), 1982, pp. 117–22.

17 R. Bahro, 'A New Approach For the Peace Movement in Germany' in E. P. Thompson et al., *Exterminism and Cold War* (London: Verso, 1982), pp. 87–116.

18 See Bahro, *From Red To Green*, p. 198.

19 Ibid., p. 202.

20 Ibid., p. 203.

21 Ibid., p. 207.

22 Ibid., p. 140.

23 Ibid., pp. 215–16 and *Building The Green Movement*, pp. 142–58.

24 Ibid., p. 169.

25 See R. Bahro, 'To Change the World Through Faith' in *Socialism and Survival*, p. 78.

26 Bahro, *From Red to Green*, p. 214.

27 See Thompson et al., *Exterminism and Cold War*, for a discussion of the concept of 'exterminism'.

28 Bahro, *From Red To Green*, p. 214; also see *Building The Green Movement*, pp. 142–58.

29 Bahro, *Socialism and Survival*, p. 130.
30 H. Marcuse, *One Dimensional Man* (London: Sphere Books, 1968), p. 130.
31 Bahro, *Socialism and Survival*, p. 151.
32 Bahro, *From Red to Green*, p. 142, and 'A New Approach for the Peace Movement in Germany', p. 115.
33 Published in *Journal of Peace Research*, 21 (2), 1984, pp. 127–39 and also published in *There Are Alternatives!* (Nottingham: Spokesman, 1984).
34 See Ibid.
35 W. Agrell, 'Small But Not Beautiful' in *Journal of Peace Research*, 21 (2), 1984, pp. 158–67.
36 Bahro, *Building The Green Movement*, p. 158.
37 The Alternative Defence Commission Report, *Defence Without The Bomb* (London: Taylor & Francis, 1983), makes too many concessions to advocates of strong conventional defence forces. For a survey of options and problems associated with non-military defence, see 'Complementary Forms of Defence: Report of the Swedish Commission on Resistance' and T. Olsen, 'Social Defence and Deterrence: Their Relationship', both in *Bulletin of Peace Proposals*, 16 (1), 1985, pp. 21–32 and pp. 33–50.
38 See E. Mandel, 'The Threat of Nuclear War and the Struggle For Socialism' in *New Left Review* (141), 1983, pp. 23–50.
39 For a critique of orthodox Marxist analyses of militarism and war see M. Shaw (ed.), *War, State & Society* (London: Macmillan, 1984), chs 1 and 2 by Michael Mann and Martin Shaw.
40 Toffler, *The Third Wave*, p. 442.
41 Ibid., pp. 442–3.
42 Bahro, *Building the Green Movement*, p. 34.
43 K. Marx, 'The German Ideology' in L. Easton and K. Guddat (eds), *Writings of The Young Marx on Philosophy and Society* (New York: Anchor, 1967), p. 409.
44 E.g. see K. Mirow and H. Maurer, *Webs of Power International Cartels and the World Economy* (Boston: Houghton Mifflin Co., 1982), and R. Burbach and P. Flynn, *Agribusiness in the Americas* (New York: Monthly Review Press, 1980).
45 Toffler, *The Third Wave*, pp. 338–58.
46 Ibid., pp. 339–42.
47 Ibid., p. 345.
48 Ibid.
49 For a good critique of Amin's theory, see Sheila Smith, 'The

Ideas of Samir Amin: Theory or Tautology?' in *Journal of Development Studies*, 17 (1), 1980, pp. 5–21.

50  Toffler, *The Third Wave*, p. 346.

51  Ibid., p. 347.

52  Ibid., p. 356.

53  Gorz, *Paths to Paradise*, p. 3.

54  Gorz, *Ecology as Politics*, pp. 197–215.

55  Gorz, *Paths to Paradise*, p. 3.

56  Ibid., pp. 92–100.

57  Ibid., p. 5.

58  For a critique of World Bank ideology, see S. George, *How the Other Half Dies* (Harmondsworth: Penguin, 1976).

59  See M. Brzoska, 'The Military Related External Debt of Third World Countries' in *Journal of Peace Research*, 20 (3), 1983, pp. 271–7.

60  See M. D. Wolpin, 'Comparative Perspectives on Militarization, Repression and Social Welfare' in *Journal of Peace Research*, 20 (2), 1983, p. 136 and R. Sivard, 'War, the Bloodstained God' in *The Nation*, 30 October 1982, p. 421.

61  For a comprehensive collection of data on the level of arms production in the Third World see M. Brzoska and T. Ohlson (eds), *Arms Production in the Third World* (Stockholm International Peace Research Institute Report published in London: Taylor and Francis, 1986); for world figures on the massive resources allocated to military–industrial complexes, see L. R. Brown et al. *State of the World 1984*, A Worldwatch Institute Report (New York: W. Norton, 1984).

62  See Brzoska and Ohlson (eds), *Arms Production in the Third World*, p. 10, and S. G. Neuman, 'International Stratification and Third World Military Industries' in *International Organization*, 38 (1), 1984, pp. 169–97.

63  Ibid., p. 169.

64  Bahro, *From Red to Green*, p. 138, and *Building the Green Movement*, p. 35.

65  Bahro, *Socialism and Survival*, pp. 41–2.

66  Bahro, *Building the Green Movement*, p. 29.

67  Ibid., p. 14.

68  Ibid., p. 17.

69  See Bahro, *From Red to Green*, pp. 179–82, and *Building the Green Movement*, pp. 123–41, for Bahro's conversations with Galtung on North–South relations.

70  E.g. see J. Galtung, *The True Worlds*: *A Transnational Perspective* (New York: Free Press, 1980).

71 The prolific output of Galtung has been partially collected in 5 volumes on peace research and 2 volumes on methodology published by Christian Ejlers, Copenhagen, 1976. Also see N. Gleditsch et al., *Johan Galtung: A Bibliography of his Scholarly and Popular Writings 1951–80* (Oslo: International Peace Research Institute, 1980).
72 Published in *Alternatives*, iv, 1978–9, pp. 277–300.
73 Ibid., pp. 292–3.
74 Bahro, *Socialism and Survival*, p. 130.
75 E.g. see B. Komarov, 'Economy and Ethics of the Gas Pipeline Deal' in *Telos* (56), Summer 1983, pp. 90–3.
76 See Thompson et al., *Exterminism and Cold War*, pp. 90–1.

## 4   REDEFINING PUBLIC AND PRIVATE SPHERES

1 See I. Reinecke, *Connecting You . . . Bridging the Communications Gap* (Ringwood: McPhee Gribble and Penguin, 1985), p.45.
2 Toffler, *Previews and Premises*, p. 22.
3 Toffler, *The Third Wave*, p. 217.
4 E.g. see S. Marglin, 'What Do Bosses Do?' in A. Gorz (ed.), *The Division of Labour: The Labour Process and Class Struggle in Modern Capitalism* (Sussex: Harvester Press, 1976), and D. MacKenzie and J. Wajcman (eds), *The Social Shaping of Technology* (Milton Keynes: Open University Press, 1985).
5 See A. Game and R. Pringle, *Gender at Work* (Sydney: George Allen and Unwin, 1983).
6 Toffler, *Previews and Premises*, p. 23.
7 P. Henkel, 'The Technology-Age Typist Works From Her Home' in *The German Tribune*, 10 March 1985, p. 7.
8 Toffler, *The Third Wave*, p. 382.
9 D. Haraway, 'A Manifesto for Cyborgs: Science, Technology, and Socialist Feminism in the 1980s' in *Socialist Review*, 15 (80), 1985, pp. 85–6.
10 Toffler, *Previews and Premises*, p. 134.
11 Toffler, *The Third Wave*, p. 227.
12 Ibid., chs 16 and 17.
13 Toffler, *Previews and Premises*, p. 134.
14 For two different versions of this massive debate (with its mountain of literature), see B. and P. Berger, *The War Over the Family* (Harmondsworth: Penguin, 1984), and M. Barrett and M. McIntosh, *The Anti-Social Family* (London: Verso, 1982).
15 Toffler, *The Third Wave*, p. 225.

16  Ibid., pp. 219–221.

17  Ibid., p. 220.

18  Ibid.

19  Ibid., p. 230.

20  A. Gorz, 'The Limits of Self-Determination and Self-Management: An Interview with André Gorz', in *Telos* (55), Spring 1983, p. 218, also included in *Paths to Paradise*, p. 66, with a different translation. For a perceptive analysis of Gorz's own socialization (as depicted in his book *The Traitor*), see A. F. Davies, *Skills, Outlooks and Passions* (Cambridge: Cambridge University Press, 1980), pp. 221–5.

21  See C. Lasch, *The Culture of Narcissism* (New York: Warner Books, 1979).

22  H. Kahn, *The Coming Boom* (London: Hutchinson, 1983), p. 195.

23  Berger, *The War Over the Family*, p. 186.

24  C. Lasch, *Haven in a Heartless World* (New York: Basic Books, 1977), and *The Culture of Narcissism*. Also see C. Lasch, 'Politics and Social Theory: A Reply to the Critics' in *Salmagundi* (46), Fall 1979. Lasch's complaint that the Left unjustly accuses him of trying to 'turn the clock back' would have more credibility if he did not, in his own words, 'often have to turn to the Right for the most penetrating criticisms of modern life' – see C. Lasch, 'Democracy and the Crisis of Confidence' in *Democracy*, 1 (1), 1981, p. 39. In claiming that a radical movement will have to stand 'for the nurture of the soil against the exploitation of natural resources, the family against the factory, the romantic vision of the individual against the technological vision, localism over democratic centralism' (p. 40 in 'Democracy and the Crisis of Confidence'). Lasch comes dangerously close to a traditional form of populist–fascist romantic politics. What kind of a 'family', 'technology', or 'politics' does he really stand for? In what way are they different from the visions of the Right that he simultaneously attacks, yet draws his critique of 'modern' life from? Will the real Lasch please stand up?

25  S. Engel, 'Femininity as Tragedy Re-examining the "New narcissism"', in *Socialist Review* (53), 1980, pp. 77–104.

26  Ibid., pp. 80–1.

27  Ibid., pp. 97–8. In a very revealing article 'The Freudian Left and Cultural Revolution' in *New Left Review* (129), 1981, pp. 23–34, Lasch misunderstands the penetrating analysis of narcissism made by Engel. While Engel shows that the category

narcissism is based on a negative view of female development, Lasch misreads Engel and thinks that she is simply advocating the 'long overdue feminization of society' (p. 31). Engel's very title 'Femininity as Tragedy' – to signify the misogynist aspects built into the psychoanalytic theory of narcissism – is thus revealingly overlooked by Lasch.

28 R. Sennett, *The Fall of Public Man* (London: Cambridge University Press, 1977).

29 J. Donzelot, *The Policing of Families*, trans. by R. Hurley (New York: Pantheon, 1979).

30 Toffler, *The Third Wave*, pp. 231–2.

31 Ibid., p. 403.

32 Ibid., p. 246.

33 Ibid., p. 335.

34 Ibid., p. 434.

35 Gorz, *Farewell to the Working Class*, ch. 9.

36 I. Illich, *Deschooling Society* (New York: Harper & Row, 1971).

37 Bell, *The Coming of Post-Industrial Society*, ch. 3.

38 See Jones, *Sleepers Wake!*, ch. 7 and Stonier, *The Wealth of Information*, ch. 11.

39 Toffler, *Previews and Premises*, p. 57.

40 Bahro, *Socialism and Survival*, p. 34.

41 See Stonier, *The Wealth of Information*, p. 180.

42 Ibid., p. 174.

43 Ibid., p. 173.

44 Toffler, *The Third Wave*, ch. 17.

45 Ibid. A similar point is made by Joel Kovel when discussing 'Narcissism and the Family' in *Telos* (44), 1980, pp. 88–100. In Kovel's view, 'the bourgeois age is, among other things, that age of a family centred upon children. It is therefore the era in which childhood emerges for the first time in history as a distinct category of existence. Pathological narcissism is then fundamentally the outcome when the family, so to speak, is not merely centred on children but collapses upon them as well, crushing them beneath its weight. It is therefore a specific disorder for that phase of capitalist development in which such a collapse occurs. Pathological narcissism is a pox of late capitalism' (p. 95). It is not clear from Kovel's analysis whether he agrees with Lasch's thesis on the importance of the Oedipal crisis, whether narcissism in its primary and secondary forms will be present in all societies, or what kind of family relations should replace child-centred families and why this family form

is peculiar to 'late capitalism'. For example, is the crushing weight which collapses upon children due to the fact that they live in capitalist societies, or to the fact that parents who have only one to three children (as opposed to ten), concentrate more of their energy on the unlucky or lucky few? Would the removal of state experts mean that parents would have to focus even more of their energy on child rearing – thus compounding, rather than relieving the crushing burden experienced by children?

46 Gorz, *Farewell to the Working Class*, p. 150.
47 Ibid., pp. 150–1.
48 Jones, *Sleepers Wake!*, p. 172.
49 D. Hawkridge, *New Information Technology in Education* (London: Croom Helm, 1983).
50 See e.g. H. Schiller, *Who Knows: Information in the Age of the Fortune 500* (New Jersey: Ablex, 1981); also see C. J. Hamelink, *Cultural Autonomy in Global Communications* (New York: Longman, 1982).
51 Toffler, *The Third Wave*, p. 362.
52 Ibid.
53 A. Feenberg, 'Moderating an Educational Teleconference' (Mimeo).
54 Ibid., pp. 14–16.
55 For a discussion of the varying responses of social movements to 'modern' social conditions, see A. Honneth, E. Knodler-Bunte and A. Widmann, 'The Dialectics of Rationalization: An Interview with Jurgen Habermas' in *Telos* (49), Fall 1981, pp. 5–31, and J. Habermas, 'New Social Movements' in Ibid., pp. 33–7.
56 A. Toffler, *Future Shock* (London: Pan, 1970), part 5.
57 Toffler, *The Third Wave*, p. 377.
58 For some representative views in recent debates on 'modernity' and 'post-modernity', see R. Bernstein (ed.), *Habermas and Modernity* (Cambridge: Polity Press, 1985); special issue of *Telos* (62), Winter 1984–5; C. Brookeman, *American Culture and Society Since the 1930s* (London: Macmillan, 1984); M. Jay, *Marxism and Totality* (Cambridge: Polity Press, 1984), ch. 15 and Epilogue; J. Walker, *Art in the Age of Mass Media* (London: Pluto Press, 1983); H. Foster (ed.), *The Anti-Aesthetic: Essays on Post-Modern Culture* (Port Townsend: Bay Press, 1983); M. Berman, *All That Is Solid Melts Into Air* (London: Verso, 1983); special issue of *Thesis Eleven* (12), 1985; special issue of *Theory, Culture & Society*, 2

(3), 1985; and special issues of *New German Critique* (22), Winter 1981, and (33), Fall 1984.

59 J. F. Lyotard, *The Postmodern Condition* (Manchester: Manchester University Press, 1984), p. 3. Using the concept 'postmodern' in a different sense, it is also interesting to read how Green movement theorists link 'postmodernity' and post-industrialism. For example, Charlene Spretnak argues that 'The spiritual dimension of Green politics, then, will have to be compatible with the cultural direction of Green thought: posthumanist, postmodern and postpatriarchal.' See C. Spretnak, *The Spiritual Dimensions of Green Politics* (Bear & Co: Sante Fe, 1986), p. 34.

60 See J. Habermas, 'Modernity Versus Postmodernity' in *New German Critique* (22), Winter 1981, pp. 3–14.

61 P. Anderson, 'Modernity and Revolution', *New Left Review* (144), 1984, p. 99.

62 F. Jameson, 'Postmodernism, or the Cultural Logic of Late Capitalism', in *New Left Review* (146), 1984, pp. 53–93.

63 M. Davis, 'Urban Renaissance and the Spirit of Post-modernism' in *New Left Review* (151), 1985, pp. 106–13.

64 J. Habermas, *Toward a Rational Society*, trans. by J. J. Shapiro (Boston: Beacon Press, 1970), p. 117.

65 Ibid., p. 118.

66 A. Huyssen, 'The Search for Tradition: Avant-Garde and Postmodernism in the 1970s' in *New German Critique* (22), Winter 1981, p. 38.

67 M. Ryan, *Marxism and Deconstruction* (Baltimore: Johns Hopkins University Press, 1982).

68 Ibid., p. 116.

69 D. Bell, *The Cultural Contradictions of Capitalism* (New York: Basic Books, 1978), p. 99.

70 Toffler, *The Third Wave*, pp. 376–7.

71 J. Casanova, 'The Politics of Religious Revival' in *Telos* (59), 1984, p. 33.

72 See A. Giddens, *A Contemporary Critique of Historical Materialism* (London: Macmillan, 1981), ch. 6, for a discussion of the relationship between the development of capitalist societies, the transformation of concepts of time and urban space.

73 See M. Horkheimer and T. Adorno, *Dialectic of Enlightenment*, trans. by J. Cumming (London: Allen Lane, 1973).

74 See Lasch, *The Culture of Narcissism* and Sennett, *The Fall of Public Man*; also see R. Sennett, 'Destructive Gemeinschaft' in

R. Bocock et al. (eds), *An Introduction to Sociology* (Milton Keynes: Open University Press, 1980), pp. 91–121.

75 Sennett, *The Fall of Public Man*, p. 260.

76 Gorz, *Paths to Paradise*, p. 84.

## 5  GETTING FROM HERE TO THERE

1 For an analysis of the conflicting priorities of workers, see K. Hinrichs, C. Offe and H. Wiesenthal, 'The Crisis of the Welfare State and Alternative Modes of Work Redistribution' in *Thesis Eleven* (10/11), 1984–5, pp. 37–55.

2 Raymond Williams calls this phenomenon 'mobile privatization' – see his analysis in 'Problems of the Coming Period' in *New Left Review* (140), 1983, pp. 7-18.

3 For a fuller discussion of this misconception, see my *Beyond The State?*, chs 3 and 6.

4 D. Held and J. Keane, 'Socialism and the Limits of Social Action' in J. Curran (ed.), *The Future of the Left* (Cambridge: Polity Press and New Socialist, 1984), ch. 12.

5 Gorz, *Farewell to the Working Class*, p. 118.

6 Toffler, *Previews and Premises*, pp. 102–3.

7 Ibid., p. 103.

8 See recent figures in *The Economist*, 1 March 1986, p. 53.

9 Jones, *Sleepers Wake!*, p. 182 and p. 24.

10 Toffler, *Previews and Premises*, pp. 194–6.

11 See e.g. R. Hyman, 'André Gorz and His Disappearing Proletariat' in *The Socialist Register 1983*, pp. 272–95, and C. Whitbread, 'Gorz, Nove, Hodgson: the Economics of Socialism' in *Capital and Class* (26), Summer 1985, pp. 125–45.

12 Both published by Beacon Books, Boston.

13 Gorz, *Farewell to the Working Class*, ch. 6.

14 Ibid., pp. 39–40.

15 Ibid., p. 67.

16 Ibid., p. 52. Marcuse's critique of Charles Reich's book *The Greening of America* is just as applicable to Gorz. 'Nobody in control of the armed forces, the police, the National Guard? Nobody in control of the outer space program, of the budget, the Congressional committees? There is only the machine being tended to? But the machine not only must be tended to, it must be designed, constructed, programmed, directed. And there are very definite, identifiable persons, groups, classes, interests which do the controlling job, which direct the technical, economic political machine for the society as a whole.

They, not their machine, decided on life and death, war and peace – they set the priorities. They have all the power to defend it – and it is not the power of the machine but over the machine: human power, political power.' See 'Charles Reich – A Negative View' in *The New York Times*, 6 November 1970, p. 41. Or as Marcuse comments elsewhere: 'Since nobody is in control, nothing can possibly be easier than the revolution, and, therefore, it is understood that the revolution will be without any violence on either side. Now I think you all agree with me that we wish that this were the case.' 'The Movement in a New Era of Repression' in *Berkeley Journal of Sociology*, xvi, 1971–2, p. 6.

17  Gorz, *Farewell to the Working Class*, pp. 68–70.
18  Ibid., p. 72.
19  Ibid., p. 74.
20  Hyman, 'André Gorz', p. 286, makes this point well.
21  See P. Adler, 'Technology and Us' in *Socialist Review* (85), 1986, pp. 67–96.
22  For a critique of Gorz which stresses the importance of union struggles in relation to new technology etc., see J. Mathews, 'Technology, Trade Unions and the Labour Process', *Working Papers in the Social Studies of Science* (Victoria: Deakin University, 1985). Despite his positive critique of Gorz, Mathews is himself too closely identified with a Fabian-neo-corporatist position which binds unions to conservative government policies implemented by Labor parties.
23  A. Gorz, 'The American Model and the Future of the French Left' in *Socialist Review* (84), 1985, pp. 101–8.
24  Bahro, *From Red to Green*, p. 220.
25  Ibid., p. 185.
26  See Bahro, *Socialism and Survival*, pp. 26, 49–50 and 63–4.
27  See Bahro, *Building the Green Movement*, p. 79, and *From Red to Green*, p. 185 and p. 205.
28  Ibid., pp. 183–4.
29  See interview with Bahro in *Undercurrents*, February/March 1983, p. 11, and *Building The Green Movement*, p. 122.
30  Ibid., p. 173 and p. 144.
31  See ibid., pp. 104–22.
32  Toffler, *Previews and Premises*, p. 84.
33  Ibid., pp. 89–90.
34  Ibid., p. 49.
35  Ibid., pp. 48–52.
36  Toffler, *The Third Wave*, p. 442.

37  Ibid., pp. 446–8.
38  A. Toffler and H. Toffler, 'Appointment With the Future' in *The Australian*, 2 March 1985, p. 6.
39  Toffler, *The Third Wave*, pp. 446–8.
40  Ibid., p. 448.
41  Ibid., p. 449.
42  Ibid., p. 450.
43  Ibid.
44  Ibid., pp. 452–3.
45  Gorz, *Farewell to the Working Class*, p. 75.
46  See e.g. *From Red to Green*, pp. 131, 133, 151 and 175; Bahro is particularly critical of Left Social Democrats such as Eppler for their 'eco-reformism' which will only keep the system going.
47  Bahro, *Building the Green Movement*, p. 211.
48  Toffler, *The Third Wave*, p. 294.
49  Toffler, *Previews and Premises*, p. 38.
50  Ibid., p. 114.
51  Bahro, *From Red to Green*, pp. 235–6.
52  Bahro, *Socialism and Survival*, p. 63.
53  Ibid., p. 50.
54  The co-option of environmentalist, feminist and peace movement slogans and language, by major parties, is a common phenomenon in the 1980s.
55  See the collection in *Building the Green Movement*, which ranges from Bahro's support for the Green Party election platform, through his criticism that the Green Party was becoming a conventional party like the other conservative parties, to his final break with the Green Party and scathing critique of the 'realists'.
56  E.g. see Bahro, *From Red to Green*, p. 177.
57  Toffler, *The Third Wave*, chs 27 and 28.
58  For an analysis of the West German Green Movement see E. Papadakis, *The Green Movement in West Germany* (London: Croom Helm, 1984), and W. Hulsberg, 'The Greens at the Crossroads' in *New Left Review* (152), 1985, pp. 5–29, for the history of the various factions and tendencies within the Greens.
59  Bahro, *Building the Green Movement*, p. 180.
60  Bahro, *From Red to Green*, pp. 181–2.
61  Toffler, *The Third Wave*, ch. 28.
62  Gorz, *Paths to Paradise*, pp. 62–3.
63  See H. Cleaver, *Reading Capital Politically* (Brighton: Harvester Press, 1979), pp. 51–66, and T. Abse, 'Judging the

PCI' in *New Left Review* (153), 1985, pp. 28–33.

64 See e.g. the special issue of *Social Research*, 52 (4), 1985, for articles by Cohen, Eder, Touraine, Offe, etc., as well as references to other literature on new social movements.

65 C. Offe, 'New Social Movements: Challenging the Boundaries of Institutional Politics' in ibid., p. 830.

66 Bahro, *Building the Green Movement*, p. 185.

67 Ibid., pp. 173–4 and 156–8.

68 Offe, 'New Social Movements', pp. 833–4.

69 Ibid., pp. 858–68.

## CONCLUSION

1 There are an increasing number of books on the micro-electronic revolution. See e.g. G. Friedrichs and A. Schaff (eds), *Microelectronics and Society For Better or For Worse* (Oxford: Pergamon Press, 1982), and I. Benson and J. Lloyd, *New Technology and Industrial Change* (London: Kogan Page, 1983).

2 A. Nove, *The Economics of Feasible Socialism* (London: George Allen and Unwin, 1983), and the Frankel–Nove debate on market socialism in *Radical Philosophy* (39 and 41), 1985.

3 Figures are from Globus and reprinted in *The German Tribune*, 27 April 1986, p. 8.

4 For an excellent discussion of some of the problems associated with democracy and equality, see R. A. Dahl, *Dilemmas of Pluralist Democracy Autonomy* vs. *Control* (New Haven: Yale University Press, 1982). Dahl favours a market socialist alternative – a general weakness in his argument despite the very important and illuminating discussions of socialist democracy.

# Index